# POLITICAL ANECDOTES

Also by Mungo MacCallum

*Mungo: the man who laughs*

*Girt by Sea*

*How To Be A Megalomaniac*
*(advice to a young politician)*

# Political Anecdotes

selected and introduced by
Mungo MacCallum

Duffy & Snellgrove
Sydney

Published in 2003 by Duffy & Snellgrove
PO Box 177 Potts Point NSW 1335 Australia
info@duffyandsnellgrove.com.au

Previous edition published as
*Mungo MacCallum's Australian Political Anecdotes*
by Oxford University Press, 1994

Distributed by Pan Macmillan

© selection and introduction by Mungo MacCallum
© extracts by individual authors

Cover image of Robert Menzies from The Fairfax Photo Library.
Cover images of Bob Hawke and Paul Keating by Peter Morris/
*The Sydney Morning Herald.* Cover image of Gough Whitlam by
Anton Cermak/*The Sydney Morning Herald*

Cover design by Alex Snellgrove
Typeset by Cooper Graphics
Printed by Griffin Press

ISBN 1 876631 74 0

visit our website: www.duffyandsnellgrove.com.au

# Contents

Editor's Acknowledgements  *vi*

Introduction  *vii*

Political Anecdotes  *1*

Sources and Acknowledgements  *277*

Index  *283*

# Editor's Acknowledgements

A number of people have helped with suggestions for material for this book. I would like to thank Geoff Bolton, Kaylene Chamberlain, Chris Cuneen, Shirley Fitzgerald, Brian Fletcher, Bill Gammage, Colin Hughes, Ken Inglis, Bede Nairn, Patrick O'Farrell, John Poynter and John Ritchie for their contributions, not all of which could be used. Katherine Steward punctiliously edited what was originally a pretty rough manuscript. Peter Rose of Oxford University Press patiently oversaw the work from start to finish for the original edition, backed up by Alexa Burnell.

Special thanks to the Richmond–Tweed Library Service, and in particular to Nicole of the Brunswick Heads branch, for help in locating material. Also to the *Byron Shire Echo* for use of its facilities.

Finally, my love and gratitude to my partner and helpmate Jenny Garrett, whose research and encouragement greatly assisted the whole project.

# INTRODUCTION

The story is told of an early sitting of the Federal Parliament in Melbourne during which a minister was being heckled mercilessly by a member of the Opposition. Eventually the heckler, who was somewhat tired and emotional, gave up and went to sleep in his place, allowing the minister to finish his speech in peace. The minister then walked across the chamber, unbuttoned his fly, and urinated in his tormentor's ear. Hansard is said to have recorded this event as: '(An incident occurred)'.

I have heard this story more than once, but no one has ever been able to give me a name or a date, so it may be no more than a political myth. But if it didn't happen it should have. Here, perhaps, is the ultimate Australian political anecdote, the quintessence of the way the rude colonials adapted the solemnity of the British parliamentary system to suit their own peculiar needs.

Of course, the rough beginnings of politics in Australia go back to long before the colonial authorities would allow a parliament of any kind. From the arrival of the First Fleet factions formed: convicts against free settlers, landholders against rent payers, Catholic against Protestant. Even within the elite group of rulers there were those who called themselves Whigs and those who claimed to be Tories. If politics is about the division of power, Australia has always been a very political country. But it is also a country that generally takes its politics casually, and which maintains a healthy scepticism about its politicians. Without question one of Australia's most distinguished political figures, Alfred Deakin, a founding father and three times prime minister, was treated not as an object of reverence, but simply as 'Affable Alfred'. The man who saw himself as Deakin's political heir, Australia's longest serving prime minister Robert Menzies, was known variously as 'Ming the Merciless' and 'Pig Iron Bob'. Australia's long-running man for all seasons William Morris Hughes desperately wanted to be seen as a statesman: the nearest he came was the nickname 'the Little Digger'. It has been claimed that Australia has never produced a great leader on the scale of a Churchill or a Roosevelt. A likely explanation is that Australians neither need nor want a great leader, and anyone who put himself forward as such would be very promptly cut down to size.

This doesn't mean, however, that the two and a bit centuries of White Australian politics have been dull or trivial. On the contrary, the cynicism with which the media and the public have regarded the whole process has produced an air of informality which has in turn produced a splendid crop of anecdotes. We see pomposity punctured and many tall poppies harvested. We meet layabouts, larrikins and liars as well as many who genuinely tried their best under extraordinarily difficult circumstances. We watch the development of the rituals of political survival, which one observer has compared to the behavioural codes of a second rate boys' boarding school – Australian politics has been, and very largely still is, an overwhelmingly male preserve.

It would be too pretentious to claim that these were the men and the events that shaped the nation; Australia is far more than the sum of its political parts. But perhaps more than in many other countries, Australia's politics and politicians reflect the real ambience of the place. This is what I have tried to bring together in this collection. In doing so I have concentrated on events rather than on the generally studied speeches of the protagonists; in any case, political speeches are usually better spoken than read. I have included a few one-liners, mainly to show that our politicians are not without wit, as is frequently claimed by their critics (especially the English). Indeed, they may be better at it than their forebears. The politician's comment in the following exchange is usually attributed to Winston Churchill:

> FEMALE INTERJECTOR   If I were your wife I'd put poison in your coffee.
> POLITICIAN   If I were your husband, I'd drink it.

In fact, according to the historian Bill Gammage, it was George Reid, New South Wales premier and briefly Australian prime minister. One for the colonies.

Australian politics is frequently rough around the edges, and often crude to the point of becoming positively scatological. But it seldom lacks gusto. If this collection proves nothing else, I hope it shows that the fire in the belly glows brightly down under.

*Notes for the 2003 edition*

In the ten years since this collection first appeared Australian politics has lost a bit of its anecdotal edge. The politicians have become greyer and more professional, the media more pompous and opinionated, the punters more selfish and cynical and the overall scene a lot less pleasant than it used to be. Updating for the past decade has generally been a grimmer task than filling in some of the gaps in the earlier edition. Australian politics has always been a fiercely competitive game, even (or perhaps especially) among nominal allies. One of my favourite yarns concerns the young politician who enters the House of Representatives for his first parliamentary sitting. Nervously taking his seat, he looks across the chamber: 'There they are,' he breathes. 'The enemy.' The crusty old veteran sitting beside him chuckles sardonically. 'No, sonny,' he corrects the newcomer. 'That's the opposition. The enemy are the ones sitting all round you.'

And this is truer today than it ever was. Politicians are supposed to be ruthless, vindictive, red in tooth and claw. The most effective taunt John Howard, arguably the most brutal of his generation, used against his more civil opponent Kim Beazley was that Beazley lacked 'ticker' – the implication being that he was a wimp and a wuss unfit to survive in the political jungle. Nice guys finish last. Only mongrels endowed from birth with the killer instinct deserve to make it to the top. Tony Abbott, a former pugilist who remains a political brawler and Mark Latham, a street fighter who brags of his hatred for those who sit opposite, are today's young hopefuls.

In this atmosphere most anecdotes tend to read more like cautionary tales than merry witticisms. All the more reason then, to record them; more than official histories do, they can give a genuine flavour of the times. In spite of one of John Howard's numerous broken promises, these times are neither comfortable nor relaxed. But perhaps this book can help to put our problems in some sort of perspective. As the anecdotal record shows, Australian politics has always been a bit of a roller coaster ride, and both politicians and public have proved surprisingly and admirably resilient.

We had intended you to be
The next Prime Minister but three:
The stocks were sold; the Press was squared:
The Middle Class was quite prepared.
But as it is! ... My language fails!
Go out and govern New South Wales!

                      Hilaire Belloc, 'Lord Lundy',
                      *Cautionary Tales for Children*

# First Contact

*When the first governor of New South Wales, Arthur Phillip, arrived at Botany Bay in 1788, his meeting with the inhabitants could not have been more promising. Captain Watkin Tench was there.*

We found the natives tolerably numerous as we advanced up the river, and even at the harbour's mouth we had reason to conclude the country more populous than Mr Cook thought it. For on the *Supply*'s arrival in the Bay on the 18th of [January] they were assembled on the beach of the south shore, to the number of not less than forty persons, shouting and making many uncouth signs and gestures. This appearance whetted curiosity to its utmost, but as prudence forbade a few people to venture wantonly among so great a number, and a party of only six men was observed on the north shore, the Governor immediately proceeded to land on that side, in order to take possession of his new territory, and bring about an intercourse between its old and new masters. The boat in which His Excellency was, rowed up the harbour, close to the land, for some distance; the Indians keeping pace with her on the beach. At last an officer in the boat made signs of a want of water, which it was judged would indicate his wish of landing. The natives directly comprehended what he wanted, and pointed to a spot where water could be procured; on which the boat was immediately pushed in, and a landing took place. As on the event of this meeting might depend so much of our future tranquillity, every delicacy on our side was requisite. The Indians, though timorous, shewed no signs of resentment at the Governor's going on shore; an interview commenced, in which the conduct of both parties pleased each other so much, that the strangers returned to their ships with a much better opinion of the natives than they had landed with; and the latter seemed highly entertained with their new acquaintance, from whom they condescended to accept of a looking glass, some beads, and other toys.

Tench, *Sydney's First Four Years* (1961), p. 35

# A Close Shave

*Relations between the Europeans and the Indians
(as they called the Aborigines) were initially cordial.*

Some young gentlemen belonging to the *Sirius* one day met a native, an old man, in the woods; he had a beard of considerable length, which his new acquaintance gave him to understand, by signals, they would rid him of, if he pleased; stroaking their chins, and shewing him the smoothness of them at the same time, at length the old Indian consented, and one of the youngsters taking a penknife from his pocket and making use of the best substitute for lather he could find, performed the operation with great success, and, as it proved much to the liking of the old man, who in a few days after reposed a confidence in us, of which we had hitherto known no example, by paddling along side the *Sirius* in his canoe, and pointing to his beard. Various arts were ineffectually tried to induce him to enter the ship; but as he continued to decline the invitation, a barber was sent down into the boat along side the canoe, from whence, leaning over a gunnel, he complied with the wish of the old beau, to his infinite satisfaction. In addition to the consequences which our sanguine hopes led us to expect from this dawning of cordiality, it affords proof that the beard is considered by this people more as an encumbrance than a mark of dignity.

Tench, *Sydney's First Four Years* (1961), p. 53

# A Flogging Offence

*When clashes did occur, Phillip administered justice impartially.*

March, 1789. Sixteen convicts left their work at the brick kilns without leave, and marched to Botany Bay, with a design to attack the natives, and to plunder them of their fishing-tackle and spears: they had armed themselves with their working tools and large clubs. When they arrived near the bay, a body of Indians, who had probably set out, and had penetrated their intention from experience fell upon them. Our heroes were immediately routed, and separately endeavoured to effect their escape by any means were left. In their flight one was killed, and seven were wounded for the most part very severely: those who had the good fortune to outstrip their comrades and arrive in camp, first gave the alarm and a detachment of marines under an officer, was ordered to march to their relief. The officer arrived too late to repel the Indians; but he brought in the body of the man that was killed, and put an end to the pursuit. The Governor was justly incensed at what had happened, and instituted the most rigorous scrutiny into the cause which had produced it. At first the convicts were unanimous in affirming, that they were quietly picking sweet-tea, when they were without provocation assaulted by the natives, with whom they had no wish to quarrel. Some of them, however, more irresolute than the rest, at last disclosed the purpose for which the expedition had been undertaken and the whole were ordered to be severely flogged: Arabanoo [an Aborigine who had been cultivated by Phillip] was present at the infliction of the punishment and was made to comprehend the cause and the necessity of it; but he displayed on the occasion symptoms of disgust and terror only.

Tench, *Sydney's First Four Years* (1961), p. 144–5.

## BRING YOUR OWN BREAD

*The wreck of the supply ship* Sirius *in 1790 almost reduced the new colony to starvation. Phillip made sure the suffering was shared equally.*

The distress of the lower classes for clothes was almost equal to their other wants. The stores had been long exhausted, and winter was at hand. Nothing more ludicrous can be conceived than the expedients of substituting, shifting, and patching, which ingenuity devised, to eke out wretchedness, and preserve the remains of decency. The superior dexterity of the women was particularly conspicuous. Many a guard have I seen mount, in which the number of soldiers without shoes, exceeded that which had yet preserved remnants of leather.

Nor was another part of our domestic economy less whimsical. If a lucky man, who had knocked down a dinner with his gun, or caught a fish by angling from the rocks, invited a neighbour to dine with him, the invitation always ran, 'bring your own bread'. Even at the Governor's table, this custom was constantly observed. Every man when he sat down pulled his bread out of his pocket, and laid it by his plate.

Tench, Sydney's First Four Years (1961), p. 166.

## The Rise of the Rum Corps

*In the early years of the colony the
officers who were supposed to uphold the law
quickly became a law unto themselves.*

The explanation of many, if not most, of the difficulties which overwhelmed the three naval governors who succeeded Governor Phillip, viz., Hunter, King and Bligh, lies in the increasing ascendancy of the officers of the [New South Wales] Corps. They not only possessed the monopoly of violence, but:

> They became an aristocracy. They were allowed to engage in trade and agriculture; gradually, they obtained control of the imports, particularly spirits; and the consequence was that, within twelve months of Phillip's departure, rum became the recognised medium of exchange. So much so that even labour could only be purchased with spirits. Under this system, the officers reaped enormous harvests.

During Hunter's governorship, the officers repeatedly smuggled convicts away from government control so as to use them in private employment, including, of course, that of the officers themselves. After Phillip's departure [in 1792], the commanding officer of the regiment, Grose, administered the colony for three years, and he was succeeded by Paterson, the next in command. Under both Grose and Paterson, 'convict servants were lavishly bestowed, not only upon commissioned officers of the Corps, but also upon sergeants, corporals and drummers, until scarcely a score of unengaged men remained for any public purpose'.

Evatt, *Rum Rebellion* (1938), pp. 26–7.

## A Liar, a Scoundrel and a Vagabond

*By 1802 Governor King had fallen
foul of the local commercial faction.*

The Governor was next engaged in a violent correspondence with a Captain Colnett of HMS *Glatton*, then at Sydney. A dozen small points aggravated the dispute, the character of which is sufficiently illustrated by the fact that King allowed his secretary, Chapman, to sign an outrageously phrased statement which was duly forwarded to Colnett by the Governor. In the statement, Chapman narrated that he had been informed by the Governor that Colnett had said that he (Chapman) had made an assertion about the date of the *Glatton*'s sailing from Sydney; and he continued thus:

> I hereby declare that Captain Colnett, or any other person who dares to say that ever I gave it out publicly and officially as Secretary to His Excellency Governor King that the *Glatton* was to sail at any particular time, is a liar, a scoundrel, and a vagabond; and that whoever he is, if he has the spirit to come forward, that I will wring his nose and spit in his face.

It is reasonably plain that, by the continuous defamation and intimidation of the officers, the Governor was being reduced to a point approaching nervous breakdown.

Evatt, *Rum Rebellion* (1938), pp. 82–3.

# The Governor and the Grazier

*The first meeting between the irascible Governor William Bligh
and the colony's largerst landowner,
John Macarthur, in 1806, was not a happy one.*

George Johnston for the military, Richard Atkins for the civil officers and John Macarthur for the free inhabitants presented Bligh with an address of congratulation. A few weeks later Bligh received a second address from one hundred and thirty-five free inhabitants of Sydney, in which they repudiated Macarthur's right to speak for the free inhabitants, and accused him of being responsible for the high price of mutton by withholding a large flock of wethers from the market till the prices rose. At the same time a further two hundred and forty-four inhabitants sent another address to Bligh also repudiating Macarthur as spokesman for the free. It so happened that at the same time Macarthur met Bligh at Government House, Parramatta, and moved the conversation round to sheep, whereupon Bligh exploded and asked him what he, Bligh, had to do with his sheep, sir, and what had he to do with his cattle, sir and was Macarthur to have such flocks of sheep and such herds of cattle as no man heard of before, and though Macarthur, sir, had five thousand acres of land in the finest situation in the country, by God sir, he would not keep it. [Former governor Philip] King wept. What Macarthur thought might be guessed from a remark in a letter Mrs Macarthur wrote to a friend in England, in which she described Bligh as violent, rash and tyrannical.

Clark, *A History of Australia*, vol. i (1963), p. 213.

# Macarthur Defies the Law

*When Bligh attempted to have Macarthur
arrested for a series of commercial offences, Macarthur simply
defied Chief Constable Oakes.*

In obedience to the warrant, Oakes proceeded to Macarthur's home near Parramatta for the purpose of making the arrest.

Macarthur looked at the warrant and then wrote out and handed to Oakes the paper:

> Mr Oakes – You will inform the persons who sent you here with the warrant you have now shewn me, and given me a copy of, that I never will submit to the horrid tyranny that is attempted until I am forced; that I consider it with scorn and contempt, as I do the persons who have directed it to be executed.
>
> J. Macarthur
> Parramatta, 15 December 1807

Macarthur told Oakes to retain the paper because it would constitute justification and said 'that if the persons directing that warrant had served it he would have spurned them from his presence'; that 'if he came a second time to come well armed, for that he would never submit until there was bloodshed'; that 'he had been robbed of £10,000,' and 'leave them alone; they will soon find a rope to hang themselves!'

Evatt, *Rum Rebellion* (1938), pp. 161–2.

# A Few Pre-Mutiny Drinks

*On the eve of the 1808 Rum Rebellion the soldiers were in a partying mood, as William Gore, an official prior to the rebellion, reported at a subsequent inquiry.*

For the first time since our arrival in this country the officers of the New South Wales Corps dined together as a mess, and the novelty of their assembling on that day was heightened by the display of their regimental colours at the door of their mess room. It was cased in the forepart of the day, and unfurled during the afternoon.

At any other time, my Lord, or on any other occasion, this circumstance would have been undeserving of notice; but from subsequent events it is to be inferred that had any one amongst the officers been waiving, this was the rallying day, when heated by wine, that was to fix them in a unanimous resolution of possessing themselves of the administration of the country.

It is very probable that, on the same Sunday evening, Macarthur conversed with Sergeant-Major Whittle and made the announcement that he was distributing, at very cheap prices and for the benefit of all the noncommissioned officers and soldiers of the regiment, large quantities of liquor from which a handsome profit could be derived. Evidence to that general effect was given by Whittle before his collapse at the court martial. And the evidence was never controverted by Macarthur. The dinner party did not conclude until a very late hour, and [George] Johnston [who was to lead Bligh's arrest] dined too well. On his way home to Annandale his condition was such that he 'tumbled out of his chaise'. Thus, on the day before Macarthur's trial, the anti-Bligh alliance was sealed in a little blood and a great deal of rum.

Evatt, *Rum Rebellion* (1938), pp. 191–2.

## The Arrest of Bligh

*On 26 January 1808, the troops stormed Government House and demanded Bligh's resignation.*

When Bligh refused, John Macarthur, John and Gregory Blaxland, James Mileham, Simeon Lord, some soldiers, and a band of the curious who were probably seeking revenge for the insults and the abuse as well as those who delighted to see the mighty taken down from their seat, entered Government House to find [Judge-Advocate Richard] Atkins with a glass in his hand, Robert Campbell behaving with dignity, and Bligh in a situation, according to [George] Johnston, three months later, too disgraceful to be mentioned. This suggestion understandably caused Bligh to burn with indignation. The three were arrested. That evening Johnston announced the arrest and told the inhabitants of Sydney and Parramatta that in future they were to obey him. All night the carousing, the cheering, and the singing went on in Barrack

Square, while no one so much as lifted a finger to help Bligh, as he raged into the night, impotent and alone except for the company of his faithful daughter.

Clark, A History of Australia, vol. i (1963), p. 220.

### The 'disgraceful circumstances' of Bligh's arrest were gleefully described by colonist W.C. Wentworth.

Dreading the resentment of the people whom he had so often and so wantonly oppressed, and having on his back that uniform which was so dishonoured before, he skulked under a servant's bed in an obscure chamber of his house, but was at length discovered in this hole, and conducted pale, trembling, and covered with flue, before the officer who had commanded his arrest.

Wentworth in Evatt, Rum Rebellion (1938), p. 224.

### Macarthur's friend General Tench was not surprised.

The concealment under the feather bed made me smile, but did not surprise me in the least, as I had long possessed the strongest testimony of a friend who had served with Governor Bligh that he was not only a tyrant, but a poltroon.

Tench in Evatt, Rum Rebellion (1938), p. 224.

### The conduct of Bligh's daughter, Mary Putland, produced a different impression, according to an eyewitness account.

The fortitude evinced by Mrs Putland on this truly trying occasion merits particular notice, for, regardless of her own safety, and forgetful of the timidity peculiar to her sex, her extreme anxiety to save the life of her beloved father prevailed over every consideration, and with uncommon intrepidity she opposed a body of soldiers who, with fixed bayonets and loaded firelocks, were proceeding in hostile array to invade the peaceful and defenceless mansion of her parent, her friend, her protector, and as she then believed to deprive him of his life. She dared the traitors 'to stab her to the heart, but to respect the life of her father'. The soldiers themselves appalled by the greatness of her spirit, hesitated how to act, and that principle of esteem and respect which is inherent in the breast of every man who sees an amiable woman in distress, and is not himself a most consummate villain, deterred them from offering any violence to her.

*Historical Records of NSW* (1892–1901), vol. vi, p. 558.

## Riot, Tumult and Insubordination

*The post-mutiny celebrations gave warning of what was to come, as William Gore observed.*

Liquor was liberally, and indeed profusely, served to the soldiers; bonfires blazed in all parts of the town; and those scenes of riot, tumult, and insubordination that are ever incident to the subversion of legitimate government and authority ensued. Macarthur, the hero of the day, paraded the streets, in the most public parts of which he was always conspicuous; and those individuals who had not lighted their houses were compelled to illuminate them by the sergeant-major and some chosen soldiers, who were detached on that particular service. The most insulting conduct and epithets were encouraged by the junto to be applied to the Governor and to his faithful officers, and such of his adherents as had persisted in refusing to exhibit outward demonstrations of their joy and approbation were carefully marked as the victims of future prosecution.

*Historical Records of NSW* (1892–1901), vol. vi, p. 560.

# Trial Without Jury

*William Gore was one of the many victims of the reign of terror instituted by Macarthur and the military. He was brought before the puppet Judge-Advocate Kemp on a trumped-up charge the following May.*

KEMP   Are you guilty or not guilty?
GORE   I have a few observations to make; I believe I have them in my hat.
KEMP   We do not wish you to say anything. We do not wish you to speak; are you guilty or not guilty?
GORE   I deny your jurisdiction.
KEMP   We are not to be harangued by you, Mr Gore; we are not come here for you to harangue us.
GORE   I will not plead; I deny your jurisdiction.
KEMP   It is not for you to deny our jurisdiction; I will pass sentence on you if you will not plead.
GORE   You are an unlawful assembly, and illegally constituted; the most disgraceful, the most rigorous sentence you can pronounce on me I shall receive as the greatest honor you can confer on me; I'll not acknowledge your authority; I deny your jurisdiction.
CAPTAIN ABBOTT   Mr Gore, you can challenge any member – you can challenge any member.
GORE   No, possessing my fealty and my allegiance to my King, I deny your jurisdiction; I will not plead – for you are an unlawful assembly.
KEMP   Clear the Court; clear the Court.
[*After an adjournment of twenty minutes, the case was resumed.*]
KEMP   We have recorded that you have refused to plead.
GORE   I have; I do.
KEMP   And we have sentenced you to be transported for seven years.
GORE   You have conferred on me the greatest honor you are capable of conferring – the only honor I could receive from such men.
KEMP   Take him away; take him off; take him away; take him away.

*Historical Records of NSW* (1892–1901), vol. vi, p. 648.

# A Very Convenient Tool

*The senior officer nominally in charge of the colony was Lieutenant Colonel William Paterson. But by early in 1809 he was having his problems. One observer reported that Paterson*

is in a very bad state of health – almost a paralytic – from former intemperance; and now I am informed from good authority that he is drunk the greatest part of his time; so that, from imbecility when sober and stupidity when drunk, he is a very convenient tool in the hands of Macarthur, or of Foveaux and Abbott, who see that his plans are executed while he keeps himself in the background to remove the offence which his actual interference would give many in the colony, who are seduced to cooperate with the rebels while they are persuaded that Macarthur has nothing to do with public business.

Historical Records of NSW (1892–1901), vol. Vi, p. 88.

# The Toll-Free Judge

*The arrival of Lachlan Macquarie as Governor in 1810 restored some sort of order, but Macquarie had problems establishing his own authority, particularly with the chief judge Ellis Bent.*

In August, Macquarie perforce began a correspondence with Bent about the payment of tolls on the turnpike road between Sydney and Parramatta. Bent had refused to pay, partly because if the Judge paid, and the Governor did not, this would contradict Bent's claim that as a judge he was the equal of the Governor, and partly because he argued that the Governor possessed no legal authority to levy taxes upon the subject. Again Macquarie was incensed by so insolent and disrespectful a letter, and told Bent that he must decline all 'further epistolary correspondence' with him. When Bent reached the toll gate on 5 September [1812], he was, as he saw it, subjected to personal outrage when the farmer of the tolls, in a state of intoxication, asked him to pay a toll. To which Bent shouted that he was the judge of this colony, that he would pay no toll while he was in it, and that if the toll-keeper did not let him go he would send him to gaol. When the farmer of the tolls reported the episode, D'Arcy Wentworth issued a summons for Bent to appear before a magistrate's court. To this Bent replied that he was not subject to criminal jurisdiction except for treason and felony.

Clark, *A History of Australia*, vol. i (1963), p. 294.

# A Matter of Decency

*Macquarie was a man of strict principles, which he applied both to the colony as a whole and to each of its inhabitants.*

In April 1816, this concern for the moral well-being of others led to actions which his enemies construed as evidence of his arbitrary disposition. The shrubbery on the government domain in Sydney was, he knew, much frequented by both men and women for most improper purposes. He had wanted for a long time to put a stop to these disgraceful indecencies, as well as, he added, to save the shrubs and the trees. To achieve this he issued a proclamation threatening to punish future trespassers. On Thursday, 18 April, Daniel Read walked across the domain on his way to work, and William Blake had also slipped into the domain. On the following morning, for an undisclosed reason, William Henshall also crossed the domain over the broken-down wall. They were arrested and Macquarie summarily ordered all three to receive twenty-five lashes. That day at noon the gaoler ordered first Read, then Henshall, then Blake to strip to receive their twenty-five lashes, and to pay the fee of a free man, three shillings per day, to the gaoler. All three found their way promptly to [Judge Ellis] Bent, where they made sworn depositions before him, in one of which Henshall, probably prompted by the learned judge, wound up with these words: 'I have no knowledge of what I was punished for than I have said, than that it was the Governor's will.' Bent promptly sent these depositions to Bathurst in a semiofficial letter on 12 June 1816. Macquarie was convinced that the punishment had had the desired effect as it had put a complete stop to the trespassers, and had prevented the breaking down of the government wall, as well as the gross indecencies.

Clark, *A History of Australia*, vol. i (1963), pp. 386–7.

## THE SOCIAL SELECTION

*Macquarie recognised, and indeed socialised with, emancipists – ex-convicts who had become settlers. The self-appointed social arbiters, such as John Macarthur's wife Elizabeth, did not approve.*

Most public social occasions, such as midday levees and dinners which started at 4 or 5pm, were for men only. As the number of respectable women increased, they were invited to official celebrations, usually joining the men after dinner at about 9pm for dancing and supper. Dancing parties, complete with military orchestra, often continued till early morning. At the King's birthday celebrations in June 1810, only four ladies, all wives of officials, were present among eighty-one people. Twelve months later the pattern was similar with five ladies joining the seventy-two men for dinner. Society was increasing and on royal birthdays there were parties at Government House for 150 people. Elizabeth Macarthur commented in 1816: 'I will not say that these assemblies have been very select.'

Broadbent and Hughes, *The Age of Macquarie* (1992), p. 28.

## A FRIENDLY WAGER

*One free settler who obviously appealed to Macquarie was the young William Charles Wentworth:*

Young William, after schooling in England where he met and admired his father's benefactor, Lord Fitzwilliam, returned to join the first expedition to cross the Blue Mountains and a blackbirding raid on Raratonga during which the ship's captain was killed and William took command and brought the ship home. He also attracted Macquarie's favour: at one stage the governor granted him the whole of Sydney's North Shore, which Wentworth promptly lost in a card game. Macquarie replaced it with deeds to the Illawarra region, which the family finally dissipated in the 1980s.

MacCallum, *Mungo: The Man Who Laughs* (2001), p.4.

## The Native Son Offends Greatly

*One of the colony's most flamboyant landholders and politicians was William Charles Wentworth, who, as he was among the first freeborn Australians, was known as the 'Native Son'. Wentworth had been a confidant of several governors including Macquarie and Brisbane, but he did not get on with James Darling.*

In September [1827] he and his friends decided to hold a Turf Club dinner at which they proposed to honour Governor Brisbane for presenting a gold cup as a prize for a horse race. Darling, sensing Wentworth and Wardell might exploit the occasion to his own pain, declined to attend. By then he was beginning to see the point of Brisbane's remark that not even an angel from heaven could get on in the colony of New South Wales. On the night of 9 November forty members of the Turf Club sat down at Cumming's Hotel. The air seemed charged with that spirit of drunken bravado and recklessness which followed Wentworth wherever he went. What he muddied, stayed muddied for life. Wentworth himself spoke to the former Governor Brisbane, who, he said, had been 'one of us'. By contrast, the present Governor had not even condescended to dine either with a gentleman, or with the members of any public body. When the time came to drink the toast to Darling a very convivial party had gathered round Dr Wardell. With his usual flair for the moment of mischief, Wentworth asked the band to play a tune appropriate to the object of their toast. One wit called for 'There's nae luck aboot the Hoose', and they laughed heartily. Then Wardell, carried away by the tendency of the tipsy to drag the mighty down to their own level, shouted 'No, not that ... play "Over the hills and far away".' And they roared with laughter, and rose to their feet and swayed and emptied their glasses while the band played merrily that tune which summed up their attitude to General Darling – this would be a much better place when that bloody Englishman went over the hills and far away.

Clark, *A History of Australia*, vol. ii (1968), pp. 78–9.

## THE GOVERNOR DEPARTS

*When Governor Darling was eventually recalled in 1831 the emancipists (of whom W.C. Wentworth was the leader) were even less restrained.*

[Darling's] departure was marked by wild jubilations from the emancipists. Hall's *Monitor* announced that an 'illumination' would rise over its editorial office the night Darling sailed, bearing the incandescent phrase 'He's off'. 'Thank God – we have shaken off the incubus at last!' Wentworth exclaimed in the *Australian*, and held open house for every emancipist in the colony on the grounds of his estate at Vaucluse, overlooking Sydney Harbour, whose perimeter had been surrounded by a shallow trench filled with Irish earth to keep the Australian snakes out. Some four thousand people converged on Vaucluse House by gig, horse, donkey and Shank's pony, and hoed into a feast more Brobdingnagian than Lucullan, involving a whole roast ox, twelve sheep, thousands of loaves of bread and incalculable quantities of ale and spirits. The pro-Darling newspaper, the *Sydney Gazette*, asked its readers to imagine

> the roaring, bawling, screeching, blaspheming, thumping, bumping, kicking, licking, tricking, cheating, beating, stealing, reeling, breaking of heads, bleeding of noses, blackening of eyes, picking of pockets, and what not ... The orgies of the lowest rabble of Botany Bay, congregated in the open air, shrouded by the curtain of night, released from the eyes of the police, and helewated by the fumes of Coopers gin ... [T]hese contemptible proceedings have excited universal disgust and abhorrence among decent people.

Hughes, *The Fatal Shore* (1988), p. 452.

# The Place for a Village

*In 1835 John Batman made a somewhat outrageous land deal for what is now the city of Melbourne.*

Through his interpreters Batman explained to the chiefs that he had come to settle amongst them on friendly terms, adding that although he was a White man he was 'a countryman of theirs' and would protect them. That day he gave the men blankets, tomahawks, knives, scissors, and looking-glasses and hung around the necks of each woman and child a necklace. They appeared highly gratified and excited. The next day he explained to the chiefs that the object of his visit was to purchase a tract of their country, since he intended to settle amongst them with his wife, his seven daughters, his sheep and his cattle. He proposed, he said, to employ the people of their tribe, clothe and feed them, and pay them an annual tribute in necessaries as a compensation for the enjoyment of the land. The chiefs seemed fully to comprehend his proposals, and much delighted with the prospect of having him live amongst them. On the following day, 6 June, after the deed of purchase was read out and explained to the chiefs, the three brothers Jaga Jaga, Jaga Jaga and Jaga Jaga, and the other chiefs, Cooloolock, Bumgarie, Yanyan, Moowhip and Mommarmalar, of the Dutigallar tribe in the district of Iransnoo and Geelong granted to John Batman 100,000 acres on which he could place sheep and cattle in exchange for twenty pairs of scissors, fifty handkerchiefs, twelve red shirts, four flannel jackets, four suits of clothes, fifty pounds of flour, and a yearly rent or tribute of fifty pairs of blankets, fifty knives, fifty tomahawks, fifty pairs of scissors, fifty looking-glasses, twenty suits of clothing and two tons of flour. By a similar deed of purchase he took possession of 500,000 acres in the vicinity of the Yarra Yarra. In return for a few knives, tomahawks, scissors and looking-glasses, and enough grog to put them in a mood to say 'yes' to anything and laugh about it, a few Aborigines had made John Batman and the other members of the association amongst the largest landed proprietors in the world. In the mood of a man feeling like a king he wrote down in his diary a few days later, 'this will be the place for the future village'. Then on 14 June he left for Launceston.

Clark, *A History of Australia*, vol. iii (1973), pp. 88–9.

## THE GREAT LAND SHARKS

*John Batman was not always successful in his attempts to acquire land; but when it came to big land claims, no one could compete with W.C. Wentworth.*

While some looked to frugal, virtuous and industrious immigrants to win the victory for civilisation over barbarism, adventurers, driven on in part by greed and in part by that dream of being giants in the land, had their moment, too, of prominence. In 1835 John Batman and his partners played for over half a million acres in the hinterland of Port Phillip and lost. Early in 1840 W.C. Wentworth and others played for no less than twenty million acres in the south island of New Zealand in return for two hundred gold sovereigns, and an undertaking to pay the same sum each year to the Maori chiefs for their lifetimes. [Governor] Gipps warned him that his treaty would be null and void and offered the chiefs ten guineas each, copious cups of tea and a cold handshake, while Wentworth filled them with rum and jokes and gave them two hundred gold sovereigns. When Wentworth refused to abrogate his treaty with the Maori chiefs, Gipps asked the Legislative Council on 28 May 1840 to pass an Act declaring that treaty to be null and void. He also announced that James Macarthur and not Wentworth would replace Phillip Parker King in the Legislative Council, having decided that Wentworth by his extravagant behaviour had forfeited the claim he had to a position he otherwise had by virtue of his vast influence in the colony and his vast possessions. Wentworth asked leave to present his case at the bar of the Council. On 30 June and 1 July he spoke for some six hours using all his gifts for rhetoric to prove that the Magna Carta and the Bill of Rights were his warranty for the twenty million acres of land in New Zealand. Broughton [Bishop of Australia] denounced his act as 'morally shameful'. James Macarthur told the Council that such wild assertions as Wentworth had uttered during those six frenzied hours could lead to nothing but disorder. The press of Sydney taunted him for his 'exorbitant rapacity', just as on previous occasions they had hinted at his promiscuity and his convict mother.

Clark, A History of Australia, vol. iii (1973), p. 176.

## LIVING HONOURABLE

*By the 1840s some ex-convicts were not only prosperous, but becoming quite snobbish about their origins.*

They, too, drove in their carriages or rode around the town mounted on handsome and well-groomed horses, the well-paid and well-fed moral policemen of the bond and the free in New South Wales. Such emancipists continued to overtop the free and respectable immigrants in the most ostentatious display of their wealth, which was said to be all the more glaring because they were driven to avenge themselves for the 'touch me not' insolence of the untainted towards all members of the convict community. The whole convict community — those in servitude, those set free from servitude, their wives, their children, and their children's children — continued to be poisoned by a silent, deep-rooted hostility to the free settlers and the 'bloody immigrants'. To the alarm and disgust of the free, the convict community gloried in their past and boasted of it. 'Thank God I'm not a bloody immigrant,' they cried. 'Thank God I came out 'onorable.'

Clark, A History of Australia, vol. iii (1973), p. 156.

# Dock Yard Society

*A clergyman's wife, Louisa Anne Meredith, was not convinced that there was any society worth the name.*

The distinctions in society here remind me of the 'dockyard people' described by Dickens ... Thus – Government officers don't know merchants; merchants with 'stores' don't know other merchants who keep 'shops'; and the shopkeepers have, I doubt not, a little code of their own, prescribing the proper distances to be observed between drapers and haberdashers, butchers and pastry-cooks ... . This pride of place is so very ridiculous and unbecoming in such a community, that were not its tendency so mischievous, it could only provoke a smile.

Meredith in Hughes, *The Fatal Shore* (1988), p. 325.

# Election Day in Sydney

*In 1842 Sydney officially became a city, and elections were held for the city corporation. Democracy ran wild.*

As election day approached the conservatives openly feared that the men of good sense and reputability were about to be overmastered by the illiterate and the vulgar. Thousands of pounds were spent by candidates in the distribution of drink. At one polling booth an infuriated drunken mob drove a police magistrate who was endeavouring to preserve order into an enclosure surrounded with high palings and pelted him with bricks, stones and large pieces of paling. At another polling booth the tent was pulled down and one of the candidates, a shipowner, was mauled by the mob. Not to be outdone, he armed the whalers on one of his ships with harpoons and whaling knives and swept his opponents away from the booth.

Clark, *A History of Australia*, vol. iii (1973), p. 191.

# The First Republicans

*By 1844 the problem of squatters taking over Crown land had become acute. Governor George Gipps decided that a vast increase in rent was the answer, but he did not reckon with the fiery Presbyterian clergyman John Dunmore Lang.*

What should be done in this moment of peril? At the very least, Lang told his readers, passive resistance to the Government had become a sacred duty, the first of all political duties, for every British subject in the colony who knew and valued his birthright. Some people, though Lang prudently denied he was one of them, went further than passive resistance. They believed that if the sovereign or his agent abrogated the constitution then all subjects were *ipso facto* absolved from the duty of allegiance. Many of the most respectable colonists, Lang claimed, were suggesting that they should throw off the British yoke altogether and assert their entire freedom and independence and, if necessary, call on the French or the Americans to help establish and maintain their freedom.

In order to give point to this claim, that many respectable colonists were in a revolutionary mood, Lang described several conversations he had had with well-to-do and responsible people. One high Tory proprietor had told him that they should *Bligh* Sir George Gipps, that is, pack him up and put him on board ship and send him off to England even if this meant flying a rebel flag and proclaiming a republic. A day or two later, a squatter told him that they should transform the Legislative Council into a revolutionary convention; it would be quite safe to do so, he said, because although the English might capture Sydney easily enough they could never penetrate into the interior and would soon be starved out for no corn grew around the capital. Another squatter told Lang that he would never pay the exorbitant additional burden of taxation which Gipps was proposing and that no one could possibly force him to do so because with his knowledge of the country and the assistance of twenty good stockmen he could defy any regiment in Her Majesty's service.

Baker, *Days of Wrath* (1985), pp. 215–16.

# A Question of Native Title

*Wentworth took the squatters' case to extremes in the
New South Wales Legislative Council in 1845.*

It was left to Wentworth to put the squatters' case. This he did in the most extreme manner, claiming that he had a right to run his stock on the waste lands of the colony without any charge whatsoever. The only legitimate charge on the squatters, he maintained, was to meet the expense of police protection – if the squatters applied for it. He rejected contemptuously the security of tenure implied by an eight-year lease; what he contended for was a totally different fixity of tenure, that right of possession due to the discoverer of the lands he occupied or one that derived from the original discoverer. This right, he said, gave him as good a title to these lands, until they were purchased for the purposes of settlement, as that possessed by the Queen herself; indeed, his right was better than Her Majesty's because it was the right of discovery and possession while hers was only an artificial title constructed out of a legal fiction.

Baker, *Days of Wrath* (1985), p. 218.

# Cutting the Ties

*In 1847 John Dunmore Lang argued for a complete separation of the
colony from Britain, in a revolutionary series of lectures.*

There came a time in the history of any colony, he believed, when the ties with the mother country should be dissolved. This political principle, universally admitted in the abstract, was always disputed in practice, for whenever a particular colony tried to assert its independence the mother country always claimed the right time for independence had not yet come. Unless the British Government changed its opinions and practice, Lang said to strong expressions of assent, the colonies would be forced to wrest their independence from the mother country and set her at defiance.

Would the colonies be able to defend themselves if they became independent of Britain and no longer defended by British troops and the British navy? Yes, said Lang; indeed Australia would be safer separated from Britain. In this way he anticipated a good deal of radical republican thought in Australia during the second half of the nineteenth century. There were three great powers, he thought, with whom Britain might go to war: France, Russia and the United States. Any one of these three, if at war with Britain, would send frigates and privateers to prowl upon our coasts, attack our towns, ruin our trade and destroy our shipping. All this would be done not with ill will to Australia, but simply to annoy Great Britain. If Australians were independent they would be free of such European depredations. What of attacks from other parts of the world? There was immense laughter when Lang enquired if his hearers were endangered by the Aborigines. The laughter continued when he suggested an invasion by the cannibals of the Pacific. Clearly nothing was to be feared from the Negroes of South Africa or from the Spanish republics of South America. There was more derisory laughter when he asked if there was any reason to suspect an invasion from China, from the empire of Burma or from Japan; laughter renewed when he pointed out that none of these people knew where Australia was so they could never find us to attack us.

Baker, *Days of Wrath* (1985), pp. 290–1.

## THE RIGHT TO VOTE

*Lang also considered the question of franchise.*

On 23 April [1847], a week after his second lecture, Lang gave a third in which he discussed such questions as the franchise and electoral boundaries. He was not confident that the Legislative Council would fix the franchise as it ought to be. He thought some people might consider his support for adult manhood suffrage to be extreme but this principle had now been recognised and acted on in the United States of America, in France and in a great part of Germany. The principle of manhood suffrage, he said, was laid down in the books of Moses by the Divine Governor of Nations. He had dictated that the adult males of any country had equal political rights and were entitled to the possession of the elective franchise. When Lang affirmed that the franchise was their natural, their inherent, their indisputable and indestructible right, given to them by their Creator, his listeners burst into cheering.

The cheering turned to laughter when he spoke about votes for women. Some people had suggested, he said, that if universal suffrage be adopted it should be extended to women. When in London he had written an article advocating universal suffrage and had been honoured by a visit from a Quaker lady anxious that he should advocate the rights of women also. Referring her to scripture, he had told her that until she could point out where holy writ endorsed votes for women he could not see his way to advocating her rights. She had gone away sadly disappointed and the audience in the School of Arts thought that very funny.

Baker, Days of Wrath (1985), p. 292.

## No More Convicts

*Lang's republicanism struck a chord with those opposed to the transportation of convicts to New South Wales.*

With tension mounting and tempers rising, over six thousand persons gathered in the Barrack Square on 16 September [1848] to demand the revocation of the Order in Council naming New South Wales as a place to which convicts could be sent. Charles Cowper was in the chair. He and the Reverend Mr Ross opened the meeting by using the language of the moralisers to denounce the sordid-minded men who worshipped golden idols. Father McEncroe asked them whether they wanted to be free men or slaves. Lang told them that if they did not want to be lickspittles and slaves, they must strike for their freedom and independence. England was in no position to retake the colony by force of arms. If England persisted in transporting convicts, he would haul down the glorious flag of England and unfurl the flag of an Australian republic. There were no cries of horror. No cries of protest, only immense cheering. A revolutionary fire was flicking around the edges of the meeting.

Clark, *A History of Australia*, vol. iii (1973), p. 445.

## The Hoary Letcher

*One who attracted Lang's wrath was Governor Fitzroy, whom Lang attacked in a scurrilous (and anonymous) pamphlet.*

The previous year, when touring the southern districts, the Governor had stayed at the Surveyor General in Berrima. The innkeeper was Ned Chalker, a champion pugilist who had saved his winnings to turn publican. Chalker had a daughter by no means devoid of personal attractions who fixed the regards of the vice-regal visitor. In due course, as she was seen to be pregnant, Chalker went to Sydney to seek redress. He got such a cold reception at Government House that he sought the help of a solicitor, William Thurlow, who preferred his claim on His Excellency in the proper manner, demanding compensation for the loss of the services of his client's child. Two hundred pounds, it was said, was given to Chalker to prevent exposure and disgrace.

'The Hoary Letcher', according to Lang's paragraph, had compounded the affair by paying only one hundred pounds, far too little for spoiling so fine a piece of *Colonial mutton*. Charles the Second, it continued, had paid his whores on a much more liberal scale but poor people are easily frightened off by authority. Then came the political point: the Governor's delinquencies would accelerate the already rapid march of the colony towards republicanism.

Baker, *Days of Wrath* (1985), p. 376.

# The Bunyip Aristocracy

*By 1853 W.C. Wentworth had lost most of his revolutionary zeal. Indeed, he had become positively anti-democratic in his desire to have Australia emulate the institutions of Great Britain.*

To achieve that end he recommended the creation of hereditary titles, leaving it to the option of the Crown to annex to the title a seat for life in the Legislative Council. Such hereditary titles would lay the foundations of an aristocracy, and the formation of an upper house modelled, as far as circumstances would admit, upon the analogies of the British constitution. He also recommended the extension of the elective franchise for the lower house to include all persons having a salary of £100 a year, all occupants of any room or lodging paying £40 a year for their board and lodging or £10 a year for their lodging only. This was, as he put it, 'a very close approximation to universal suffrage'.

*His recommendations were greeted with derision.*

Outside the walls of the Legislative Council howls of anger and moral indignation greeted the proposals. In the *Empire* Henry Parkes charged Wentworth with presenting a 'wretched patch work of political absurdities', whose tendencies were all oligarchical, a constitution 'more atrocious than ridiculous', 'mummery' with which to 'befool the old ladies of Macquarie Street'. It was a measure, Parkes said that, while it kept them slaves, would make them the laughing-stock of every civilised nation. On 6 August the poet Charles Harpur, in a letter to the *Empire*, was cheeky and irreverent. What, he asked, would be the criterion for being a lord? Would it be drunkenness, or money, or the possession of 'a thumping great nose'? The Wentworth upper house would be one more cobweb which the broom of the future revolution would sweep utterly away.

> The ultimate ridicule came from radical political
> orator and writer Daniel Deniehy:

'Here', he said, 'they all knew the common water mole was transferred into the duck-billed platypus, and in some distant emulation of this degeneration, he supposed they were to be favoured with a bunyip aristocracy.'

Clark, A History of Australia, vol. iv (1978), pp. 36 ff.

## The Master Spinner

> By the 1850s a new breed of populist politicians had appeared. Jack
> Robertson (later premier of New South Wales) was one.

In his private life he was a paragon of the laws of his tribe. In the company of men his conversation was distinctively Australian rather than Rabelaisian. He often invited his opponents to smell his arse: he once said to the mayor of a country town 'See here Master bloody Mayor: if you think I'm a bloody spider to go and spin spiders out of my bloody arse you're bloody well mistaken, that's all.'

Clark, A History of Australia, vol. iv (1978), p. 138.

## The Man with the Big Shelala

> The battle for land continued as free
> selectors (small farmers) moved further west.

Squatters sometimes treated selectors as a plague of locusts which had to be exterminated or driven away if the grass was to be preserved for their stock. Near Yass in 1865 George Glendinning and his sons took up selections on the squatting-run of T.S. Hall, the magistrate for the district, who was leasing eight hundred square miles from the Crown. Hall wrote Glendinning a threatening letter: 'I am Exceedingly sorry to Hear', he wrote in August 1865, and understand of the way you and your Family are annoying and endeavouring to Injure Our St. Helier's property for I am quite sure you nor your Family never received any Injury at my Hands. And more than that, wile you kept away from me I was quite Determined not to Interfere with you – But Rest assured that If you continue to annoy us that we will take steps to protect Ourselves – All the Land Round about your First Selections is useful Greasing Land, as Good as a Good deal of the land we have bought, and there is nothing to stop us From Buying Every inch of the Land in Neighbourhood of your Selections – and take my word, this course will be adopted. And further I will Find Shepherds that will not be afraid Even of your Big Shelala – My motto has always been to live and let live and I wish to continue in that course – I am your Obedient Servant, Thomas S. Hall.

Clark, *A History of Australia*, vol. iv (1978), p. 169.

## THE ROYAL VISIT

*In August 1867 Australia received its first royal visit, from His Royal Highness Prince Alfred Arthur George, Earl of Ulster, Duke of Edinburgh, Prince of Saxe-Coburg-Gotha, second son of Her Gracious Majesty Queen Victoria.*

Women and children pelted the carriage with flowers, public dignitaries presented the Prince with declarations of loyalty, veneration and affection for the Queen and her empire. Then the Prince was driven in an open carriage through the streets of Adelaide, which were decorated with huge portraits of him, portraits which caused him to whisper to the man next to him, 'I do not think Mother would recognise me in some of these illustrations.'

*In Melbourne the mood was somewhat less restrained.*

As the carriages of the members of high society rolled towards their gorgeous palaces in Toorak and the bayside suburbs of St Kilda and

Brighton, the houses of the lower orders were already astir, for 8 November was the day when the people met their Prince at a free banquet to be held on the bank of the Yarra River. It was one of those hot, north wind Melbourne days in late November, when the dust and the heat of midday frayed the nerves. When thirsty members in the crowd called for drink, the brazen broached a tub of wine and began to hand out goblets to their friends. Inflamed by drink, a hungry mob rushed the tables on which the food was laid out. A saturnalia began. Men and women rolled about in the grass and the dust on the river bank fumbling with each other's bodies, while mothers frantically urged their children to look the other way. Some men and women rushed across the fields with bottles of wine, legs of lamb, and loaves of bread tucked under their arms or held in their hands. Others lay on the grass dead to all the world, with their mouths open, their clothes stained by the wine, while flies crawled over their faces feasting on the scraps of food and drink that had not found their way to those all too capacious mouths. Next day the *Argus* declared that a more 'miserable day' had 'never been witnessed in Victoria'.

Clark, *A History of Australia*, vol. iv (1978), pp. 249, 251–2.

## THE TERRORIST STRIKES

*Prince Alfred's experience in Sydney was the last straw.*
*On 12 March 1868 he was shot.*

Alfred's main engagement after the Hunter trip was to patronise a picnic to raise funds for a sailors' home and it was here that the shooting took place. After lunch in the official marquee the prince strolled out to mingle with the crowd – when a man suddenly drew a revolver and fired into his back. A shocked picnicker grappled with the assailant and deflected a second shot, as it happened, into an unfortunate bystander's foot. 'We heard two faint sharp reports', wrote one who was there, 'and saw smoke. Before *one minute* had passed there was such a scene as I never witnessed.' Alfred fell forward, exclaiming 'Good God, my back is broken,' and hysteria seized the crowd. To cries of 'string him up' gentlemen and ladies fell upon the assassin, tearing his clothes, battering and bruising him. They were prevented from killing him only by the stern determination of the police, sailors from the *Galatea* and the chief justice, Sir Alfred Stephen, who in a wild mêlée rescued the assassin from his would-be lynchers, dragged him to the wharf, flung him on to the steamer *Paterson* and despatched him to Darlinghurst Gaol.

Martin, *Henry Parkes* (1980), p. 135

*The assassination attempt was made by an Irishman named Henry James O'Farrell. According to another account of the event, he was saved from the mob by John Dunmore Lang.*

Lang heard the shooting and saw the smoke from the revolver. He thought at first some boys were amusing themselves by shooting at birds. In a moment, though, when the seriously wounded Prince was carried past Lang to a tent, Lang realised what had happened. The Chief Justice, Sir Alfred Stephen, rushed up. He had had Lang in his court often enough, in various capacities, to know who he was. He now asked him to try to restrain the crowd from lynching O'Farrell on the spot. This unfortunate man was now in the hands of the enraged mob which was ripping his clothes off and almost pulling him limb from limb. Telling the multitude that the prolongation of his life was the likeliest way in which the police could ferret out his accomplices, Lang entreated them to do O'Farrell no violence.

Baker, *Days of Wrath* (1985), p. 358

*Yet another version suggests that the colony's leading men led the lynch mob.*

After lunch Sir William [Manning] asked the Prince if he would be interested to see the display the Aborigines were about to put on for the White man. Before he could reply, a man of fair complexion, whose eyes wore the signs of a man who had suffered much, stole up to within six feet of the Prince, pulled out a revolver, and fired at his back. The Prince had been wounded, but not mortally. The man then tried to shoot William Manning, but missed. Then before he could fire again a Mr Vial pinioned his arm, so that the bullet entered the foot of George Thorne who was carried away by Mr Hassall.

Alexander Stuart, a pillar of the Presbyterian Church, seized a carving knife and attempted to stab the assassin. Alfred Stephen, possibly swayed by the prospect of a field day when he had the assassin in the dock, urged Stuart to let the law take its course, but, somewhat to his surprise, the god-fearing Stuart still declared he wanted to 'rip the scoundrel up'. The president of the Legislative Council gave way to the feeling that the assassin should be taken hold of and strung up on a tree. Respectable lawyers called on the mob to hang the wretch there and then; hysterical voices were heard shouting 'hang him', 'lynch him', 'string him up'. Excited men tore the clothes off the back of the assassin and blackened his eyes and bruised his lips, as women screeched and yelled out, 'Cut him to pieces with scissors.' The police shielded him as best they could and carried him slowly to the wharf where he was put on board the police launch for Circular Quay.

Clark, *A History of Australia*, vol. iv (1978), pp. 254–5

## PARKES STIRS THE POT

*Henry Parkes, then Colonial Secretary of New South Wales, decided there was a chance to exploit the anti-Irish sentiment that followed the assassination attempt.*

Believing there was some political advantage to be gained in the heat of the moment by a whack on the drum of sectarian sentiment, Parkes decided to exploit the hysteria stirred up by the attempted assassination of the Prince and the arrival of Fenian convicts in Western Australia. He wrote to the Chief Secretary of Victoria, James McCulloch, to tell him his government was in possession of information which left no doubt of the fact that the man O'Farrell was one of a band organised for the diabolical purpose of taking the life of the Prince, and that he had accomplices in Victoria and probably in Ireland. A few days later news reached Sydney that sixty Fenians had landed in Perth. Judging the time ripe for a 'man of the hour' to appear as the saviour of the people, seven days after O'Farrell fired at the Prince, Parkes rushed through both houses of parliament, on 19 March 1868, a bill for 'the better suppression and punishment of seditious practices and attempts'. He was supported by Sir William Manning, who still believed that in the eyes of Irish Catholics the end justified the means, and that anything was lawful if it helped to get rid of the oppressor. The *Sydney Morning Herald*, deploring the Irish tendency to look on traitors as patriots, and murderers as martyrs, applauded him for taking steps to protect the government and the nation against the daggers, the brand and the pirates. Parkes was once again 'the man of the hour'. Only the Irish and the Catholics withheld their approval and their affection. The *Freeman's Journal* pointed out that there was no disenchanted party here, that the power of Great Britain was not likely to be undermined by talking nonsense and drinking rum in Sydney. O'Farrell on 20 April denied he had been connected with any person or any organisation. [Roman Catholic Archbishop John Bede] Polding denounced Parkes as a man who had wantonly and wickedly imported enmities and miseries into their public life. By July the only traitors snared in the Parkes net were some drinkers who had amused the lounge lizards of Sydney with comparisons between the life of the Prince and the life of blackfellows.

Clark, *A History of Australia*, vol. iv (1978), p. 259

## An Irish prayer

*The Irish never forgave Parkes.*

The Treason Felony Act of 1868 marked him as the enemy. From the Irish-Australian homes of the Bathurst district flowed such maledictions as this 'Prayer' composed apparently at a time when Parkes was laid low with illness: 'If he's bad today, may he be worse tomorrow; may he be dead, damned and into Hell rammed, and may the hearthstone of Hell be his eternal pillow and that is my prayer for him this blessed and holy day. Amen.' So the wrongs and grievances of the Old World were joined to those of the New.

Crisp, *Ben Chifley* (1963), p. 4

## THE NATIVE SON COMES HOME

*W.C. Wentworth's stature grew over the years. Although he died in England, his body was brought back to Sydney with great pomp and ceremony.*

On 6 May 1873 the first state funeral in the history of the colony was accorded to Wentworth. The government proclaimed a public holiday; shops and business houses closed down for the day; thousands thronged the streets to see or take part in the ceremony. For the memorial service in St Andrew's Cathedral admission was strictly by ticket: only men were admitted. The clergy were there in their gorgeous robes, the consuls of foreign powers, the military and the judges were attired in their brilliant uniforms and colours. After the service the pageant, headed by a sarcophagus of a grandeur of size and design similar to that deemed appropriate for the Duke of Wellington and Burke and Wills, proceeded to Vaucluse. There the police moved the people away from the vault where the sarcophagus was to rest. The clergy, members of the armed services, judges, members of parliament, city councillors, university professors, members of the bar, private gentlemen and volunteer officers heard the bishop recite the prayer of thanks to Almighty God for being pleased to deliver William Charles Wentworth out of the miseries of this sinful world. Then to a Gregorian chant in the minor mode a choir sang a version of Psalm 39, intoning with a wistful melancholy the words 'How vain a thing is man' over the remains of a man who had begun his public life as a Byron of Botany Bay, and ended it with a shy interest in the life of the world to come.

Clark, *A History of Australia*, vol. iv (1978), p. 233

# Alfred Deakin's Teachers

*The Victorian Liberal Alfred Deakin was to be three times prime minister of Australia, but in his younger days held somewhat unusual views.*

In August 1880 Deakin began what he called 'A Spiritual Diary – Personal and Mundane'. In it he recorded, until September 1881, the results of his 'communication with unseen intelligences' through various women mediums in seances. The mediums were worthy but not highly-educated suburban housewives; this, it seemed to him, made their communications the more remarkable, since they contained matter beyond their power to invent. The 'Spiritual Diary' is mainly concerned with prophecies about the political situation in Victoria, his own investments in mining companies, the personal affairs of 'K.S.' (probably his sister) and of one 'E.M.', apparently a friend of his own age. The 'intelligence' who specialised in the discussion of Victorian politics was supposed to be Richard Heales, a former premier who had died in 1864. His was a rather specialised field, and he was perhaps lucky to find a young man who was interested in it. His companions in the other sphere could hardly have been deeply interested in colonial politics; they included Sophocles, John Knox, J.S. Mill, Macaulay and Edmund Burke, who also communicated with Deakin through the mediums. No details of the methods of the seances were recorded – whether, for example, the mediums spoke without prompting or in answer to Deakin's eager questions – and it is impossible to tell whether this nonsense was imposed upon him, or half-suggested by himself. At some later time, against a list of 'Names given by controlling intelligences' which he scored through, he very properly wrote 'Rubbish'. The last record was dated 1 September 1881. On 14 January 1882 he added the sentence: 'Instead of the arrant nonsense with which I have filled the first part of this book I will now try and put the remaining pages to better uses – recording thoughts in place of superstitions.'

La Nauze, *Alfred Deakin* (1965), pp. 61–2

# The Sydney Stoush and Cabbagegardenopolis

*By the 1880s politics had become a power struggle, and the rivalry between Sydney and Melbourne had emerged as a permanent feature.*

In politics men were divided not by principles but by sordid struggles for such spoils of office as salary, patronage and social prestige. In the Legislative Assemblies proceedings were sometimes interrupted by disgraceful brawls as drunken members knocked the stuffing out of each other and kicked each other in what *Table Talk* called a 'most sacred part'. In Sydney one member of the Legislative Assembly suggested the erection, within the vicinity of the house, of a 24–foot ring for the more convenient settlement of 'hon. gentlemen's political differences', so that in future the dignity of the house would not be affronted at the expense of parliamentary crockery. Some members were said to be drunk for weeks on end. Politicians clowned in public about the superiority of free trade over protection, or the superiority of protection over free trade. In 1883 the *Bulletin* sneered at the Victorians' surprise on finding that the government offices in Sydney were 'larger and more luxuriantly appointed than those of "Cabbagegardendopolis"'. In the same year James Service, the premier of Victoria, accused Sydney-siders of being 'dead' on all the great issues of the day. The Sydney-siders replied that they were as far above Victorians as the heavens were above the earth.

Clark, *A History of Australia*, vol. iv (1978), p. 376

# 'We Are a Rabble!'

*The New South Wales Legislative Assembly debate on the tariff bill in 1886 produced some amazing scenes.*

[George] Dibbs, manager of the house and equally adamant that the Bill would go through, had bedding put in the anterooms for the use of government supporters, refused to adjourn and set out to wear the Opposition down. The climax came during a continuous sitting which the Government forced between Thursday 8 July and the early hours of the following Sunday. Disorder on the second night led the chairman of committees to clear the galleries and the Opposition, having incorrectly anticipated an adjournment, decided to treat the sitting as illegal. Chaos followed. One member sat on the table and shouted: 'There is no house' and 'We are a rabble!' Another crowed like a cock and a third threw himself on his back and cried 'Damn the chair!' And when Jennings walked to the table to speak [Henry] Parkes rushed up to him, shook his fist in his face, and exploded: 'You d–d bugger–you fenian–who are you?' The speaker, [Edmund] Barton, called in urgently by a desperate chairman, managed with difficulty to restore order and proceedings continued, until at midnight on Saturday Parkes strode out of the chamber at the head of his followers, throwing on the table a protest at parliament's desecration of the Sabbath! The rump – the triumphant government supporters – then put all clauses through with despatch.

Martin, Henry Parkes (1980), p. 357

## LOOKING FOR A STRAIGHT MAN

*Henry Parkes had some difficulty forming a Free Trade ministry in 1887.*

In asking Thomas Garrett to join the ministry, Parkes felt he must 'speak plainly' about the man's 'infirmity of losing himself at times in drink':

> I said 'Can you in this respect keep straight?' He replied: 'Give me till 10 o'clock tomorrow to think over it and see my wife.' I replied to this: 'Oh, be a man, and make up your mind at once, for the sake of yourself, your family and the country!' He then said with much feeling, 'I will, old man! – By God's help I will! and on your broad Free Trade policy I will fight with you to the death.'
> *But alas, it only lasted 18 months.*

In July 1888 poor Garrett, succumbing after all to his weakness and 'knowing how very much I am to blame', obeyed a request from Parkes to resign.

Martin, *Henry Parkes* (1980), p. 362

## A Real Live Man in London

*Australian politicians were finally preparing to strut the international stage. Alfred Deakin put Australia's views to the Colonial Conference of 1887 and impressed Lord Onslow, the co-president:*

I well remember … the first time that a native born Australian statesman appeared in England. It was at the Colonial Conference of 1887. There were arranged on one side of the table the rulers of England, both past and present, and on the other the representatives of the colonies – 'grave and reverend signiors' – who delivered themselves of many platitudes, in excellent language and well of, with regard to their loyalty to the mother country, and hoping for the success of the colonies. At last it came to the turn of Mr Deakin, the Chief Secretary for Victoria. He struck an entirely different note. He told us at once what Australia thought of England. He said that when he took up the paper he learned that Mr Gladstone had a cold, or Lord Salisbury the gout – but when he took up the Australian [sic] papers in England he could find nothing from Australia except that one man had won a sculling race, or a pugilist had beaten another. He told us how we had given the Islands of the Pacific to the French, and Samoa to the Germans, and he told it with such *bonhomie* that we could not help realising that we had before us a real live man.

Onslow in La Nauze, *Alfred Deakin* (1965), p. 94

# A Knighthood for a Name

*Henry Parkes as Premier of New South Wales and Lord Carrington as Governor were jointly in charge of the 1888 Centenary Celebrations. Parkes saw them as an opportunity to boost New South Wales, but Carrington was able to restrain him.*

[Parkes] almost got off to a bad start at the end of 1887 with a Bill to mark the coming occasion by changing the name of New South Wales to 'Australia'. It was pressed on him by Sir Alfred Stephen and heartily approved by diehard old colonists like Sir John Robertson ('We introduced civilised man', he wrote. 'Also all kind of suitable agricultural products, as well as horses, cattle, sheep and all the livestock of commercial value, before any of our neighbours had existence. If this colony is not Australia I should like to know what colony is'). But the Bill raised the hackles of colonists elsewhere on the continent, provoking a protest to the Colonial Office and a prickly correspondence between Parkes and Gillies, the Premier of Victoria. Lord Knutsford [the Secretary of State for the Colonies] told Carrington that since representatives of the other colonies, in England at the time for the Imperial Conference, were 'vehement in their denunciations', he hoped the proposal would be dropped. On 19 January Carrington seized on Parkes's new knighthood to apply pressure to him: 'Offered Sir Henry Parkes the GCMG', he noted in his diary, 'which he accepted with pleasure promising to send me a letter abandoning the change of name …' True to his word, Parkes wrote that 'Though I could easily have carried the Bill I think it had best be dropped', adding that in fact he personally cared little about the name: it was just that 'the hasty, hectoring spirit in which the other colonies have interfered has set my back up a little, and other people, and very important people too, have the same feeling'.

Martin, *Henry Parkes* (1980), pp. 368–9

# THE CURTAIN GOES UP

*By 1889 Lord Carrington was urging Henry Parkes to proceed with Federation as quickly as possible. In a letter to his daughter Annie, Parkes revealed that he was ready.*

I have very much changed of late in my views of human life and I have my former relish for Parliamentary work. I am trying hard to get into a systematic disposal of my time with a view to employing in the best way whatever portion of life remains to me. I have definitely planned a political history in two octavo volumes under the title of 'Chapters of Autobiography'. I dare say you have heard me speak of it. Also a collection of my Political Writings – Letters, Despatches and a work on Parliamentary Government. I am declining, in response to repeated suggestions and invitations from the other colonies, of offering myself as Leader in a great movement to federate on a solid basis all the Colonies. So you see if a few years of strong life are left I am likely to have work enough.

Earlier on that very day Carrington and Parkes had had, in the words of the former, 'long conversations on Australia', during which, beyond doubt, Parkes's change of direction away from local issues towards Federation crystallised. The Governor had recently entertained a Canadian delegate from the Imperial Federation League, George Parkin, to lunch with [Sir William] McMillan, [Sir George] Reid and Bruce Smith. Carrington did not think much of Parkin's case: 'The idea', he wrote, 'of a huge Council representing England and the colonies, debating whether we are to go to war &c. seems to me absurd.' In discussing this with Parkes he 'remarked how different the position of Lord Knutsford is in Canada to what it is in Australia. "That must be so," was the reply, "until we federate." Sir Henry then said, "I could confederate these colonies in twelve months." "Then why don't you do it?" said I, "it would be a glorious finish to your life." He smiled and said, "There are difficulties."' Next day Parkes wrote confidentially to the Victorian Premier, Duncan Gillies, offering to take 'some prominent or leading step in the cause of Australian federation'. He told

Carrington, though not his ministerial colleagues, at once. 'Events move quickly', the Governor noted in his diary. 'And so the curtain goes up on what may be a very great dramatic performance.'

Martin, *Henry Parkes* (1980), pp. 382–3.

## VERBAL MUD

*Alfred Deakin was never short of a phrase to describe his enemies.*

Alfred Deakin in an article in the *Australasian Critic*, once called 'Ivan' Fairfield, of the *Argus*, 'criticaster, new Münchhausen, erratic Daniel, disguised troubadour, swearer at large, *advocatus diaboli*, rattling propagandist, untrustworthy and incompetent, as incoherent as unfair, pelican in the wilderness'. Alfred always had a pretty turn for verbal mud.

*Bulletin*, 5 August 1893.

## ENTER 'THE LITTLE DIGGER'

*The roaring nineties produced many memorable politicians, but none more colourful than William Morris 'Billy' Hughes (also known as 'the Little Digger'). Hughes was to remain a key figure in Australian politics for more than half a century. His description of the way he was originally preselected for the safe Labor seat of Lang in 1894 is worth quoting at length.*

In due course the night fixed for the selection came round. There was a full house and all the candidates were lined up on the stage. The chairman, a Liverpool Irishman named MacDermott, who in private life was a coal-lumper, solemnly outlined the procedure, which to my ears bore a terrifying likeness to that which greeted the ears of the early Christians as they were being thrown to the lions. Each candidate was to address the meeting for fifteen minutes, and at the close of the speeches a ballot on the preferential system would be taken. The candidates were to speak in alphabetical order. The publican took the floor first. His name began, most appropriately, with a B.

He was greeted with tumultuous cheers, which he had thoroughly earned, for he had kept 'open house' for some weeks past. Encouraged by his reception, he started off in great style, but as he knew rather less than Tutankhamen about the Labour movement he ran out of ammunition in less than five minutes and subsided in a splutter of moist excitement. When the other four floundered in his train, I began to understand why my intrusion had so disturbed. They knew nothing whatever of the Labour platform, whilst I was one of those who had helped to draft it. The five took rather less than half an hour to say all they knew or could think of. I spoke for a full fifteen minutes, which in itself produced a distinct impression. Then came the ballot, which lasted till after midnight. No one had a majority on the first count and efforts to allot the preference votes were frantic but futile. The preferential system was new to my prospective constituents, who were completely baffled by its diabolical subtleties. Motions for a recount were repeatedly moved, and the results, which were entirely inconclusive, were greeted with howls of rage and derision. As a last resort it was decided that only one of the candidates should fall out. Happily I just missed being at the bottom of the poll; I was still in the running, but only just in.

The entertainment ran for three successive nights, feeling rising higher at each performance, which invariably ended in wild confusion. One man fell out each night, but I still kept my place, gathering my strength daily from the supporters of the defeated aspirants – for as each of these took the count, the great bulk of his followers, bitterly resenting their champion's downfall, came over in a body to my standard. When the fateful night fixed for the final ballot came round the odds were only very slightly in favour of my opponent.

An hour or more before the proceedings began the neighbourhood of the Mission Church – which both parties had chosen as a fitting temple for a contest in which, after a desperate struggle, right was to emerge, perhaps bleeding, but certainly triumphant – was a stirring sight. Large and desperately earnest men came hurrying towards it from every point of the compass. Not all were electors, for the news of these historic preliminary ballots had sounded like a trumpet call in the ears of many enthusiastic lovers of liberty in the remoter parts of West Sydney. Every moment the crowd grew in numbers and animation. And because they were not only lovers of liberty, but men who sniffed the promise of battle joyously, they hoped that those who officiated at this historic ballot would not prove themselves dogs in the manger by declaring the aftermath to be a private fight, but would throw the portals wide open and bid all the world join in. Buoyed up by this pious hope, they had raced through their evening meal, leaving about their mouths and on their chins and moustaches traces of eggs and dubious gravies, and suggestions of crumbs. And some of them, fresh from their work on the wharves, had their wool hooks stuck in their belts.

The place was packed at seven o'clock, when MacDermott – his hair cropped close, his great moustache yellow and curved like that of an ancient Viking – took the chair and called the assemblage to order in a voice that could be heard blocks away. There was an air of intense excitement; every man felt in his bones that he was going to have his money's worth – and perhaps something over. Mac's opening remarks were keyed to the right pitch. He said there had been a lot of sparring and scrim-shanking going on. He didn't hold with these preferential votes – no one could make head or tail of them. Anyhow, they'd done with the damn thing now, and when they went out of the hall that night the Lang division would have elected its candidate (deafening applause). Mac went on to say, 'Gentlemen, we're going to have everything fair and above board' – terrific applause. Only electors of the Lang division could vote, and in order to make sure that none others did, Mac looked round and observed in a casual way 'I notice a lot of our friends from the Rocks and Pyrmont here. We're glad to see them, but they can't vote, because' – and here Mac smiled broadly – 'every elector must produce his "electric right".' (Loud, but not extravagantly loud, cheers.) 'Each candidate', Mac went on, 'has the right to appoint two scrutineers.' This seemed to me quite inadequate, but making the best of a bad job I chose the two biggest of my supporters. I noted with some satisfaction that they both carried wool hooks. If I went down I felt reasonably sure that I should not be unavenged.

And then the votings began. I shall not forget that night in a hurry. I have never found life dull; I like life, bustle, movement, and I thrive on excitement; but, after all, one can have too much of a good thing. From the word go the electors of the Lang division made it willing – they poured into the little Mission Church like flood waters rushing down a mountain gorge. They wanted not the spur of compulsory voting. The trouble was not to get them to vote, but to induce them to leave off. They were so desperately in earnest that it was only by unwearying vigilance backed by *force majeure* that they were prevented from voting again and again. They would go out, refresh themselves with beer, rearrange their hats, turn up the collars of their coats, and jauntily re-enter and once more endeavour to record their vote. Baulked in one direction they tried another. Since they could not vote twice on the same 'electric right' – or vote at all unless they had one – they immediately set out in search of loose or unattended rights. Some sneaked furtively into their homes and lifted the old man's right while he was at tea. The tedium of those stretched in beds of sickness was relieved by numerous callers, who, oozing sympathy at every pore, sought to coax from the invalid 'the loan of your electric right'. And many a man dead these six months and more put in his little vote that night through the hand of one who had not forgotten him, or where his elector's right was to be found.

At nine o'clock MacDermott announced in thunderous tones that the ballot had closed, and that the result would be declared as soon as possible. The narrow street was crowded, an air of suppressed excitement prevailed. I waited near the door, trying to give a lifelike imitation of a man serenely confident of victory. I indulged in airy persiflage with some of my friends who had come down to the war zone to see how things were going. What we talked about I do not know. Words just dropped out of my mouth mechanically. I was waiting for the verdict, straining my ears to catch the first murmurs that meant that the numbers were up. But, for what seemed to me an eternity, an ominous silence remained unbroken. Then, suddenly, the end came! The crowd, which had been unnaturally quiet, sprang into life. A roar burst upon my ears. 'What is it?' I asked. 'Run for your life,' said one of my friends, 'you have been selected.'

There was something about his words, and particularly about the way he said them, that spurred me to instant action. While the words still hung upon the air I was racing across Kent Street, then up Bathurst Street I tore at full speed, and, turning into Clarence Street, came in less than thirty seconds to the police station, unto which I rushed as if pursued by Chicago gunmen.

'Hullo!' said the sergeant, who had been peacefully reading the evening paper, 'What's the matter?'

'There's trouble, sergeant, down in the Mission Church,' I said breathlessly.

'Trouble?' repeated the sergeant, eyeing me curiously. 'What sort of trouble?'

This was some question because when one looked at the thing calmly, I was the trouble. But as it was of no use trying to go into a long, laboured explanation, I said shortly, 'They're fighting.'

'Fighting, are they?' said the sergeant. 'All right, I'll send a man down.'

'One man's no good, sergeant,' I said.

'Oh,' said the sergeant, 'it's that kind of a fight, is it?'

'It is,' I replied earnestly.

'Very well! I'll send down a couple of men.'

'Thank you!' I said, and then raced back to the hall again without loss of a moment.

As I entered a mighty roar shook the building, which again reminded me of the hungry lions impatiently awaiting the arrival of another Christian. Somehow I managed to fight my way to the pulpit around which a knot of my staunchest supporters were gathered. One of these, Ringer Byrnes, summed up the situation in a nutshell, 'They've got the numbers,' he whispered hoarsely, 'but we've sent out scouts, and our mob'll be here in a few minutes.' I quite understood, and with an injunction to Ringer not to let them get me from the side – the hall was shaped like an L – I stepped into the pulpit and turned to face the crowd, which howled savagely, and seemed on the point of rushing the pulpit in order to tear me limb from limb. As far as I could judge, we were outnumbered by at least two to one. Things looked very ugly. Our only chance was to stall off an immediate rush in order to give our reinforcements time to get up.

Taking advantage of a momentary lull, I held up my hand. 'Gentlemen,' said I, in my best Chesterfieldian manner. I got no further. To be defeated when they had counted so confidently on victory was bad enough, but to be addressed in this fashion was not to be borne. They gibbered with fury; they covered me with abuse. My band of supporters gathered more closely around; those who had wool hooks grasped them firmly. As for me, my eyes never left the doorway, through which the reinforcements were trickling in. I noted with satisfaction that the two constables had arrived. Pandemonium reigned for some minutes. Again and again I attempted to speak, but in vain. Every time I opened my mouth the crowd howled with fury. I stood there, apparently impassive, but with my eyes glued on the doorway through which a steady stream of men was coming. At this rate the tables would soon be turned. The back of the hall was now densely packed with my supporters.

At last, Ringer leaned over to me and shouted, 'We've got 'em', and surging forward, closely followed by his band, he made his way towards the most turbulent of the crowd, shouting madly, 'Three cheers for Billy Hughes!' And that was the end of the famous ballot for the Lang division, which had lasted for many nights, and at length resulted in this glorious triumph for the cause of right.

All this happened many years ago, but once bit twice shy. One such ballot was more than enough for me, and from that day to this I have never had another.

Hughes, *Crusts and Crusades* (1947), pp. 112 ff

## A Squatter's Coat Of Arms

*Billy Hughes told many stories about his early days in Parliament in the 1890s and his colleagues there. This one illustrates the hostility that still existed between the squatters and the free selectors.*

New England, as became its name and economic circumstances, had chosen for its member Mr G.A. Cruickshank, a typical representative of what was then referred to by the *hoi polloi* as the 'squattocracy'. In dress, demeanour, speech and outlook on life, he was a *de luxe* edition of the pastoral oligarchy of his day. Had Fate called him to play his part in the halcyon aftermath of the Norman Conquest, he would have made an ideal feudal baron; as it was, his coming was delayed so that he was destined to tread the first steps of the squatters' decline from greatness.

Through the mists of the years I can see him as he stood in his place in the back row of the horseshoe bend, a fine figure of a man, speaking with a clipped Oxford accent, forcefully, but with studied restraint, of the deplorable effects of the policy which cloaked its nefarious purpose under the resounding name of 'closer settlement'. It was a good speech, but a still better one was to follow. John Haynes, the man who made it, had been for many years a notable figure in the public life of the State. A master of incisive speech, he was one of the wittiest men I have known. If the member for New England was the typical squatter, John Haynes was the ideal spokesman of the free selector. As he was a man that laid about him with a will, the good news that 'Haynes was up' ensured a full House. He began, as was his wont, very quietly. He paid the member for New England many compliments, eulogising the matter and the manner of his speech, and then, having cleared the way for an effective thrust in tierce, he paused, and, turning towards the Chair, said:

'But, Mr Speaker, the honourable member did not do himself justice. The honourable member did not tell the House that he is entitled to a coat of arms. A coat of arms, Mr Speaker.' Members wriggled in ecstasy; everyone felt in his bones that something really worthwhile was coming. They were not disappointed. 'A coat of arms, Mr Speaker,' repeated John, looking around a House hanging on his words.

'What is his coat of arms?' shouted Mr W.P. Gick. 'Does the honourable member know?'

'Yes, Mr Speaker,' said John, 'I will tell the honourable member. The coat of arms of the honourable member for New England is a branding iron and a moonless night.'

Hughes, *Policies and Potentates*, (1950), pp. 8–9

# Wully Meets Phylloxera

*John Haynes figured in another of Billy Hughes's many stories. This time his victim was a parliamentarian named William 'Wully' Affleck.*

Wully Affleck, whose speech was marked with a heavy Scottish accent, entered Parliament in late middle life, and in affairs political was as unsophisticated as Alice in Wonderland. The forms of the House, the range of matters discussed and the speeches delivered were to him a never-failing source of wonder. He approached every subject before the House with the zest of unspoilt youth. To watch him listening with rapt attention to [James] Gormly who, although born and bred in Australia, spoke with a most pronounced Irish brogue, was an entertainment that made the highest flights of the Tivoli sound like a penny whistle. When Gormly was telling the House that 'Lake Cargellico was one of the foinest lakes in the country, Mr Sphaker, barring the want of a dhrop of wahter', Wully looked around with a strained expression on his face, and as his fellow members roared with laughter, shook his head and sank back in his place, utterly unable to understand what it was all about.

At that time the *phylloxera vastatrix*, that terrible little green fly, was getting in some dirty work among the vines in the grape-growing districts of the State, and the Government had introduced a Bill to eradicate the pest. Wully was keenly interested in this measure, for although grape-growing was not one of the staple industries of his electorate, as a country member he took a keen interest in the matter. When in due course he rose to speak he said that he was wholeheartedly in favour of the Bill; he had heard a great deal about the ravages of the *phylloxera*, although he admitted that he 'had never seen one'.

At this admission, John Haynes, who had been told of Wully's intention to speak and had prepared an 'exhibit' which he hoped would prove to be of service to neophytes, said, 'What! the honourable member has never seen a *phylloxera!*'

'No,' replied Wully, looking hopefully towards him.

'Very well,' said John, whipping out his exhibit – a full-grown Sydney prawn, neatly pasted on a strip of cardboard, with the legend *Phylloxera vastatrix* in large letters beneath it – 'There it is.'

Wully took the exhibit, stared at it in astonishment, and after wiping his glasses carefully again examined it attentively; then, handing it back, he said in an awed voice, 'Well, Mr Speaker, I can well understand that such a fearful beastie would do great damage to the vines.'

Hughes, *Policies and Potentates* (1950), pp. 12–13

## Let Them Eat Flour

*Another prominent politician of the 1890s was George Reid, Premier of New South Wales and later prime minister of Australia. Jack Lang, later to achieve political fame in his own right, described Reid's style on the hustings.*

Reid, who had a very portly figure, measuring as much around the girth as he was tall, was a favourite butt of the cartoonists of the day. *The Bulletin* invariably depicted him as a buffoon in cap and bells. He was an adept at repartee and his meetings attracted huge crowds as he was a good public speaker. He was good-tempered and didn't mind a joke against himself provided he could get in the last word, which was invariably effective. For example, addressing a meeting shortly after he became Prime Minister, someone in the crowd threw at him a bag of flour, which spread right across his waistcoat. Reid simply dismissed the incident by turning to the crowd saying, 'When I was elected to lead a government in this State, people could not afford flour with which to make bread. Now they can afford to throw it away, all over me.'

Lang, *The Turbulent Years* (1970), p. 15

## A Wake-Up Call

*George Reid was no respecter of rank.*

His obesity no doubt contributed to his disturbing tendency to fall asleep at any time or place. In his memoirs he observes that, at a banquet during the 1897 Imperial Conference, finding himself seated between the Prince of Wales and the Archbishop of Canterbury, he was compelled to ask the latter to make certain that he stayed awake, a request which the Archbishop thought had never been made to any occupant of the See of Canterbury before.

Hughes, Mr Prime Minister (1976), p. 38

## An Each-Way Bet

*Reid's views on Federation were, to put it mildly, confusing.*

At the close of the convention Reid had returned home and agreed to speak on Federation at a meeting in the Sydney Town Hall. It was destined to be a speech that made him famous for all time. He started off by saying that he proposed to address himself to the problem as if he was a judge summing up for the benefit of a jury. Then he carefully enunciated the arguments in favour of Federation. Then he switched sides and just as carefully set out the case in opposition. In all, he spoke for two hours and when he had concluded, his audience was completely in the dark as to whether he was for or against the proposition. From that time on he became known as 'Yes-No Reid'.

Lang, The Turbulent Years (1910), p. 23

## Votes for Whom?

*As Federation approached, the women's suffrage movement, led in Victoria by Vida Goldstein, campaigned more vigorously for the vote. One of its most outspoken opponents was the Chief Justice of Victoria, Sir John Madden.*

He had declared in 1895 that women's suffrage would abolish soldiers, war, racing, hunting, football, cricket and all manly games. Sir John based his stand on the Bible: 'Thy desire shall be to thy husband, and he shall rule over thee.' He spoke of the women's movement as a threat to conventional morality. 'Women suffragists', he believed, 'are the worst class of socialists. Their idea of freedom is polyandry, free love, lease marriages, and so on. Are those qualifications for the franchise? Are we going to allow women who would sap the very foundation of the nation to have votes?' The *Australian Woman's Sphere* replied with a list of the men who were not disqualified from voting: effeminate fops, drunkards, larrikins, drunken savages, opium-smoking Chinese, prize fighters, 'Fat Man' politicians and wife kickers.

Clark, *A History of Australia*, vol. V (1981), p. 192

## Talks Like a Book

*Meanwhile the Federation movement, after stalling briefly, was gathering pace again with public meetings around the country.*

Early in 1896 the President of the Australian Natives Association, James Hume Cook, arrived in Charters Towers, Queensland, to preach the gospel of Federation. The chairman of a meeting to promote Federation, a Northerner, and as such suspicious of southern 'swells', especially educated gents such as Hume Cook from 'Smellbourne', opened proceedings with these remarks: 'Well! Boys! They're 'ere! Bein' strangers – we've got to give 'em a fair 'earin'. Anyone as don't like wot they've t'say can leave; and anyone as kicks up a row I'll 'andle meself.' When Hume Cook rose to speak a giant of a man jumped up and said: 'There 'e is boys! not much to look at! But by Christ 'e can talk!' Concluding that he was making quite a good impression Hume Cook decided to splash the colour about, to indulge in those purple passages beloved of Melbourne liberals. He was encouraged by the remark of an interjector: 'That's right! Give them some fireworks.' So Hume Cook concluded by declaring that the federation of Australian colonies would send 'the fiery Cross of Union from the Gulf of Carpentaria to the Great Australian Bight, and from Melbourne clear across to Perth'. This delighted his audience. The man with the big voice was quite overcome and shouted to the audience: 'What'd I tell yer?

Ain't 'e a beauty? Talks like a book! Hey! You fellers, I noo'm in Brunswick; and the drinks is on me w'en the meetin's over!'

Not long afterwards down in Hobart at the southern extremity of the Australian colonies, another barracker for Federation was assuring the locals:

> Gentlemen, if you vote for the Bill you will found a great and glorious nation under the bright Southern Cross, and meat will be cheaper; and you will live to see the Australian race dominate the Southern seas, and you will have a market for both potatoes and apples; and your sons shall reap the grand heritage of nationhood ...

Clark, A History of Australia, vol. V (1981), p. 129

## MY PARTY, RIGHT OR WRONG

*By the end of the nineteenth century the party system was becoming established in Australian politics, to the annoyance of many idealists. Ada Holman, wife of the New South Wales Premier, described her own disillusionment.*

If ever oratory could convince it should have done so by the most stirring speech surely ever made in the Parliaments of New South Wales. Mr W.M. Hughes spoke against Australia sending a contingent to fight against the Boers. W.A. Holman was admittedly a finer orator than W.M. (his senior in the House and in politics) but he himself always declared that Hughes's speech on this occasion was unsurpassable. 'It reached the heights of the sublime,' was my husband's verdict. 'Not Burke, nor Grattan, nor Gladstone, nor O'Connell, nor any of the magicians of the spoken word ever got near its magnificence.'

I sat in the Speaker's gallery throughout that night and heard the three-hour speech. It was nearly midnight when Hughes got a hearing, but time stood still while the magic words came pouring out from seemingly inexhaustible depths. The speaker was by times passionate, by times logical, presenting the situation of the heroic Boers with irresistible force, by times sparkingly witty, tearing the racketeers to bits with biting rancour, scathingly cutting up their 'patriotism' which evinced itself by crushing a small nation to death for the possession of its gold.

'He's got them now, he's got them!' I reflected, as cheer after cheer went up from the throats of opponents, as tears ran down hardened cheeks, as breathless silence followed every syllable.

'How right he is,' said a bitter antagonist of Hughes to me. 'How unanswerably right!'

When the division was taken about 3am, Hughes had secured seven votes in a House crowded to capacity. So much for oratory, so much for the right, when party is at stake.

Holman, *Memoirs of a Premier's Wife* (1948), p. 11

## THE FEDERATION WALTZ

*The final details of Federation were wrapped up in London in May 1900, when the Colonial Office approved the draft constitution. Alfred Deakin led the Australian delegation which negotiated the last sticking point, the method of appeal to the Privy Council.*

It was now restored to Australian jurisdiction. 'This is all we want and if we get this we shall secure a great victory,' Deakin told [Sir Charles] Dilke. On 17 May the details were settled with [Colonial Secretary Joseph] Chamberlain and Finlay, the Attorney-General. 'Splendid' was the entry in Deakin's diary, an entry expanded a few months later into a description of the curious scene that followed: 'when the door closed upon [the Australians] and left them alone, they seized each other's hands and danced hand in hand in a ring around the centre of the room to express their jubilation'.

La Nauze, *Alfred Deakin* (1965), p. 190

# A Final Error

*On the eve of Federation the Governor-General, Lord Hopetoun, ignored local advice to appoint Edmund Barton as the first prime minister, and instead sent for the senior premier, Sir William Lyne of New South Wales. It was a major error.*

The story of the Hopetoun blunder is well known. Barton was the first man invited by Lyne to join his Ministry, and the first to refuse. After [Frederick] Holder of South Australia and [George] Turner of Victoria had publicly rejected their invitations and indicated that Deakin would probably take the same view, Lyne's prospects were hopeless. The commission he received on 19 December 1900 was returned on Christmas Eve and given the same day to Barton who within twenty-four hours was able to tell the Governor-General that he had a Ministry.

Hughes, Mr Prime Minister (1976), p. 18

# A Far-Flung Election

*The first federal election in 1901 was a long and complicated process, as Alfred Deakin reported anonymously for the* London Morning Post.

The fact that, though all the elections closed on March 30, the Western Australian declaration of the poll has only just taken place, we in New South Wales are still waiting for the ballot papers from a remote hamlet called Five-Day Creek, and that the official [result] of the Queensland poll, even with the aid of railways and the telegraph, may not be officially ascertained six weeks later is in itself worthy of note. It may help to convey to the minds of Englishmen some sense of the enormous areas and distances which make the problems of government in Australia so much more complicated than they appear to Londoners, who approach them with all the preconceptions which are necessarily misconceptions begotten of old-world experience in a small, compact, and thickly-settled country. Another striking circumstance of the late election is the number of ballot papers rendered ineffective by the multitude of candidates to the Senate. In New South Wales nearly forty thousand votes were wasted in the attempt to strike out exactly forty-four names from a list of fifty so as to leave six, and six only, unerased. Many other incidents equally unsuspected by critics beyond our borders will require to be allowed for by them if they desire to do justice to our public men. The standards set up for them must differ from those of Westminster, because the conditions, often entirely different, are always ruder and cruder. There must be boundless opportunities for blundering somewhere in the endeavour to deal with so vast a territory lightly sprinkled with population along its interminable coastline. No capital wherever situated can keep in touch with more than a fraction of its dominion, and must be so remote from the rest as to permit the presence of but a few qualified representatives from its outlying regions. Yet its Government and legislature must needs speak, act, and provide for the whole. Truly the Commonwealth, like an infant Hercules, will need to fight even from its cradle.

Deakin, *Federated Australia* (1968), pp. 52–3

## THE FIRST PARLIAMENT

*Although lawyers predictably had the largest presence in the first Federal Parliament in 1901, there was a fair spread of occupations, as the following analysis shows.*

Lawyers predominate in both houses of the Federal Parliament. There are eleven legal gentlemen in the Senate (seven barristers and four solicitors), and fifteen in the House of Representatives. The total number of lawyers in the two houses is therefore, twenty-six, rather less than one fourth of the aggregate of one hundred and eleven members. In the New South Wales Assembly there are fourteen lawyers, or about one ninth of the total number of members. In the British House of Commons of six hundred and sixty-nine members, there are one hundred and forty lawyers. The avocations of the Senators are: barristers, seven; solicitors, four; merchants and commercial life, six; journalists, three; miners, three; pastoralists, two; contractors, two; banker, one; tin-worker, one; surveyor, one; ship's fireman, one; market gardener, one; wharf labourer, one; labourer, one; property-owner, one; carpenter, one. In the House of Representatives there is an even greater variety of occupations, for there we find – barristers, twelve; solicitors, three; merchants and commercial life (including agents, accountants, etc.), eleven; pastoralists and graziers, seven; miners, five; auctioneers and land and estate agents, four; journalists, four; farmers, three; surveyors, three; shipowner and shipping manager, two; hotel-keepers, two; mining speculators and mine owners, two; storekeepers, two; labourer, one; sharebroker, one; umbrella-maker one; compositor, one; legal manager, one; doctor of medicine, one; hatter, one; watchmaker, one; shearer, one; general agent, one; property owner, one; minister of religion, one; wharf labourer, one; ship engineer, one; retired civil servant, one. There will, unless members are designated in correct parliamentary fashion, by the names of the constituencies they represent, or by initials, be some confusion, as several sets of members bear the same surnames. Thus there are two Smiths in the House of Representatives, and one in the Senate. There are two McLeans, both in the House of Representatives. There is one Cooke, and there are two Cooks, all in the House of Representatives. Two Grooms sit in the same House, also two Edwards. There are two Ewings, one in the Senate and one in the House of Representatives; two Camerons, one in each House; and in the House of Representatives there is a Solomon and also a Solomons. The surnames of several members likewise stand for what, in the school days of the present generation, used to be called 'common objects of the country'. Thus, there is a Fysh, a Salmon, a Page, a Forrest, a Fisher, a Fowler, a Drake, a Turner, Cooks, Grooms, a Holder, a Chanter, a Fuller, a Baker, a Walker, Sawers, a Lyne, a Reid (and a strong one, too), and a Harper; while adjectives are represented by a Best, a Brown, and a Quick. Happily, also, Zeal (though he is on the wrong side fiscally) is not absent from the parliamentary galaxy.

*Braidwood and Araluen Express*, 19 April 1901.

# A Flag of Our Own

*One of the early acts of the Australian government was to search for an Australian flag. The competition produced some bizarre entries.*

The Government decided that a new nation required a new symbol, and in September 1901 the 30,000 entries in the national flag competition were displayed in the Exhibition Building, Melbourne. Described by one observer as 'a monotonous Study in Jacks, an all-pervading symphony in ensigns, with variants of stars, bars or stripes' (*Bulletin*, 14 September 1901), the show resulted from the offer of £200 for the best design for a new national flag. Five entries subsequently shared the prize, whilst two others shared the prize for a national Seal. The exhibition revealed some ingenuity among the competitors – one incorporated the Union Jack on the bottom of a corrugated iron tank, another a kangaroo shooting at the Southern Cross and another the Jack draped in leg-irons. One competitor had a couple of emus galloping towards the North Pole; one had six index fingers pointing towards a seated Britannia; and one a six-tailed kangaroo. The great majority of the entries included the Union Jack and the Southern Cross. The final version contained: 1. The Union Jack on a blue or red ground. 2. A six-pointed star, representing the six federated states of Australia, immediately underneath the Union Jack, and pointing direct to the centre of the St George's Cross, of a size to occupy the major portion of one quarter of the flag. The Southern Cross in the 'fly', as indicative of the sentiment of the Australian nation.

Crowley, *Modern Australia in Documents*, vol. i (1973), pp. 18–19

## Uneasy Truces

*The first few years of Federation saw a series of minority governments and loose alliances between the Free Traders, the Protectionists and the Labor Party. George Reid, leader of the Free Traders, found the constant switching of partners amusing.*

The then Deakin administration [1903–4] having been defeated, or having resigned, a ministry came in which represented a party to which the honourable and learned Member for Ballarat [Deakin] had up to that time made no pointed reference, except to compare it to one of three cricket elevens. But the moment that an administration was formed by my honourable friend the Member for Bland [Watson, Labor] a new set of things was created. The honourable and learned Member for Ballarat, on the basis of a fiscal truce which had been decreed by the people, rushed into my arms, and suddenly developed a very pointed spirit of antagonism to his former allies. He found that the voters who had returned them were pawns, that the members who were returned were dummies, and that the ministers of that party were figureheads. He also discovered that their methods of organisation outside, and their methods inside, were such as were subversive of the true principles of parliamentary government. I cordially agreed with him in that view.

Reid in Crisp, Federation Fathers (1990), p. 401

## To the Death

*Reid also recalled the clashes between the South Australian radical Charles Kingston and the Western Australian conservative Sir John Forrest.*

The two fought tooth and nail in Cabinet; now they have renewed the deathgrip outside ... Both the combatants abandon science and go in for rough and tumble methods ... Mr Kingston almost chokes with rage when his fiercest denunciations only provoke laughter ... Mr Kingston is splenetic, ferocious at times, and always finds forcible language in which to clothe his thoughts – but he is weary and wasting ... Sir John is vigorous, crammed full of vitality, just as hard a hitter, but he can last. The contrast between the two is very marked – the South Australian, white, stuttering, hurling out epithets and innuendos with the ear-splitting shriek of a shell; the Western Australian red-faced, fluent, strident, raspy, replying with the nerve-destroying crack of a Maxim.

Reid in Crisp, *Federation Fathers* (1990), p. 363

## AFFABLE ALFRED AND PUFFING BILLY

*Alfred Deakin, leader of the Victorian Protectionists, and Billy Hughes, then a Labor militant, clashed repeatedly. Edward Beeby, a journalist, recalled one of Hughes's most effective moments.*

He was a brilliant debater, brilliant in repartee. And one of his best retorts was given in the first Commonwealth Parliament [in 1903]. Hughes, as a Labor member, was making a most ferocious attack on some of Deakin's policies, and one statement brought Deakin to his feet with the cry, 'I deny it! I deny it! I deny it!' There was dead silence in the House. Hughes stood in his place with his hand to his ear, and the silence lasted so long that the Speaker asked whether the Honourable Member had finished his remarks. Then Hughes looked round at the House and looked at the Speaker and said, 'Oh no, Mr Speaker, I was just waiting for the cock to crow.'

Thompson and Counihan (eds), *On Lips of Living Men* (1962), pp. 82–3

*But after Hughes spoke in Deakin's own electorate of Ballarat, Deakin hit back.*

At the end of a speech defending his conduct in general terms, he referred, suddenly, to the attack so recently made upon him in the city in which he was now speaking: 'And as for the gentleman in the Academy [at Ballarat] who devoted so much time to me and my works, I do not propose to reply to him except by saying he presents to you as undignified a spectacle as does the ill-bred urchin whom one sees dragged from a tart-shop kicking and screaming as he goes.' It was so unlike Affable Alfred that the delighted reporters looked up in astonishment.

La Nauze, *Alfred Deakin* (1965), p. 378

## Encouraging Labor

*Henry Bournes Higgins, later famous as President of the Commonwealth Conciliation and Arbitration Court, was a liberal colleague of Deakin. But he was prepared to go where he was needed.*

When Labor leader Watson was forming the first federal Labor Cabinet [in 1904], it was natural, then, that given his party's lack of an experienced lawyer he should ask Higgins to be Attorney-General. Higgins accepted, believing, as he told Deakin, that 'the poor fellows need encouragement'. As Attorney-General he maintained a low profile, which provoked some criticism; but he was angered by the tactics used to expel the shortlived Labor Government. 'We came into office without cadging,' he said, 'and we shall go out without cringing.'

Rickard in Kramer et al. (eds), *The Greats* (1986), p. 123

## A Matter for Trembling

*In 1908 one issue for the Labor government was the establishment of a Commonwealth Bank. The flamboyant American expatriate King O'Malley felt strongly about it.*

'Its importance', he said, 'is so overpowering that I tremble. Hope sees a star and listening love hears the rustle of a wing.'

Ellis in Kramer et al. (eds) *The Greats* (1986), p. 142

## Stuffing the Boxes

*King O'Malley's campaign for the Commonwealth Bank was opposed by Billy Hughes, who was not the most scrupulous of politicians. Labor activist Dorothy Catts recalled one of Hughes's tricks that misfired.*

[Hughes] never managed to get along with King O'Malley, and one of the things they disagreed about was the establishment of the Commonwealth Bank. King fought for several years to get a majority in caucus to bring his Bank policy before caucus, to have it put on the fighting platform of the Labor Party. The first thing he had to do was to put a notice of motion in the leader's box, because all business to be dealt with had to be put as a notice of motion in the box. King got the notice of motion ready and he handed it to his office boy. 'There you are, lad,' he said, 'put that in the leader's box.' But when the boy came out into the passageway, Billy Hughes had been watching and he came out and said to the boy, 'Here you are, lad, give me that, I'll put it in. I'm going to put something else in.' So the boy handed the piece of paper over and went back into the office. He didn't say anything about it. But King was dismayed when the caucus commenced, to find that his notice of motion about a Commonwealth Bank was not on the agenda paper. So he raised the question, but he was told, 'Oh no! There is no notice of motion about the Bank.'

At the dinner adjournment King went back to his home in Albert Park in Melbourne, and he and a few of his colleagues put their heads together to see how they could outwit Hughes. King decided to antedate another notice of motion to the date of the original one, and then, as he was going into the caucus room, he slipped it into the box. When he got into the room he stood up and said, 'Mr Chairman, I'm very concerned about that notice of motion because I've made inquiries and I find my office boy handed it to you, Mr Hughes, and you put it in the box yourself, so it must have been in the box, since you put it there. I suggest that we open the box again and make sure that it isn't stuck in the box.' So of course, Billy Hughes couldn't say anything about that, except agree to it. They opened the box and the notice of motion was in it, and it got before caucus, and with a majority of one it was put on the fighting platform, and the Commonwealth Bank was founded. King and Billy Hughes often clashed and Billy would come up to be friendly with King, wanting a bit of the jollity that King always had around him, but King would just be civil and say 'Good day, brother,' but he wouldn't talk to him at all. But when Billy Hughes died twelve months before King, the newspaper reporters went to King and said 'Well, Mr O'Malley, we see your old arch-enemy is dead. Have you any comment to make?' And King shook his head and he said 'Brothers, this is one occasion when there's no comment.' He wouldn't speak ill of the dead.

Thompson and Counihan (eds), *On Lips of Living Men* (1962), pp. 84–5

## A Bitter Fusion

*In 1909 Deakin's Protectionists formally withdrew their support from the minority Labor government and went into what was called a 'fusion' with the Free Traders. It was not a course favoured by all Deakin's colleagues, especially Sir William Lyne.*

When the House met on the afternoon of 27 May there were a few brief questions, briefly answered. He arose to address the Speaker. As the ill-assorted ranks behind him applauded, the bowed figure of Lyne in the Corner straightened itself. 'Judas! Judas! Judas!' he roared. And again, in the sudden silence, 'Judas! Judas! Judas!' The cries of 'Order' momentarily drowned the voice of the Speaker; then he was heard demanding a withdrawal. Lyne muttered ungraciously while Deakin stood faintly smiling; but again and again he burst into furious interjection.

*Billy Hughes did not let the opportunity to get at Deakin pass. Next day he told the House:*

Last night the honorable member abandoned the finer resources of political assassination and resorted to the bludgeon of the cannibal. Having perhaps exhausted all the finer possibilities of the art, or desiring to exhibit his versatility in his execrable profession he came out and bludgeoned us in the open light of day. It was then that I heard from this side of the House some mention of Judas. I do not agree with that; it is not fair – to Judas, for whom there is this to be said, that he did not gag the man whom he betrayed, nor did he fail to hang himself afterwards.

La Nauze, *Alfred Deakin* (1965), pp. 566, 568–569

## Death in Fusion

*After fusion the political gloves came off.*
*There were unforeseen consequences.*

The standard of debate in the Commonwealth Parliament fell to a low level after the fusion had been completed. The political atmosphere in the House of Representatives was electric as members threatened vengeance against their opponents and 'fights with the gloves off'. The Prime Minister was to be 'hunted to his political death'. Ministers were 'to have no peace' or 'to be shown no quarter'. It was to be 'a war to the knife', with 'a stiletto finish'. Shouts of 'Judas' echoed across the chamber as members engaged in postmortems on 'the Great Betrayal'. Much that was said never reached the ears of the reporters, let alone the pages of *Hansard*. And at the end of a lengthy all-night session the Speaker of the House, Sir Frederick Holder, fell prone from his chair muttering 'Dreadful! Dreadful!' He was dead before breakfast.

Crowley, *Modern Australia in Documents*, vol. i (1973), p. 140

## Pluck versus Brains

*Despite his three terms as prime minister and his ability to align himself with any faction that suited his purpose, Deakin often exasperated his colleagues. The bluff former explorer Sir John Forrest was an admirer with reservations.*

For all his urging, it had never been assumed by Forrest that in any Government that might replace Labor the leader would be anyone but Deakin. He might be tried, to a point of exasperation dangerous to a large man of sixty-one, by the scruples, hesitations and lack of backbone of his former chief. He might say with feeling, 'What a pity Deakin has not got some of my pluck and that I have not got some of his spare brains, we would both be very much better men.' But he knew that Deakin was in a different class. Though he had left him on a matter of principle, he did not suppose for a moment that if they came together again there would be any question about who would lead.

La Nauze, *Alfred Deakin* (1965), p. 543.

## Hideous Disclosures Hidden

*Deakin never wrote his memoirs. Like many politicians, he preferred to hint rather than reveal, as a note written in 1913 shows.*

During my thirty years in politics I have often been amused by the permanent difference — not seldom the amazing difference between the newspaper stories of the 'why', the 'how', and the 'by whom' and the facts as I have known them at first hand. I have occasionally thought of putting my testimony on record and it was one of the first projects that suggested itself in my final resignation. I have a great many valuable materials and had a very trustworthy memory so that I felt exceptionally equipped for the task. Further reflection modifies my intent and if I write anything at all it will be either merely illustrative or pithed of all really personal matters. Some of the disclosures I should have to make would be scorching, some of them hideous — not that politicians as a whole or the people with whom they associated were exceptionally untrustworthy, corrupt or salacious — so far as I have seen while practising at the Bar and in general society the same shames and horrors occasionally occur though they are usually cloaked out of recognition. But much has been missed as to some of the most prominent politicians in this State and in the Commonwealth while the true grounds for Cabinet actions and dissensions have been displaced by inventions and falsehoods. One ought not to pick exposures or become exposed when the witnesses are dead. After all the silence that sometimes follows a storm suggests that since the whole truth about all cannot be written the references to the shady past should be omitted in detail and even in the exceptional instances treated as ashes to ashes.

La Nauze, *Alfred Deakin* (1965), pp. 629–30.

## THE NAMING OF CANBERRA

*After years of acrimonious debate about the site of the national capital, Canberra was finally selected. There was, however, still controversy about the name.*

On Wednesday, 12 March 1913, a large number of politicians and official guests gathered on the slopes of Capitol Hill to witness the Governor-General, Lord Denman, lay the foundation stone of a federal capital column. Shortly afterwards, those present joined in the singing of the hymn 'All people that on earth do dwell' and Lady Denman then said 'I name this capital of Australia Canberra.' A great shout went up. The residents of the territory were delighted that the original name of the place had been retained and that the capital had not been given some unpopular or ridiculous name: the Minister of Home Affairs, Mr King O'Malley, wanted it called Shakespeare, and one of many hundreds of other suggestions was Sydmeladlperbriho. The occasion called for numerous patriotic speeches. The Prime Minister, Mr Andrew Fisher, hoped to see Canberra become the seat of learning and the arts, as well as of politics. The Governor-General pointed out that the choice of the site had been a necessary compromise, but that compromise was the essence of British self-government, and, furthermore, that the people should not cavil at the expense of creating another city because Sydney and Melbourne were already overcrowded. King O'Malley took the opportunity to declare his belief that God had commanded the English-speaking peoples to secure the control of and constitutionally govern the earth in the interests of civilisation, whilst Mr W.M. Hughes, the Attorney-General, pointed out that Canberra was the visible sign of a continent – 'The people are incapable of nourishing abstract ideals. They must have a symbol.' He also noticed that there was no trace at the ceremony 'of that race we have banished from the face of the earth'.

Crowley, Modern Australia in Documents, vol. i (1973), p. 194

## AN APOLOGETIC PRIME MINISTER

*Sir Joseph Cook was no match for Billy Hughes, according to that later master parliamentary tactician Fred Daly.*

Sir Joseph Cook ([in 1913] The Honourable) was prime minister of Australia for fourteen months but he only had a very slender majority – two or three votes – over the Labor Opposition. W.M. (Billy) Hughes, then a member of the Labor Party Opposition, related the story of how it was decided by the Labor Party that he should 'insult' Prime Minister Cook during a debate, which would result in him being suspended by the House. The incident, if properly exploited by the Opposition, might bring on an election.

    In accordance with the Party decision Billy did his act. In a bitter attack on Prime Minister Cook he said, 'The Prime Minister is both cowardly and contemptible.' The Speaker called on Billy to withdraw and apologise to the Prime Minister for his offensive remarks. But Billy refused to do so, having in mind the object of the performance. The Speaker then sent for Prime Minister Cook and requested him to move the usual motion, 'That the Right Honourable Member be suspended from the service of the House'. The Prime Minister rose in his place, but before moving the motion he asked, 'In what way did the honourable member intend the remark? Was it personally or politically?'

Billy later explained it this way: 'Like a bloody fool I said, "Politically, of course."'

'In that case,' said the Prime Minister, 'I take no offence whatever.'

'And,' said Billy, 'the Prime Minister then apologised to me.'

Daly, *The Politician who Laughed* (1982), pp. 60–1

## The Bulldog Breed

*There was no lack of support for Britain at the start of the First World War in 1914. A rally in Adelaide was apparently typical.*

The Police Band struck up 'Australia', and as the melody pealed forth the people sang lustily. Rousing cheers followed. That cleared the way for the Commissioner of Public Works to say a few words.

Sir Richard, who was given a most cordial reception, remarked: 'Gentlemen – His Excellency the Governor has sent a message that he wished to be associated with this gathering. (Applause.) Sir Henry asks the people of South Australia to keep a stiff upper lip. (Applause.)'

A Voice: 'We'll do that all right.'

Sir Richard called for cheers for the King, and they were given with deafening heartiness.

The band rendered the National Anthem, and at the close of the inspiring music further cheering was indulged in.

A Voice: 'Three for the British Navy!' There was a mighty response.

Someone also made a remark which was drowned in the noise, but it was the right kind of sentiment, and the thousands of throats were again exercised to the full, and hats were whirled round and round in the air with excitement.

'Rule Britannia' was sung, and then the instrumentalists played it.

A Voice: 'Hurrah for France!' It was the introduction for 'The

Marseillaise' by the band. Once again the gathering was convulsed with cheering.

A Voice: 'For the Russians!'

Sir Richard Butler: 'Three cheers for the allies of Great Britain!' There was a grand reply.

'See the Conquering Hero' and 'Rule Brittania' were contributed by the instrumentalists amid further outbursts of applause.

Voices: 'The Empress of the Waves!' 'Sons of the Sea!'

Sir Richard Butler: 'Three cheers for the Governor."

The Crowd: 'Hurrah, hurrah, hurrah!'

The band then struck up the National Anthem, and to its accompaniment the people sang –

> God save our gracious King,
> Long live our noble King,
> God save the king;
> Send him victorious,
> Happy and glorious,
> Long to reign over us –
> God save the King.'

Justice having been done to the occasion, the gathering dispersed. 'Wasn't it grand to be there?' He was one of the bulldog breed.

*Register*, Adelaide, 6 August 1914.

## A Colourful Campaign

*During the Great War the conscription issue split the country, and more particularly the Labor Party. The first referendum led to some vicious appeals to racism:*

Against this, the NO campaign included a simple patriotic appeal to race prejudice:

> The ruling powers would import servile and cheap colored labor if it became lawful to send white men out to be shot down, led like sheep to the slaughter to make a fat man's holiday. This lonely outpost of the white man's civilisation

would be deprived of its scanty garrison and left open to the cheap Asiatics, reduced to the social and economic level of Paraguay or some other barbarian country.

When it was learned that several hundred Maltese immigrants were coming to Australia, although at their own expense and on their own initiative, the NO campaigners gave this as proof that Hughes and the 'fat men', wanting a flood of cheap coloured labour, could not wait even until after they had won the referendum. One of the most popular NO posters said: VOTE NO AND KEEP AUSTRALIA WHITE.

Horne, *In Search of Billy Hughes* (1979), p. 80

## THE LITTLE DIGGER WALKS OUT

*In 1916 Billy Hughes, a pro-conscriptionist, was the Labor Prime Minister. However, he decided to abandon the party — or at least the anti-conscriptionists — and attempt to govern with Opposition support.*

When his time came to speak, using his jaunty style, he made points designed to come in handy in his coming battle against former comrades. He said his attackers were not speaking for themselves, but on instruction from an outside organisation. He was establishing the argument he would use for years afterwards that he had been a good Labor man, but he would not accept dictation from a 'junta' outside the party. He now provided the climax of the anecdote: he picked up his papers, and said 'Let all who support me follow me.' To a derisive cheer, he walked out of the room followed by twenty-four of the sixty-five members of the party. (One changed his mind, and went back.)

Horne, *In Search of Billy Hughes* (1979), p. 80

# THE NEW FUSION

*By the end of 1916 Hughes was ready to sever his last ties with Labor and formally join with the conservatives. But he forced the conservative leaders to approach him first. James Hume Cook, the Liberal leader, met Hughes at Parliament House to offer a coalition. Hughes temporised; he would have preferred a National Labor Party, but admitted he had neither funds nor support.*

Hume Cook had a brainwave. He would ask Alexander Peacock, the Premier of Victoria, to approve of a new organisation, to be called the National Party. [Thomas] Ryan, the Labor Premier of Queensland, should be excluded. Peacock arranged the meeting for 8pm on 13 December. Peacock, without telling Hume Cook or Sir William Irvine, invited Hughes. Hughes was truculent: 'Well, gentlemen! What have you got to say?' The premiers told him a fusion of National Labor and the Liberals would mean a victory for 'Winning the War'. Hughes, impatient as ever, said: 'Well! We all seem to be agreed, so there's no use wasting time in discussion.' With that he picked up his hearing aid and stalked out of the room. As they walked together down Collins Street Peacock said to Hume Cook: 'But Great Scott! What a victory!'

Clark, *A History of Australia*, vol. Vi (1987), p. 43

# THE WARWICK EGG

*The second referendum campaign in 1917 was even more bitter than the first. As a result of one demonstration, Hughes established a new enforcement agency.*

Speakers were regularly shouted down and meetings broken up, eggs, bottles and road metal were thrown and the police sometimes drew their batons. Among these reports of disorder a meeting Hughes addressed at a Queensland country railway station provided what for several decades remained one of the best remembered anecdotes about him. The anecdote had many versions. In the most extreme (improvised by Hughes and some of the newspapers on the day) Hughes was in great danger. Desperadoes armed with spanners and hammers stood threateningly; he was assaulted in a sudden tumult by a number of men in what virtually amounted to a riot. From this he emerged, gallantly dishevelled, his knuckles bleeding. In the least extreme version (and also, perhaps the truth) an egg hit his hat and when he ran from the platform a sergeant in plain clothes caught hold of him and tried to quieten him down; the men 'armed with hammers and spanners' were a train examiner with his wheeltapping hammer and a railway workman with a spanner, both on their normal job. In all versions of the anecdote Hughes ordered the sergeant to arrest two men and the sergeant refused, so, after a public squabble with [Premier Thomas] Ryan, who supported the sergeant, Hughes founded the Commonwealth Police.

Horne, *In Search of Billy Hughes* (1979), p. 92

## THE WAR PRECAUTIONS ACT

*In 1917 the Hughes Government announced a huge number of new crimes for which offenders could be fined or jailed. Among them were:*

Selling or offering for sale commodities at a price in excess of the maximum fixed by Regulation [216 cases].
Obstructing an officer in the course of inspecting books of firms.
Falsely representing to be returned soldiers.
Wearing returned soldiers' badges without title to them.
Misleading a military officer.
Being in possession of a forged military discharge certificate.
Wearing a soldier's uniform without right to do so.
Being in possession of official documents.
Failing to register as an alien [about 650 cases].
Selling badges without authority.
Selling uniforms without authority.
Making unauthorised use of military and naval uniforms.
Offences in regard to passes, certificates, &c.
Exhibiting the red flag [31 cases].

Evasion of censorship of letters for enemy countries.
Attempting to transmit letters from the Commonwealth otherwise than through the post.
Accepting assignment of allotment certificates from female dependants of soldiers.
Breaches of active service moratorium regulations.
Using, for purpose of trade, names other than those by which the accused were known at the date of the commencement of the war.
Being in unauthorised possession of wireless apparatus.
Using a code for secretly communicating naval information.
Disclosing information with regard to the movements of ships.
Using the word 'Anzac' without permission for purposes of trade.
Selling goods issued by the Red Cross Society.
Collecting for patriotic purposes without authority.
Failure to furnish information required by a competent authority.
Short delivery of coke to Navy Department.
Advocating action calculated to prevent the production of warlike material for purposes connected with the war.
Making statements prejudicial to recruiting [about 150 of such cases]: –

> 'Any man who puts on a uniform is a fool. A German has as much right to live in this country as an Australian.'
> 'Do not enlist to fight for a man like "Billy" Hughes. He owes me a quid. I am a German and proud of it.'
> 'Poor fools are going to the war because they have no sense.'
> 'England is decaying. She wants Australia to go. Australians are fools to go.'
> 'These men in khaki are hired assassins and murderers. They are only a pack of mugs who put on khaki.'
> 'Our men are nothing but murderers and baby killers.' …

Exhibiting disloyalty or hostility to the British Empire.
Making statements likely to cause disaffection to His Majesty.
Publishing information which might be of use to the enemy.
Spreading reports likely to cause alarm. Spreading a false rumour that a transport with Australian troops on board had been torpedoed.
Publishing and printing matter which had not been previously submitted to the Censor.

Printing matter in such a way as to suggest that the omissions indicated had been due to the action of the Censor.

Attempting to cause sedition or disaffection among the civil population.

Having in possession prohibited publications.

Making false statements likely to prejudice the judgment of voters in connection with military service referendum [these prosecutions were launched by the district military commandants]. Making statements likely to prejudice relations with foreign powers.

Disturbing referendum meetings.

Taking part in a meeting of a number of persons exceeding 20 in the open air in a proclaimed place on the pretext of making known their grievances [the convictions in these cases were quashed by the High Court].

Showing, in printed matter, alterations made by the Censor.

Distraining on property and raising rent on female dependants of soldiers.

Refusing to supply a foodstuff in the quantity demanded on tender of payment at fixed price.

Addressing a public meeting after being ordered to refrain from doing so.

Harbouring an unnaturalised German.

Wrongfully dyeing military overcoats.

Scott in Crowley, *Modern Australia in Documents*, vol. i (1973), pp. 302–4

## No Tipping, Please

*Hughes's attempts to keep on friendly terms with Labor supporters were seldom successful, as a meeting with the young John Curtin in 1917 proved.*

The hostility which Hughes aroused among some sections of the Labor movement was demonstrated when he visited Western Australia during the election campaign. Accompanied by journalists (including Curtin) Hughes travelled to Pemberton to meet the timber workers there. After watching one worker fell a mighty tree with an axe, Hughes laid a pound note on the stump as a tip.

'Keep it,' said the unionist.

'Don't you drink?' asked Hughes.

'No.'

'Don't you want to buy some tobacco?'

'No.'

'Even amongst the trees', Curtin wrote, 'Mr Hughes found politics persisted in the west.'

On this trip, as Curtin told the story later, Billy Hughes sent for him. It is not known what passed between them, except for one exchange which Curtin mentioned. Hughes said: 'You don't like me, do you? I know you don't. I've been reading some of your articles. Why do you attack me so bitterly?'

Curtin replied: 'You are trying to smash the Labor Party.'

Hughes said: 'I couldn't do that. No one can smash the Labor Party. I couldn't. You couldn't. Not even some of the people in it now ... '

Ross, *John Curtin for Labor and for Australia* (1971), pp. 59–60

## A Prime Minister Without Peer

*At Bendigo, during the second conscription referendum,*
*Hughes had promised to resign if the vote went against him.*
*It did, but he had no intention of keeping the promise.*

The first step was to have the parliamentary party behind him. On 3 January [1918] the party began a two-day meeting. On the first day Hughes pulled a bold face, spoke solemnly of the best interests of the country and of the empire, and after five hours got a confidence vote of sixty-three to two. Overnight some of the malcontents gave each other enough courage to have another go: when the meeting resumed on the next day and they moved that Hughes be replaced by a candidate of their own the number ready to vote against him went from two to seven. There were more than this who wanted to get rid of Hughes, but they weren't yet ready to put up their hands and say so. For the moment Hughes could still look as if he had the party behind him. Now, so that he could look as if he cared about his pledge at Bendigo, Hughes formally resigned to the Governor-General and, one after the other, seven taxis dropped political leaders at Government House while the Governor-General 'sought advice'. The seventh visitor, the Treasurer, Sir John Forrest, was bold enough to give the advice that he, Forrest, should replace Hughes. Forrest spent two hours putting his case: Hughes was too autocratic ... he was a muddler and a meddler ... his real concerns were not with the business of Government, but 'limelight exhibitions'. The Governor-General was sympathetic: he thought that by staying in office Hughes was losing face. Taxis then brought back to Government House two of the National Party leaders who had already been there. They stuck by Hughes. After dinner Hughes was told that he was again prime minister. As a reward for disloyalty, Hughes quickly caused Forrest to be made a peer – 'Lord Forrest of Bunbury' was the first Australian elevated to the House of Lords – then took a gnome's delight in telling Forrest that one so elevated now had to resign from Australian politics.

Horne, *In Search of Billy Hughes* (1979), p. 93

## LORD FORREST OF BUNBURY

*Billy Hughes's own version of how he got rid of
John Forrest in 1918 probably gained something in
the telling. Norman Cowper's recollection of it went like this:*

I used to enjoy his stories. One of the best was his story about Lord Forrest. He told it something like this: 'Ah, you see,' he began, 'you see, during the war, the first war, you know, we formed a coalition Government. Oh it was a wonderful team, a ministry of all the talents. There was Watt, former Premier of Victoria; Forrest, former Premier of Western Australia; there was Pearse, there was ...' Oh, he enumerated the whole team. And he said 'Oh, they were a wonderful team on paper, but they fought among each other intolerably. Things got to such a stage, such a pitch at one time, that I threatened to resign for the lot of them. That shook them. For a time all was well, but after a while they were as bad as ever, things were as bad as ever. Watt and Forrest were constantly at one another's throats. They fought like a couple of Kilkenny cats, and I didn't know what to do. I was at my wit's end, until one day I said to Watt "I know what to do." "Oh," said Watt, "what's your plan, William?" I said "I'm going to make him a lord." "Oh," said Watt, "I don't think you can do that, William." I said, "I'm going to do it." He said "You know, you'll have to put it over the powers that be." I said I was going to do it, I was going to see the Governor-General. I went to the Governor-General, I told him what I wanted to do. He said "Oh, I don't think you can do that, Mr Hughes." I said "I'm going to do it, I'm going to." He said "Oh well, you'll have to get on to Downing Street." I got on to Downing Street. They were horrified. They nearly had a fit. They said it hadn't been done and it couldn't be done and it wouldn't be done. I said "It's going to be done. I'll make a national issue of it." "Oh well," they said, "if you feel so strongly about it, you'll have to show us some jolly good reasons." So for three days Watt and I sat down and composed the most wonderful epitaph for that silly old beggar Forrest. Oh, we sent it off. It evidently made the desired impression for after a time word came through that His Majesty had been pleased to create Forrest "Lord Forrest of Bunbury". I went to find Forrest, to break the news to him. He wasn't in, but I saw Lady Forrest. I congratulated her on this spontaneous recognition by His Majesty of her husband's wonderful desserts. Oh, she was deeply affected, she was in tears. She said she always knew that someday John's wonderful merits would receive their due meed of recognition.

'So I left her and I went off and I found Forrest. Oh, I congratulated him on this spontaneous recognition by His Majesty. He took it very calmly. Ah, very calmly indeed. So after a while I said to him "Well, Forrest," I said, "I expect we'll be losing you soon. You'll want to go overseas and take your rightful place in the House of Lords." "Oh, no fear I won't," he said, "oh no, I like this country. My work is here. I'm not going over there." You could have knocked me over with a feather duster. "Oh," I said to him, I said, "now look here, Forrest," I said, "you've got to look at this thing from my point of view. I'm the head of a coalition Government in which I represent the Labor wing. How can I have a lord in my cabinet?" I said, "Some fellow will get up in the House of Representatives and he'll ask me a question and I'll have to – am I going to refer to the noble Lord in the Senate? Not on your life, Forrest, I'm not going to be put in that position," I said. Oh I didn't make any impression on him, not that I noticed it. So I went off and found his physician, a fellow named Berge or Bird or whatever it was, oh, a most distinguished man, a man of the most distinguished eminence in his profession. A man of such eminence that he was dignified by the name of "Mr". Oh, I said to him, "Now look here, Berg or Birch or whatever your name is," I said, "you know as well as I do, that every day that the silly old fool remains in political life, shortens his life, and it's up to you," said I, "Berg or Berch or whatever your name is, to give him the right advice in this matter." Oh I made a considerable impression on him. So I went off. And evidently Berg or Berge or whatever his name was, he gave him the right advice. For after a time Forrest announced that he was going overseas. He went. Everything in the garden was lovely. Peace reigned supreme. Oh, I'd have made him a bloody duke if necessary!'

[*Forrest in fact had cancer, from which he died on the voyage.*]

Cowper in Thompson and Counihan (eds),
*On Lips of Living Men* (1962), pp. 106–7

## An Instant General

*As a wartime leader, Hughes had to go 'home' to England for conferences. He used unorthodox tactics to make sure Australia's interests were represented, as his driver Alf Bachili recalled.*

Talking of the First World War, Billy once told me 'When I was Home,' he said, 'after I became prime minister, Australia wasn't represented on the War Council. I said to Lord Kitchener that we should be represented, but Lord Kitchener said, "Well," he said, "you can't be represented, Mr Hughes, you have no General."' So Billy said 'I'll soon get one!' So he said 'I picked out a very upstanding, fine-looking Major,' he said, 'and I made him a General. He was a General overnight. He looked the part too,' he said, 'and we were on the Council all right. Oh yes, yes, yes, of course we were.'

Bachili in Thompson and Counihan (eds),<br>
*On Lips of Living Men* (1962), p. 87

## Deaf to All Pleas

*Later, at Versailles in 1919 to discuss postwar arrangements, Hughes was no less self-confident.*

The impenetrable shell of his designs was buttressed by masterly use of his deafness and the deficiencies of the large and primitive hearing aid he carried which figures in one of the best 'Billy Hughes' anecdotes. At Versailles, during a discussion of the projected mandates system, Hughes (backed to some extent by Massey of New Zealand) insisted that details of the mandate system should be available before Australia could agree. Woodrow Wilson demanded to know if this was an ultimatum, and amid protestations of other delegates that this could not have been meant, Hughes allowed that it was. Wilson then delivered himself of an especially Wilsonian reproof:

> Mr Prime Minister of Australia, do I understand your attitude aright? If I do, it is this, that the opinion of the whole civilised world is to be set at nought. This Conference, fraught with such infinite consequences to mankind for good or evil, is to break up with results which may well be disastrous to the future happiness of eighteen hundred millions of the human race, in order to satisfy the whim of five million people in the remote Southern continent whom you claim to represent.

Hughes, who had pushed his machine towards the President while he spoke, answered:

> Very well put, Mr President, you have guessed it. That's just so.

(In an improved version of the story Hughes first makes the President repeat his pomposity, and then says: 'Mr President, that's about the size of it.')

Hughes, *Mr Prime Minister* (1976), pp. 60–1

## COOK'S COMMON SENSE

*Another delegate to Versailles was former prime minister Joseph Cook, a man of few words.*

As Minister for the Navy he travelled to England with Hughes and sat with him in the Imperial War Cabinet, and after the war he was a delegate to the peace conference where his service on the committee on Czechoslovakia produced the observation of Sir Harold Nicolson:

> Old Cook is all right. He has sense. The French the other day started an endless argument about the Delbruck nationalist laws. When the whole thing had been translated into English, old Cook was asked to record his views. 'Damn Delbruck' was what he said.

Hughes, *Mr Prime Minister* (1976), p. 50

## FIRST, THE GOOD NEWS

*John Latham, later a major figure in conservative politics and Chief Justice of the High Court, was also there as an adviser. Former Liberal MP Sir James Killen talked to him many years later.*

After World War I Latham accompanied Prime Minister Hughes to the Versailles Peace Conference as a legal adviser. The President of the United States was Woodrow Wilson, who was heartily disliked by Hughes. Sir John Latham gave me the following account of a breakfast at the end of the conference.

'I came down to breakfast to see Hughes crumpled over an

egg and a piece of toast. I said: "Good morning, Prime Minister." He pretended not to hear me, I repeated the greeting. "Well, Latham, that's a matter of opinion," was his reply. I asked: "Sir, is something wrong?" His reply was: "Well, you're in a most inquisitive mood, Latham, aren't you?" I ignored the insult and persisted with my question. Hughes eventually said to me: "Well, Latham, you have heard the news, haven't you?" I said: "No, Sir, I have not." Hughes said: "Well, you know Latham, Woodrow Wilson came to this country on board a United States battleship," I told him that I understood that was the case. "Well, Latham, the ship has sunk with a loss of all life." I gasped and said: "Oh, Sir, that is dreadful news, dreadful news indeed." Without batting an eyelid Hughes looked at me and said: "Yes, Latham, it is; but there is worse to come. It is not bloody true."'

Killen, *Killen in Company* (1989), pp. 133–4

## THE FIRST WOMAN

*In 1894 South Australia had legislated for women's suffrage, and for the right of women to sit in parliament. In 1921 the first woman legislator, Edith Cowan, was elected to sit in the Western Australian Legislative Assembly, which had given women that right only a year earlier. Her maiden speech began:*

I stand here today in the unique position of being the first woman in an Australian parliament. I know many people think perhaps that it was not the wisest thing to do to send a woman into Parliament, and perhaps I should remind Hon. Members that one of the reasons why women and men also considered it advisable to do so, was because it was felt that men need a reminder sometimes from women beside them that will make them realise all that can be done for the race and for the home. I have been sent here more from that standpoint than from any other ...

Then, again, the Scriptures tell us that it is not good for man to be alone. I appreciate the honour that was conferred on me in asking me, though not the youngest member in this House, to move the Address-in-reply. I look on it as an honour conferred on the women of the country, and I therefore thank the Government for it.

HON. W.C. ANGWIN   They only wanted your vote.

> Western Australia, Legislative Assembly 1921, *Debates*, vol. 64, p. 15

## BACK ON THE TRAM

*Jack Lang, known to friends and enemies alike as the 'Big Fella', played politics tough. In 1927 he resigned as Premier of New South Wales to call a snap election and catch his Labor rivals by surprise. As he told it:*

It was a shock move that took my opponents completely by surprise. For example, Harry Hauptmann, roundsman for the *Sun*, went down to the Education Department to interview Tom Mutch. He casually inquired how his leadership plans were proceeding, to which Mutch gave him an equivocal reply only to have Hauptmann say, 'Haven't you heard the news? Lang has resigned and you are no longer even a minister.'

Making certain to look after all the small details of the transfer, I issued instructions that all ministerial cars should return to their garages immediately, to await instruction from their new ministers. The wife of one of the displaced ministers was attending a select function at the Hotel Australia, and after it was finished went out on the footpath in Castlereagh Street to wait for her husband's car and chauffeur. After waiting a considerable time for it, her attention was directed to a *Sun* poster containing the news of the dismissals. So she had to go home by government tram, instead of the chauffeured car.

> Lang, *The Turbulent Years* (1970), p. 70

# Billy Juggles the Bills

*In Canberra the National Party, led by Stanley Bruce, and the Country Party, led by Earle Page, had formed a coalition.*
*Billy Hughes, though still nominally a National, was plotting its downfall, as his private secretary H. V. Howe recounted.*

The facts of the fall of the Bruce–Page Government [in 1929] have never been told. I am probably the only one alive today who knows them. Hughes was determined to bring about the fall of the Government on the Maritime Industries Bill, which he contended would have abolished the Arbitration Courts throughout Australia. He'd mustered all the support he could get, and he was still one man short of the number necessary to beat the Government. The only possibility was that he might be able to win over a member of the Government side who was bitterly opposed to his own party on the question of taxation of cinema films, which was shortly to be introduced into the House. It was a big issue for the film industry and the film interests had been trying to contact Hughes and get his support against the Government, but Billy would have nothing to do with them. The member whose support Billy wanted would have nothing to do with Billy on the Maritime Industries Bill.

The principals in the film industry had been ringing Billy nearly every day but he never happened to be near the 'phone when they rang. The morning of the day on which the vote on the Maritime Industries Bill was to be taken, Billy said to me 'If so-and-so (naming one of the film principals) doesn't ring by ten o'clock this morning, you ring him and tell him to ring me as near as possible to half past three this afternoon.' It so happened that just before I was going to ring Sydney, the man in question rang. I gave him Billy's message to ring at half past three in the afternoon and I said 'Mr Hughes will be here.'

About a quarter past three, Billy came into the room with the member whose support he'd been seeking. He'd invited him to afternoon tea. At half past three the Sydney leader of the film interest rang. Billy spoke to him. He said 'No, I could not vote against the Government on an issue like the taxation of films. You have no possibility of defeating the Government on that issue. There is only one issue you can defeat the Government on, and that is the Maritime Industries Bill.' And he said 'It so happens that your man is in my room now.' He said 'If you persuade him to support me on the Maritime Industries Bill, we'll defeat the Bruce-Page Government and the question of the taxation of cinema films will never come before the House.' The Sydney man persuaded the member to support Billy on the Maritime Industries Bill, and that night the Bruce-Page Government fell.

[*The defector was Walter Marks.*]

Howe in Thompson and Counihan (eds),<br>
*On Lips of Living Men* (1962), pp. 99–100

## An Australian Governor-General

*The Labor government that followed the 1929 federal election was headed by James Scullin. Scullin, in many ways a waverer, confounded his critics by insisting that the former Chief Justice, Sir Isaac Isaacs, be appointed the first Australian-born Governor-General.*

Jimmy Scullin forwarded the name of Isaac Isaacs to the King. The King was not amused. Cables were exchanged. Through his private secretary the King wanted to know who Isaac Isaacs was. The King wanted to retain his right of choice: he wanted a list of names from which he would make the final choice. Ramsay Macdonald asked Jimmy Scullin to wait until he arrived in London for the Imperial Conference. But Jimmy Scullin did not bow to all this pressure. In cables to the private secretary to the King he informed his most Britannic Majesty that Isaac Isaacs had had 'an exceptionally long and honourable public career', that he was a 'man of splendid qualities', that his probity and impartiality had earned for him the unstinted admiration and respect of his fellow citizens. The manner of his private life afforded 'additional reassurance that his elevation to the high office of Governor-General would occasion no offence to any section in the community'. Jimmy Scullin did not want to do anything 'which might occasion His Majesty any difficulty or embarrassment'. The King would not budge: Jimmy Scullin would not budge.

Clark, *A History of Australia*, vol. vi (1987) p. 343.

*Eventually Scullin, in London on an official visit in 1930, insisted on seeing the King in person.*

They met at Buckingham Palace on 29 November, only a few hours after Jimmy Scullin had bidden an emotional farewell to his relatives in the village of Ballyscullin. The King said he wanted to say something to the Australian Prime Minister: 'We have sent many governors, Commonwealth and State, and I hope they have not all been failures'. Scullin said 'No', they had not all been failures. He then unfolded the reasons why they had nominated an Australian. It was clear Jimmy Scullin was not going to make any concessions. It was fourteen years since Billy Hughes, another Labor prime minister, had been a guest at Buckingham Palace, fourteen years since the *Labor Call* had exclaimed, 'Ye gods!' But this time no Labor man need have any qualms about treachery or betrayal. This time the King-Emperor gave way. After explaining to Mr Scullin that the last thing he wanted as King was to be the centre of a public controversy, the King said: 'I have been for 20 years a monarch, and I hope I have always been a constitutional one, and being a constitutional monarch I must, Mr Scullin, accept your advice which, I take it, you will tender me formally by letter.'

Clark, *A History of Australia*, vol. vi (1987), p. 359

## ACT NOW AND WORRY LATER

*Scullin was not always so bold. A protracted dispute between mine-owners and miners resulted in the owners staging a lockout in 1930. While the Commonwealth argued, Jack Lang had an easy solution.*

Scullin agreed to call an industrial peace conference in an effort to settle the dispute. The Federal Government was represented by

Scullin and six ministers. [The New South Wales Premier Thomas] Bavin was in attendance as well as representatives of the employers and unions. I was invited to attend and arrived at the Commonwealth Bank building about 10pm to find everyone in a state of dejection. I was asked if I had any suggestions. I replied: 'Yes. Seize the mines. You have a mandate to open them within a fortnight, and if the coal owners persist in defying the law, you must show that you are the Government. Seize the mines starting with the Richmond Main and Pelaw Main, two of the richest mines in the world. If they are paid proper award rates, the miners will be glad to work them.'

The Federal Attorney-General reacted as if he had been shot. He said: 'Good God, man, you must be mad. It wouldn't be constitutional.' I replied: 'It's no use giving me empty lawyers' arguments while people are starving. Act now and worry about the constitution later.'

Lang, *The Turbulent Years* (1970), p. 81

## TRADITIONAL BRITISH STANDARDS

*The up-and-coming conservative Robert Menzies would not have agreed with this approach. He vigorously supported the rights of British bondholders whatever the cost to Australians.*

Probably the most quoted speech of this phase in Menzies' career was an address on 'Politics and the Church', reported in the Melbourne daily papers on 4 May 1931. One sentence was to be quoted again and again by left-wing propagandists, because it seemed to epitomise the attitudes of a man and a class incapable of understanding the plight of their fellow countrymen. 'If Australia was to surmount her troubles only by abandonment of traditional British standards of honesty, justice, fair play and honest endeavour, it would be better for Australia that every citizen within her boundaries should die of starvation during the next six months.'

Hazelhurst, *Menzies Observed* (1979), p. 74

# Mr Moneybags

*The onset of the Great Depression meant that the Scullin Government was simply unable to counter the arguments and threats coming from the banks, both local and foreign.*

At the Premiers' Conference in August 1930 all Australian governments agreed 'to tighten the belt' by balancing their budgets and raising no more overseas loans for the time being; they also agreed to finance only reproductive public works. They had listened to lectures by Sir Otto Niemeyer of the Bank of England, and Sir Robert Gibson of the Commonwealth Bank of Australia, who advised them that only by a strict attention to economy could the nation weather the economic storm. Sir Otto had been invited to Australia by the Scullin Government, and was not welcomed by many trade union officials and State Labor politicians. They were even less impressed when he told the premiers that Australia was 'off Budget equilibrium, off exchange equilibrium, and faced by considerable unfunded and maturing debts ... ', and that 'There is also evidence to show that the standard of living in Australia has reached a point which is economically beyond the capacity of the country to bear'. He also said, 'I assume that everybody in the room is in agreement that costs must come down.' From that point onwards many Labor spokesmen, and especially J.T. Lang of New South Wales, warned of the danger of Australia becoming a pawn in the hands of High Finance and of Mr Overseas Moneybags. But the warning was not necessary for most Australians, because the myths and the illusions of the twenties had already been shattered.

Crowley, *Modern Australia in Documents*, vol. i (1973), p. 475

# On the susso

*The Depression led to widespread unemployment and left governments virtually powerless. In 1931 a deputation called on Victorian Premier E. J. Hogan for assistance. He said he would do what he could.*

The Premier said he sympathised with the men, and would continue to do everything possible to assist. They had to remember that there had been a drop of £100,000,000 in the national income, and that they were spending £30,000,000 less loan money. He explained at length the Unemployed Relief Act, and stated that the Act specified that the men were to be paid the basic wage, and not 12/11 a day. No figure was mentioned in the Act. The Government had fought for the preservation of the basic wage. The Unemployment Relief Board would be appointed immediately, and would comprise the Premier and Messrs Jones, Monk, Hancock, McKay and Hunt. The board would go into the detail of the Act. Men who did not secure their four days' work in one week would have the time given to them in the following week. Tents would be provided by the department, the men would be supplied with a messroom, and they would be charged cost price for the food. By co-operation the Government hoped to be able to supply the food at 12/- a week. The fares to the place of employment would be paid by the Government. There would be no limit to the number of weeks of work to be given. If a man gave satisfaction there was no reason why he should not remain on the work until the job was finished. Relief works would be started in Melbourne, Geelong, Bendigo, Ballarat and other country centres. The Government intended to pay to each council £2 for every pound expended on work to provide employment for the workless. In the year just completed the Government had expended more than £1,000,000 on relief work, and had provided employment for 41,938 men.

*Labor Call*, Melbourne, 15 January 1931.

# Out of the Domain

*The* Labor Daily *had earlier found New South Wales Premier Bavin less sympathetic when he stopped homeless men from camping in the Domain.*

Visitors may be offended at sight of derelicts!

Police boot enforces Bavin order. They have no home, but they must go.

Evicted and harried like dogs in city.

Govt makes war on starving. Mighty Ukase goes forth to 'Clear off.'

Outcasts in last stages of distress.

They who have no home save the caves or cliff shelters of the Domain; whose only beds are those made of old newspapers – those unfortunates whom the denial of work had made outcast in this city – are to be 'evicted'.

The landlords of private dwellings are callous enough in all conscience, but can their callousness match that of the landlords of the Domain, who set their agents, the police, to hound out the distressed from even the refuge of a cave?

The ukase of the mighty has gone forth to the humble and harmless 'dosser', who asks of the night nothing but cold stone on which to lay his head:

'Get out!'

Last night, ere it was quite dark and when the unfortunates were preparing to make up the 'beds', an officer of police paid them a visit and told them to be ready to 'clear off'.

The police had orders, he said, to shift them out of the Domain as soon as the fine weather came.

The homeless and shelterless, it appears, are permitted to seek the comforts of the windswept caves and the rain that drives in upon them when the weather wears the icy aspect of winter, but when fine weather comes, they must 'beat it' – to where?

'Anywhere, anywhere – out of the world', for all the authorities care, who will neither shelter nor feed these unfortunate fellows.

It is plain that such derelicts cannot be tolerated within the borders of the city. With the advent of the fine weather, what a sight that would present to the increasing number of visitors to the Domain! ...

Two men who had been compelled for weeks past regularly to 'doss' in the Domain visited the *Labor Daily* last night to tell us of the ukase that had been issued.

They were decent looking, manly men, wonderfully clean in appearance, considering their distressful circumstances, and they asked that we should inform the public that they were to be ordered off the Domain.

'We come to the *Labor Daily* because you are our last and only hope,' said one of them.

'We have no other place to sleep besides the Domain. We do not loaf about in the day, but only go there for some sort of shelter in which we can sleep at night. Can't they leave us there?

'They say that people walking in the Domain do not like to see us there. We are in the caves right over at Lady Macquarie's Chair, and in nobody's way.'

A simple and pitiful plea!

But Mr Bavin will have these ragamuffins out of it, all the same.

Bravo, Mr Bavin!

GET OUT!

*Labor Daily*, Sydney, 27 August 1930.

## LISTENING OUT

*Eventually the problems of the Great Depression became too much for Scullin, and indeed for the Federal Labor Government as a whole. Journalist Warren Denning recalled the gathering crisis in the caucus.*

It was no uncommon spectacle to see Mr Scullin walk out of party meetings profoundly distressed. So terrific became the tumult at times that all Parliament House was aware of it, although there were double and padded doors separating the party room from the lobbies. While ministerial sentries patrolled the passages to keep prying ears from encroaching too closely, Opposition members passed with sly and cheerful smiles, and such pert observations as 'I see the party is unanimous again.' Journalists, far from attempting to 'listen in' to forbidden places, were embarrassed in their efforts to get far enough away from the disturbance to be able to proclaim that they were making no effort to overhear it. Indeed, there was no need to try and overhear it. When the party doors opened after another of the innumerable truces had been called, most members of the various factions were only too willing to meet newspaper correspondents in any of the scores of places where the latter obtained their accounts of what was happening, and pour into listening ears their tale of woe. Indeed, it was possible, had we cared to do so, at times to sit in our own rooms behind the press gallery, one floor above that on which the party meeting was being held, and hear snatches of argument hurled into the night by the stentorian voices of the vociferous antagonists.

Denning, *Caucus Crisis* (1937), p. 94

## THE MAN FOR THE JOB

*In Sydney, New South Wales Premier Jack Lang was having trouble with the New Guard, a right-wing-paramilitary organisation that was challenging his authority. Lang told how he went to his chief secretary, Mark Gosling, to find a tough cop.*

So I asked Gosling who the strongest man was in the force in his opinion. He suggested the name of Superintendent W.J. MacKay, Superintendent of the Criminal Investigation Branch. I knew MacKay by reputation. He had been the chief police witness in the Industrial Workers of the World cases where he acted as police shorthand writer obtaining information that had sent most of them to gaol. The next time I had heard about him was at the time of the Rothbury mine riots. He had led the police sent up from Sydney by Weaver to protect the mine. During the disturbance the deputy leader of the Labor Party and later Minister for Mines, Labour and Industry, J.M. Baddeley, had been hit on the skull by a police truncheon. It was generally believed that the policeman wielding the truncheon had been MacKay. I decided that MacKay was the kind of man to take charge of the situation that was developing, so I sent for him.

Lang, *The Turbulent Years* (1970), p. 157

## CUTTING THE RIBBON

*Lang's most famous confrontation with the New Guard was at the opening of the Sydney Harbour Bridge in 1932. Lang recalled that MacKay proved his worth.*

One of the members of the New Guard's City Locality was a former officer of the Irish Guards, a Captain De Groot, who was in business in the city as an antique dealer. He was the man who conceived the plan for disrupting the ceremony and beating me to the ribbon and accepted responsibility for executing the plan himself. His idea was to attach himself to the Governor-General's escort of the Light Horse, drawn from Victoria Barracks. The Governor-General was staying at Government House, and whether De Groot joined the escort at Victoria Barracks, at Government House or *en route*, was never made clear.

As the escort came trotting down the road towards the official stand where the Governor-General was to take his place, observers might have noticed in the rear a figure mounted on a horse that was ungroomed and had none of the polish of those used by members of such an official party. He was dressed in an officer's uniform that did not belong to any of the units stationed at the Barracks. It was ill-fitting and had obviously seen better times. He was carrying his sword stuck through his belt because the polo saddle he was using did not have any rings for the sword frog.

I was walking towards the ribbon when the strange figure dug his heels into his mount, drew his sword and yelling something incoherently dashed up to the ribbon and severed it with a stroke of his sword.

Standing beside me was Superintendent MacKay and he

didn't hesitate one fraction of a second. He seized the mounted figure by his foot, snatched it out of the stirrup, lifted him into the air and dumped him hard on his back on to the hard concrete of the roadway. The shock must have shaken every bone in De Groot's body.

Mark Gosling came rushing up to me to ask me what happened. I looked around to find MacKay, but he had disappeared. He had grabbed his man, rushed him down the tunnel at the side of the bridge and placed him in a police car, and taken him off to the Reception House. That was quick thinking and the cleverest thing he could have done as it gave everyone a good laugh at the expense of the New Guard.

Lang, *The Turbulent Years* (1970), p. 173

## Hunting the Reds

*The New Guard's activities were frequently violent, according to press reports.*

Reds were harried last night at Wollongong, Leichhardt, and Ballarat (Vic.).

In both the NSW cases New Guardsmen were the attackers.

At Wollongong last night the Communists were hunted over fences, across fields, and down lanes, in a long, wild chase. Eleven were arrested by the police and charged with riotous behaviour. Others were forced to flee the town.

Mention of Colonel Campbell at a Communist meeting precipitated the mêlée, in which the Reds were swamped by over a thousand New Guardsmen and local citizens. The Reds were prepared, however, and many drew heavy batons at the first sign of attack. A knife was flashed by one, but he was quickly overpowered.

Many were injured in the fight, a 16-year-old boy being struck on the forehead at the outset.

Returning from the hunt the Guardsmen and citizens burnt every scrap of Communistic literature they could find, and stood round the flames singing 'God Save the King'.

Some time later a crowd of 500 besieged a house where L. Sharkey, the Communist Senate candidate, had gone to escape the mob.

Only on the intervention of the police were Sharkey and another man allowed to leave the house.

Led by an ex-AIF officer who is a Military Cross winner, eighty employees of the Ballarat Freezing Works determined that the five Communists, whom they blamed for all the trouble at the works, must leave the city.

One Communist was seen in Sturt Street. He bolted into a dairy and was seized there. Two others, who had taken a boat out on Lake Wendouree, were grabbed when they landed.

Two more were also captured, but as they pleaded for time in order to settle domestic matters, they were given until this morning to leave Ballarat.

The police took over the three men who had been secured, and drove them to their lodgings, where they packed up their belongings, and left Ballarat last night.

When the Communist candidate for Dalley, J. Sylvester, attempted to speak at the corner of Flood and Marion Streets last night a crowd of nearly 1,000, amongst whom were many New Guards from Dulwich Hill and Summer Hill, surged forward and upset the platform.

Free fights followed, and it took a posse of police, under Sergeant Jaeger, some time to restore order and rescue the Reds.

A quantity of Communist literature was burnt in the gutter while the crowd sang 'Keep the Home Fires Burning'.

*Daily Telegraph*, Sydney, 10 December 1931.

## A Safe Drive Home

*Jack Lang was eventually dismissed from office in 1932 by the Governor of New South Wales, Sir Philip Game, but not before the New Guard had hatched a desperate plan to kidnap him and hold him in Berrima gaol until he resigned. Lang foiled them easily.*

Volunteers were called for and then sworn in with an oath of secrecy to participate in the actual kidnapping and then act as armed guards at Berrima.

My movements were regularly observed and reported on to headquarters. It was customary for my car driver, Arthur Fitzsimmons, to pick me up either at Parliament House or at the premier's office in Macquarie Street, and drive me home along Parramatta Road. The actual date was finally selected and I was duly warned about what was afoot. The secret was so badly kept that my brother-in-law, Billy McNamara, came rushing out to Auburn to warn me about what was intended and couldn't understand it when I failed to register any great concern.

When I finished my work for the day, I sent for Fitzsimmons and told him that his services were no longer required for the day and he could go home as I had brought my own car into the city and would be driving myself.

The New Guard plan was to station key members of the organisation along Parramatta Road, with instructions to watch for my official car and at a given signal, to drive their cars across the road to block it and then seize me.

As I drove through Burwood, Strathfield, Homebush and Flemington, I noticed a large number of cars parked on the side of the road without lights and an unusually large number of cars parked in side streets.

I was a very careful driver and proceeded slowly on my way. I was concerned only that some of them might recognise me at the wheel and act on their own initiative. But they were too intent on looking for the official premier's car to be worried about just another old limousine travelling at a leisurely pace along the road. So I reached my home without challenge of any kind, went inside, had my dinner and retired to bed where I had a very sound sleep.

Lang, *The Turbulent Years* (1970), pp. 180–1

# The Dismissal (1)

*Lang's dismissal prompted near riots in Sydney, but the public — and the Labor Party — later endorsed it.*

J.T. Lang, Labor Premier of New South Wales, was dismissed from office by the Governor, Sir Philip Game, on 13 May 1932 for a breach of federal law. The dismissal of a premier for any reason other than the loss of his majority in Parliament was an exceedingly rare event. Lang's dismissal also appeared extraordinary to those who thought that State governors had long since become titular figureheads. Lang's long-standing disagreements with the right of the national Parliament to enforce the Financial Agreement of 1927, and with ALP official policy on the correct cure for Australia's economic problems, had led him to defy the Federal Conference of the ALP, the Commonwealth Government, the Commonwealth Parliament and the High Court of Australia. All of them had declared that Lang's policy of refusing to pay interest due on overseas loans, and refusing to hand over revenues due to the Commonwealth Government, was illegal. Lang's supporters demonstrated in thousands under the slogan, 'Lang is right!' His demagogic oratory called on his supporters to affirm his leadership by acclamation, and Sydney had never seen such mass political rallies. At one great rally 'Mr Lang marched with his people', ahead of the column of Labor veterans, tableaux and floats lauding the achievements of Lang's regime. Constitutionally, the Governor had been entitled to dismiss the Premier for his illegal actions, but it was fortunate for the Governor that the electors of New South Wales overwhelmingly endorsed his action: Labor was reduced from fifty-five to twenty-four seats against a Government coalition of sixty-six, in the Legislative Assembly. Lang never again took office, although the Langism which had helped to destroy the Labor Party's unity persisted for several years in both state and federal politics.

Crowley, *Modern Australia in Documents*, vol. i (1973), p. 516

# The Pay Envelope Stunt

*The election that followed Lang's dismissal was a nasty one.
The business community was determined to prevent
Lang resuming office, as he recalled.*

On June 6th [1932], we had no idea that our opponents had one desperate last keg of dynamite which they planned to throw into the political bullring before voting day. It was their pay envelope stunt. In the pay envelopes of their employees in the final pay before voting took place, employers had inserted notices warning them that if Lang won on the Saturday there would be no guarantee that their jobs would be available to them in the following week. That caused panic in thousands of homes and made many workers change their minds.

The President of the UAP, Sydney Snow, carried it a step further. In his store at the corner of Liverpool and Pitt Streets on that Friday he had huge packing cases carried in and members of the staff were informed that if Lang won, the store would be closed down, the business moved to Melbourne and there would be no necessity for them to report for work on the Monday as their employment would be terminated.

Lang, *The Turbulent Years* (1970), p. 218

# When Ben Chifley was Hated

*The split Lang caused in the Labor Party endured for some years, with
political Labor candidates standing against Langites in
state and federal elections. In 1935 Lang was opposed in his own seat
of Auburn by Ben Chifley. Meetings were stormy.*

Chifley himself used to tell a story about one such meeting where he was speaking from a box on a kerbside under a shop verandah. The air was sometimes filled with more substantial objects than mere abuse. All through Chifley's speech a raw-looking old character with eyes nearly glazed and mouth sagging open was standing in the gutter leaning against the next verandah post. As the meeting progressed a drizzling rain commenced and before long the water dripped off the edge of the verandah onto this beery-looking reprobate's cap, whence it pursued its course down his nose and finally dribbled over his stubbly chin to his faded coat. He seemed hypnotised by Chifley and the latter found himself willy-nilly addressing almost all his remarks to him. Finally, as the meeting closed and the crowd broke up, the rapt listener detached himself from the verandah post and as he shuffled away past Chifley he remarked: 'Godstruth, it must be bloody lovely to be hated like you are.'

Crisp, *Ben Chifley* ( 1963), p. 96 (note)

## IF AT FIRST YOU DON'T SECEDE ...

*Western Australia had never been happy as part of the Federation. In 1933 its citizens voted to get out.*

Since 1901 many Western Australians had believed that they would probably do better out of the Australian Federation than in it, but they had been able to see no practicable way by which they could escape from it. In 1906 the Parliament in Perth had supported secession in principle but had done nothing further. In 1927 witnesses before the Royal Commission on the Constitution had complained bitterly about the harmful effects of federal economic policies, especially tariff protection, which raised the cost of living in the West. So did decisions of the Commonwealth Arbitration Court. The onset of the Depression gave the secessionists a more receptive audience, and most of the non-Labor politicians climbed on to the secession bandwagon. In April 1933, Western Australians decided by 138,653 votes to 70,706 to secede from Australia and form a separate self-governing dominion; all the wheat-growing districts voted overwhelmingly in favour, all the gold-mining districts voted against. When the Commonwealth Government did not express sympathy with the idea, the Western Australian Parliament appealed for help to the British Parliament at Westminster. Their petition was rejected on the grounds that its acceptance would have violated the constitutional conventions of the Empire. By then the state was beginning to recover from the dark days of the Depression and, as nobody wanted to organise a Fremantle Sugar Party after the fashion of America's Boston Tea Party, the matter was shelved. It was obvious that the differences of interest between West and East were far outweighed by the common interest of Australia in relation to the outside world, and that 'it was not necessary to cure prickly heat by amputation'. Western Australians readjusted to their isolation, and, as previously, continued to vote at federal referendums in favour of increasing the powers of the Commonwealth Parliament; on the day of the secession referendum the voters threw out of office the politicians who had advocated it.

Crowley, *Modern Australia in Documents*, vol. i (1973), pp. 526–7

## Prohibited Immigrants

*As Hitler and Mussolini gained power in Europe, some Australians sought to alert their country to the dangers of Fascism. The authorities did not take kindly to their efforts.*

In November 1934, a congress of the Movement Against War and Fascism was held in Melbourne. The main guest speaker was Egon Kisch, a Czechoslovakian-born journalist of international repute. He was declared a prohibited immigrant on his arrival by ship from Fremantle; he continued his journey to Melbourne, where a challenge against the actions of the authorities was dismissed in the Supreme Court; he temporarily settled the matter by jumping on the wharf and breaking a leg. There were more legal actions and more demonstrations. Kisch travelled to Sydney and was arrested as an illegal immigrant; on appeal, the High Court in December 1934 decided that Scottish Gaelic, in which he had been tested, was not a European language within the meaning of the Immigration Act. Kisch toured Australia, holding his first rally at the Sydney Domain on 18 November before a crowd of 5,000 people. Among the speakers was the much-admired and respected veteran of pacifist protest against Australian participation in the Boer War and World War I – the Reverend David Rivett. After a short attack on militarism, he collapsed and died on the platform. Participating in these exciting events was Gerald Griffin from New Zealand. Refused admission to Australia by failing a language test in Dutch, he returned secretly and for some months he and Kisch led the police a merry dance around Australian industrial centres. Much publicity was thereby obtained for the Movement Against War and Fascism. In November 1934, a labourer from Collingwood, Victoria, was prosecuted for offensive behaviour for distributing antiwar pamphlets to the crowd that gathered at the Botanical Gardens in Melbourne to hear the Duke of Gloucester dedicate the Shrine of Memory to those who died in the Great War. The struggle for collective security thus became linked with the demands for freedom of discussion leading, with other developments, to the conversion of key union leaders to the ideas of the Left.

Ross, *John Curtin for Labor and for Australia* (1971), pp. 158–9

## Taking the Pledge

*When James Scullin resigned as federal Labor leader in 1935 Frank Forde was tipped as his successor. His only rival, John Curtin, had a problem.*

[Labor MP] E.J. Holloway believed that only one who had opposed the Premiers' Plan would be acceptable as a Labor leader, especially to the trade unionists of New South Wales and Victoria. He supported Curtin – but was Curtin to be trusted? Holloway, or someone acting on his behalf, approached Curtin about his drinking.

'Do you think you have it conquered, Jack?' Curtin was asked.
'Yes,' he replied.
'I have been asked by the Party to invite you to stand for an important position.'
'What is it?'
'The chaps want me to guarantee that you will keep sober.'
'Of course I would – what is the position?'

Curtin did not seem to have had any doubts, either that he could keep sober or that the subject needed a long discussion. 'What is it?' he repeated.

'Leader of the Party.'

'Me!' At last Curtin was aroused. 'Not me – I wouldn't have a chance.'

'Oh yes, you would. I've a team prepared to vote for you, if I pass on your promise that you have given up the drink.'

'You tell them – I promise, and I will carry out my promise.'

Ross, *John Curtin for Labor and for Australia* (1971), p. 147

## Not If, but When

*Curtin was elected in 1935, and took a far more pessimistic view of the country's future than most of his colleagues.*

Curtin was watching the Indian Ocean from Cottesloe, as he often did when thinking out a problem, letting his mind flow as freely as the waves … His daughter Elsie was with him.

'Thinking of the election, dad?' Elsie asked.

Curtin looked up at her quickly. 'No, not the election,' he answered unsmiling.

'Then what?'

He hesitated a moment. 'I was just thinking', he said quietly, 'what would we do, what our reactions would be, if we saw the Jap fleet coming in past the island now.'

'Do you think they ever will?'

'I've stopped wondering if they ever will,' said her father. 'The only question to be answered now is, when?'

Chester in Ross, *John Curtin for Labor and for Australia* (1971), p. 172

## WHAT MAKES POLLIES TICK

*Even during the late 1930s there was no obvious hostility
to or from Germans in Australia, as the Country Party
politician Arthur Fadden recollected.*

Families of German extraction were prolific [in the Darling Downs]. At one meeting a couple of lads were having some fun at the expense of the hard-case German who chaired my meeting. One of them, employed by a local stock and station agent, asked him if he could explain the difference between politics and cattle ticks.

'Vell, yes,' said the chairman, 'poli-tics, dot is Mr Fadden. Cattle ticks vos nasty little parasites vot hangs on to the cow and sucks her blood vich reduces her milk; and dot young fellow who asks der question is another parasite vot lives on the dairymen and is a lunatick.'

Fadden, *They Called Me Artie* (1969), p. 40

## HUGHES ON HITLER

*The United Australia Party Prime Minister Joe Lyons
was keen that Australia do nothing to offend
Hitler's Germany during the prewar years. John Paton,
secretary to Billy Hughes, told how the Little Digger
got around the edict in 1938.*

I remember once, when we got to Inverell – and this portrays both his personality and also his refusal to be one of the Cabinet team – Lyons had telegraphed him that under no circumstances was any Cabinet minister to make a statement on foreign affairs. We were in the lounge at the hotel, and the local reporters asked Hughes what he thought of Hitler. Hughes was still smarting under this telegram that he had had, and he said 'I'm only Minister for External Affairs – I'm not allowed to say anything – so therefore I cannot comment. I will, of course, say that if you paved the way from here to Broken Hill with Bibles, and if that man Hitler swore an oath on every one of them, I wouldn't believe a goddam bloody word he said.'

I spent the rest of the evening trying to keep that out of the Sydney press because at the time Australia and Britain were playing ball with Germany — or, rather, trying to avert the obvious war — and if that had come from Australia's Minister for External Affairs, it would probably have created quite a sensation.

Paton in Thompson and Counihan (eds),<br>
*On Lips of Living Men* (1962), pp. 108–9

## TRADE COMES FIRST

*The Country Party leader Earle Page took a more pragmatic view, as the records of a 1938 Cabinet meeting showed. He believed that*

not until Germany had been satisfied ... Would [there] be any prospect of easing down on the armament race, or any change from the policy of autarchy which the German Government were at present following, or consequently any general revival of world trade ... Germany had formerly been one of Australia's most important markets for her wool and other raw materials, and there could be no revival of this market until more normal trading arrangements with Germany were possible. What Australia desired, therefore, was a politically satisfied Germany which would be ready to take her share in the peaceful development of the world. Would the German Government be satisfied if they got the Sudeten Germans, and if they would be satisfied, would it not be wise to give the Sudeten Germans to them?

Martin, *Robert Menzies* (1993), p. 233

# Righteous Wrath

*A 1938 speech by Robert Menzies on the subject of leadership was seen as a direct attack on Prime Minister Joe Lyons — especially by his wife Enid.*

Suddenly I was electrified.

'Joe,' I exclaimed, 'have you seen what Bob Menzies said in Sydney yesterday?'

'Yes. Why?' he answered mildly.

'Why?' I almost shouted. 'Why? Can't you see it's a direct public hit at you?'

'Not at all,' he replied. 'Bob wouldn't be guilty of such a thing. It's just the way it's reported.'

'Don't be a fool, Joe,' I adjured him. All my fighting blood was up. I could not accept any theory of misreport or misinterpretation. The attack on Joe's leadership had for weeks, yes, even months, filled columns of the daily press. He would be a naive person indeed who would expect such a speech at that time to be taken at its face value, and Bob was not noted for naivete. I was brimming over with righteous wrath.

Lyons in Martin, *Robert Menzies* (1993), p. 243

# Pig Iron Bob

*In 1938 Menzies' attitude to trade with Japan earned him an unwanted nickname.*

Waterside workers at Port Kembla refused to load pig iron bound for Japan, on the grounds that it was going to be used for war purposes against the Chinese and might conceivably be used to manufacture munitions for later use against Australia. The Attorney-General in the Commonwealth Government, Mr R.G. Menzies, then threatened to invoke the 'Dog Collar' (Transport Workers) Act against the unions if they did not behave themselves, and thereby earned the sobriquet 'Pig Iron Bob' which stayed with him for the rest of his political career. Mr Menzies claimed that the quantity of pig iron involved was almost microscopic compared with that involved at the time when the Government prohibited the export of iron ore from Australia. He also said that there was no shortage of foundry pig iron in Australia; that if pig iron were not sold to Japan, then neither should wheat and wool used by Japanese troops in China be sold to Japan; that the League of Nations had not imposed economic sanctions on Japan; and that, in any case, as he told Parliament,

> while problems and differences of opinion undoubtedly exist in relation to the supply of raw materials to foreign countries in certain circumstances, such problems must be faced by the Government and the Parliament of the Commonwealth. They cannot be determined by independent industrial action by any union or group of men. This is the place for discussion and decision in regard to the question of the supply of raw materials to foreign countries. With the assistance of the good offices of organised industrialists, I hope that we shall succeed in establishing that these problems must be determined by the Parliament.

Crowley, *Modern Australia in Documents*, vol. i (1973), pp. 588–9.

## BRING BACK BRUCE

*Menzies resigned as Attorney-General after Earle Page and the Country Party (who were governing in coalition with the United Australia Party) blocked his plans for an insurance scheme. When Joe Lyons died in office in 1939, Page and others were determined to prevent Menzies from succeeding him as prime minister. UAP supporter Roy Curthoys explained the position in a letter to his friend J.R. Darling.*

Your Melbourne Club friends in the National Union and their opposite numbers in the Union Club in Sydney, aided and abetted by Page, who not unnaturally hates Menzies for the devastating stories Menzies so openly and so tactlessly spreads about Page's leadership of the trade delegation in London; and by [Richard] Casey, who, in the opinion of most people, comes out of the whole business very badly, made a dead set on Menzies. He was held to have disgraced himself by his resignation on the national insurance issue, which, as he himself has said, was one of the more respectable actions of his life ... I think the National Union also felt that Menzies would not be sufficiently amenable to its orders. Hence the first move was to try to get [former prime minister Stanley] Bruce back. Casey had sounded the Party and having found that he could not command more than a handful of votes, he backed the move. Page, determined to have anyone but Menzies, offered Bruce his seat.

Martin, *Robert Menzies* (1993), p. 269

## An Extraordinary Attack

*After Joe Lyons's death the Country Party leader Earle Page became prime minister for a short period. The United Australia Party elected Robert Menzies as its new leader, but Page would not accept him.*

Parliament met on April 19, and then, after party leaders and a number of individual members paid tributes to Lyons, adjourned as a mark of respect. On the afternoon of the next day Page paid the conventional visit to the Governor-General, Lord Gowrie, to tender his resignation as outgoing Prime Minister and to say to whom the commission should pass. But that morning, in the House of Representatives, he took the unprecedented step of announcing beforehand what his advice to Gowrie would be. At the beginning of his short period of office, Page reminded the House, he had committed himself to retire in due course in favour of whoever the UAP elected in Lyons's stead. He would do so now, but since the new leader was Menzies, he and the Country Party were not prepared to serve any longer in a coalition government with the UAP. In explaining why, Page launched an attack on Menzies which the *Sydney Morning Herald* next day described as 'a violation of the decencies of debate without parallel in the annals of the federal Parliament'.

With war threatening, said Page, this was a time when the

country demanded above all a prime minister capable of leading 'a united national effort', but Menzies's public record certainly did not suggest he had the right qualifications for that. Three incidents – one 24 days ago, one 24 weeks ago and one 24 years ago – 'give me no basis of confidence that he possesses the maximum courage or loyalty or judgment'. Twenty-four days previously, he had resigned as Attorney General, at a time when it was crucial that the Cabinet be held together as it prepared for war. Twenty-four weeks previously he had made in Sydney 'a speech on leadership which was taken by a large section of the people of Australia as an attack on his own leader. I do not say it was, but … '

At this point uproar developed as Sir Frederick Stewart, the member for Parramatta, interjected angrily that six members of his party had had an assurance from Lyons that he did not regard the speech as such. But this was as nothing to the excitement when Page came to his third charge: that 24 years previously, when Australia was in the middle of the Gallipoli campaign, Menzies, after being in the military forces for some years, resigned his commission and did not go overseas.

Uproar and cries of 'shame' from both UAP and Labor benches greeted this declaration, but Page pressed on: 'I am not questioning the reasons why anyone did not go to the war. All I say is that if the right honourable gentleman cannot satisfactorily and publicly explain to a very great body of people in Australia, who did participate in the war, his failure to do so, he will not be able to get that maximum effort out of the people in the event of war.'

Martin, *Robert Menzies* (1993), p. 273

# BEHAVE NORMALLY

*Menzies' advice to Australians on the declaration of the Second World War in 1939 was surprisingly low-key.*

I appeal to all citizens to go about their affairs in characteristically normal and cheerful fashion. I hardly need to say that it has never been our habit to be rattled, to lose our sense of proportion, or to exaggerate our dangers. I have been a little criticised for talking optimistically, but as an Australian, I have never believed that Australians have to be frightened into taking a realistic view of things. If we were, at this stage, to allow our anxieties to get the better of us, the only effect would be that business would be disturbed, that many people would lose their employment, and that our internal problems would, as a result, become exaggerated. Your best contribution is, therefore, to behave normally.

*Sydney Morning Herald*, 26 August 1939.

## THE ENEMY WITHIN

*The outbreak of war saw swift action by the police, the press reported.*

Moving swiftly early yesterday morning, police patrols, working under the direction of the military intelligence service, rounded up a large number of enemy aliens in Sydney and other centres in New South Wales.

The plans had been carefully organised, and the police made their arrests in accordance with lists of wanted men and women, based on the secret dossiers in possession of the authorities.

The persons detained were taken to selected police stations, where they spent the night in cells. Subsequently, they will be interned in prisons in country centres of New South Wales. A fleet of cars was used to take them to the stations, which had been prepared for their reception.

The movements of wanted persons had been checked carefully for some time before the orders were given for the roundup. An elaborate system of watchers and telephone posts was designed to keep the authorities informed of any suspicious movements among aliens, indicating that when the time for their arrest came, they might not be found in their usual places of residence.

Moving scenes were witnessed in the night and early dawn as men were ordered to leave their families and accompany the police.

The internees reacted in accordance with their various temperaments; some with blustering indignation, some with sullen acquiescence, and some with apparent resignation to one of the inevitable consequences of war.

In several cases, wanted persons were in possession of revolvers. The police were armed to guard against any contingency that might arise.

Large sums of money – in one case about £500 – were found in the effects of a number of those arrested. The persons wanted were permitted to dress and say farewell to their relatives, but were kept continuously under police supervision.

The raids were the culmination of many months of carefully coordinated effort between the military organisation, the State police, and the federal authorities.

Prominent Nazis had been kept under secret surveillance in a manner which enabled the lists of wanted persons to be revised and extended from day to day.

Details of preparations for the roundup were so worked out that the motor transport fleet, manned and ready to move off at a minute's notice, was standing by, not only throughout Sunday night, but also all Saturday night, in case war had been declared then.

The word to move was not received from Melbourne until after midnight, but when it came the organisation functioned with impressive smoothness.

'The people of New South Wales would be amazed and gratified,' an authority said last night, 'if they could know the full history of this thorough and dramatic action for the protection of Australia against enemy activity within our borders.'

*Sydney Morning Herald*, 5 September 1939.

## Putting in the Boot

*In 1940 the United Australia Party–Country Party coalition was eventually reformed under Menzies with Arthur Fadden as the new Country Party leader. Not everyone was happy.*

Fadden became deputy leader and acting leader of his party. Two of the alternative leaders, [John] McEwen and [Earle] Page, went into the ministry; the third, [Archie] Cameron, did not, and ultimately moved over to the UAP. His refusal of office warrants retelling:

> Cameron's reception of my invitation could have been heard at Sydney Heads as he abused Page and others. I attempted to get a word in and persuade him to discuss the proposition on a reasonable basis. He cleared his throat, spat the whole length of the wall-to-wall carpet, pulled off one elastic-sided boot, then the other, and as he threw one into the furthest corner of the room he swore that he 'would not be found dead with the Country Party mob'.

Fadden in Hughes, *Mr Prime Minister* (1976), pp. 115–16

## Fixing the Election

*During the early years of the war Menzies and Opposition leader John Curtin agreed to form a joint War Council with members from all parties. Fadden (acting PM while Menzies was abroad) recalled how he and Curtin cooperated to solve each other's problems in 1941.*

About this time, on 12 March, the Curtin-led Labor Party and the Beasley group healed their differences and merged as a single party. As a consequence positions in the Opposition camp were declared vacant and refilled by an election in the party room. After the voting, Curtin came to see me.

I could tell, as soon as he sat down, that he was gravely worried. He always carried two pairs of glasses and, when agitated or distressed, would remove one and replace it with the other. This he was doing – I can see it now.

He told me that in the party ballot for positions on the War Council, Beasley, who had been a member because of his leadership of his group, had been defeated. Evatt had been elected in his place. Beasley had been a member of the council since its inception, and, although difficult at times, had proved a useful member. To lose him now, Curtin thought, would be a danger not only to the expression of Labor's viewpoint but also for the government of the country if so vigorous a critic as Beasley were to be left on the outside. In any case Curtin undoubtedly preferred Beasley to Evatt.

I suggested to Curtin that he write me a letter immediately stating that because of the gravity of the situation which the country faced, membership of the council should be increased by two.

'Why two?' asked Curtin.

'I would like to appoint Jack McEwen,' I replied. 'Jack has ability and he can also be difficult at times.' Curtin wrote the letter and the two appointments were made in due course.

Fadden, *They Called Me Artie* (1969), pp. 55–6

# The Whitest Man in Australia

*Menzies gained widespread admiration when he confronted striking coal miners in 1940. Even Rowley James, the Labor member for the electorate of Hunter, was impressed.*

When Menzies arrived at Kurri Kurri he found an almost empty theatre: the miners' leaders had organised a boycott, providing buses for adjournment to a mass counter meeting at the Newcastle sports ground. Menzies forthwith drove the thirty miles to the Newcastle meeting where, from a boxing ring set up in the centre of the ground, the northern miners' leader, 'Bondy' Hoare, was addressing a crowd of strikers and their sympathisers, drawn from the districts surrounding Newcastle and estimated to number more than 4,000. Shouldering his way on to the ground through jeers and boos, Menzies sat at the foot of the ring, heard out the speeches of the miners' leaders, then asked to be allowed to speak himself. Hoare asked the crowd for a decision, and a great roar of 'No!' went up. But Menzies, sitting unmoved, heard out more speakers, the crowd wavered, and a new vote gave permission. Reporters at the scene thought he was listened to with good humour, despite bursts of noisy interjection. The latter, of course, were to his taste. Asked ironically, for example, where his bodyguard was, Menzies replied, quick as a flash: 'The only bodyguard I have here is composed of two or three thousand Australian citizens, who, I believe, will listen to me. I am the grandson of a working miner, who was thrown out of a job because he formed a union.' Eloquent words followed, asking the men to return to work and apply to the court for a variation of the award – the advice in fact which Curtin, though he did not go personally to the coalfields, was giving them. But after Menzies had spoken, the audience carried a motion repudiating 'the attempt by ... The Prime Minister to break the loyalty of the miners to their leaders' and expressing their determination to carry on the strike.'

A little over three weeks later, as strike funds dwindled, a series of conferences brought the strike to an end, with the union representatives agreeing to an undertaking to abide by court awards for the duration of the war. Menzies took the occasion to revive a proposal, so far rejected by the union movement, that it form an advisory panel to assist the Government on industrial matters and Curtin agreed to press the unions to reconsider the matter. Meanwhile one man at least, while remaining a political opponent, never forgot Menzies' trip to Kurri Kurri. In 1945 Rowley James, in a private conversation, called Menzies 'the whitest man in Australia today', and in explanation declared that Menzies had 'done a thing that Curtin dare not do and that is go to the coalfields ... I will not hear a word against Bob Menzies, who is a genuine Australian, and probably the best that this country has raised for a long time'.

Martin, *Robert Menzies* (1993), pp. 298–9

# A Slide Evening

*Menzies spent much of 1941 abroad, on errands that many of his critics perceived as unnecessary. The Canadian Prime Minister, MacKenzie King, described one evening in Ottawa.*

I took Menzies to my room, where he met members of the War Cabinet. We discussed matters until nearly six. I then went with him to his car, he taking a moving picture of myself from the steps. While there, he thought of the pictures he had taken in England, and spoke of using them after tonight's dinner. I promised to get lantern and screen and told him to bring along the slides.

... Had dinner for about 60, – the Governor-General being present, also the Chief Justice. After the GG proposed the King's health, I then proposed Menzies. He replied and, later, we withdrew into the adjoining room, where he showed coloured views of his journey from Australia, through Africa, the Holy Land, his visit in England, etc. When concluded, we adjourned into an adjoining room for conversation.

It was almost midnight before we could get Menzies to leave. I felt sorry for the GG, who was thoroughly tired out, and really, in a way, treated with discourtesy by many of the guests leaving before he did. He was, however, nice about it all.

King in Hazlehurst, *Menzies Observed* (1979), pp. 224–5

# A Grave Return

*Menzies finally arrived home in August 1941, having been warned by colleagues about the discontent within his party. Minister for the Army, Percy Spender, wrote:*

Menzies was already on his way home, but I wrote to reach him en route. To put it briefly, I told him how his political grave was being dug.

When he arrived he stayed briefly in Sydney before 'going into smoke' for a few days at a friend's place near Moss Vale, some 100 miles or so south of Sydney, preparing a major speech which he was to deliver at the Sydney Town Hall. He did not communicate with me.

The town hall meeting was a tremendous success.

After the meeting a reception for a small group of people was held by the Lord Mayor in his rooms. Menzies was surrounded by his admirers. He made no attempt to speak to me until he saw my wife and myself standing rather apart. We had been watching what was taking place with, perhaps, sardonic detachment, because one of the themes of the evening had been the loyalty his colleagues in Cabinet had given him during his absence! He broke off and strode over to us. Without ado he said: 'Well Percy, where is this grave you wrote about!' My reply was: 'It's been dug all right Bob: it is only waiting for you to be pushed into it.' He made some remark to the effect that I must have a vivid imagination, and strode away.

Spender in Hazlehurst, *Menzies Observed* (1979), pp. 241–2

## A Little Lie Down

*When Menzies eventually returned to
Canberra later in August 1941, it was made clear to him that
his only course was to resign, which he did.*

A resolution thanking Menzies for his services was carried. 'Many members of the party were plainly stunned and upset by what was happening, but there was no real attempt to discourage me from the indicated course.'

The Country Party members were sent for and the joint meeting now took place. Hutchinson and Marr nominated Fadden as the new leader; there was no other nomination. At this point Menzies records, simply: 'Issued statement to press, and went home.'

His private secretary, Cecil Looker, later remembered that it was somewhat less matter-of-fact than that. He and Menzies, he said, left the party meeting just after midnight. With his arm around Looker's shoulders and tears in his eyes, Menzies blurted out words which Looker recollected as 'I have been done ... I'll lie down and bleed awhile.'

Martin, *Robert Menzies* (1993), p. 382

## HE'LL BE BACK

*Menzies' resignation appeared to put an end to
his prime ministerial career. There was one member of parliament,
however, who saw it differently.*

Only Archie Cameron, sitting in his shirtsleeves, with one brace hanging loose over his left shoulder and his elastic sides on a government-owned table, divined the truth: 'Finished? He'll be back. The bloomin' big cow's only stepped off the road to clean the muck off his boots and cut himself a new waddy.' And then he summed up the reasons for the late (not much lamented) prime minister's failures: no new chum can drive a team of mixed bullocks bogged in blacksoil and panicking, when he doesn't speak their language. A big whip blooming well makes it worse.'

M.H. Ellis in the *Bulletin*, 22 March 1961.

## AN INDEPENDENT NATION

*Arthur Fadden took over as wartime prime minister in
August 1941, but sometimes had difficulty asserting Australia's
independence, as a clash over North Africa showed.*

There were still more than a thousand Australian troops in Tobruk. Blamey, the officer in charge, had first recommended their relief in July 1941. The War Cabinet had decided to notify Britain that the men were in poor physical condition and ask for their relief. On 11 September, Churchill sent a personal cable to Fadden ending: 'I think ... that you will weigh very carefully the immense responsibility which you would assume before history by depriving Australians of the glory of holding Tobruk till victory was won, which otherwise by God's help will be theirs for ever.' But in Fadden's view, history was not as important as the health of Australian troops. Cabinet supported Blamey, who discussed the matter with General Auchinleck, the British Officer in Command of the Middle East. After Auchinleck had given the reasons why Tobruk should not be relieved, Blamey spoke:

'Gentlemen, I think you don't understand the position. If I were a French or an American commander making this demand what would you say about it?'

'But you're not,' Auchinleck replied.

'That's where you are wrong,' Blamey said. 'Australia is an independent nation. She came into the war under certain definite agreements. Now, gentlemen, in the name of my Government, I demand the relief of those troops.'

'Well, if that's the way you put it, we have no alternative.'

Ross, *John Curtin for Labor and for Australia* (1971), p. 229

## The Fall of Fadden

*Fadden's Government was short-lived. With the government depending on the support of two Independents, it was only a matter of time before the Opposition moved. In October 1941, Labor leader John Curtin formally opposed Fadden's budget. Fadden later wrote:*

On the day the vote was to be taken Curtin called on me on his way to lunch. 'Well, boy,' he said, 'have you got the numbers? I hope you have but I don't think you have.'

I replied, 'No, John, I haven't got them. I have heard that Wilson (the other Independent) spent the weekend at Evatt's home, and I can't rely on Coles.'

Curtin said, 'Well, there it is. Politics is a funny game.'

Wryly I replied, 'Yes, but there's no need for them to make it any funnier.'

I had no lunch. My table was piled with files and I worked on these to give my prospective successor a reasonable start. As I worked Jos Francis, my old Queensland colleague, came to my office and said he had just left [Arthur] Coles, who was annoyed that I had not seen him to ask for his support.

I replied that I had not condescended to do so, whereupon Jos said, 'I have reason to think it might pay you to have a yarn with him.'

I told Jos that if it would please him I would be willing to see Coles.

Jos left the room hurriedly and returned with Coles so quickly that he must have been very close to my office door. Jos left and Coles began the conversation by asking for a cigarette. I told him, pointing to my box, to have the lot.

Coles then told me that he agreed with the Budget by and large.

I answered, 'That being so, Arthur, you will not find it very difficult to support it.'

He looked at me and said, 'But I want the Cabinet reconstructed.'

I replied, 'That might be on the cards. Where do we move from there?' He tapped himself on the chest and looked at me inquiringly. 'You mean,' I said, 'with you included?'

He nodded but I gave him no encouragement. When he got to the door he turned round and said, 'I do not intend to vote with the Government.'

I replied, 'And I'll tell the House why.'

Just as the House was about to meet, Jos asked how I had fared with Coles. I told him and asked him to let Harold Holt know, for Harold had effective material to reply to Coles.

When he spoke, Coles referred to his meeting with me saying that he had told me frankly that I could no longer regard him as a Government supporter.

I interjected, 'Unless I put you in the Cabinet.'

Coles denied my allegation. It was my word against his.

Fadden, *They Called Me Artie* (1969), pp. 68–9.

# Curtin and his Circus

*Curtin inspired great trust as prime minister. Allan Fraser, a journalist who later became a politician, described his rapport with the press.*

I've never known a man who was better able to handle the press than he was. Off the record information, as you know, is information which is given in confidence to pressmen but never for publication. Curtin poured out more off-the-record information than any other prime minister would dream of doing, and yet he was never once betrayed by any of the pressmen; nor, so far as I know, was there any even accidental disclosure of that information. A great feeling of friendship and mutual trust existed between Curtin and the members of his Circus. He frequently used the well-known and good political trick of preventing the publication of things that he didn't want published by telling them in confidence to the members of his Circus.

Fraser in Thompson and Counihan, *On Lips of Living Men* (1962), p. 65

# Nothing to Say

*Another close friend, Victor Courtney, recalled Curtin could also be tough under pressure.*

Soon after he was made prime minister he was telling me of some of the pressure groups that he had to put up with. Most forceful of all was one man, a big newspaper man since dead, who was very wealthy and powerful at the time. 'I'm afraid I had to talk very straight to him,' said Curtin, describing the interview, 'and he never came at me again.' I asked Curtin what he had said and I remember Jack spoke very slowly in reply. 'I said to this man, "I want you to understand that I obey nobody else but the people of Australia. You may as well know now that you have nothing in the world that I want."' And the man to whom he was speaking was a millionaire. That was my finest memory of John Curtin.

Courtney in Thompson and Counihan, *On Lips of Living Men* (1962), pp. 66–7

# Feeling the Strain

*Curtin had a great sense of personal responsibility for the decisions he had to make. Allan Fraser and Frank Green, Clerk of the House of Representatives, recounted his fears at the recall of the 9th Division from the Middle East to Australia in 1942.*

ALLAN FRASER   Curtin was a man extraordinarily sensitive. In the first place he was sensitive to criticism, which was an unusual quality in a man who had gone through the mill in politics as he had. A leader in the *Sydney Morning Herald* could hurt him, where it would be like water off a duck's back for Ben Chifley or any of the others who were around him. He felt the strain and responsibility of everything that he did. For example, it was through his personal decision, finally, that the 9th Division was returned to Australia instead of being sent to Burma, as Winston Churchill wished. I think the Division was about fourteen days on the water coming back to Australia without any naval escort. Most men could, I think, and would have said, 'Well, I've made the decision which I believe was right. If something untoward happens as the result of it, it's not my fault. I've done what was right.' Curtin, I've no doubt, realised that. But at the same time you could tell throughout that fortnight, both from his conversation and his attitude, that he felt himself personally responsible for the lives and safety of those thousands of young men on those ships, and I doubt if he ever slept more than an hour or two a night during that fortnight. The strain upon him was intense and when the 9th Division was safely in Australia and the news that they were back could be released to the Australian people, John Curtin was as a man released from great darkness and unhappiness.

FRANK GREEN   Of course we knew nothing about it at that time, but the minister's chauffeur, Tracey, whom I knew very well, dropped me a hint that night after night the Prime Minister was not going to bed. He was just walking about all night. Well, knowing him very well, I took the liberty of finding out what was the trouble. That night I was going home after midnight – after the rising of the House – and when I got to the Lodge I got through the wire fence (there was no guard there in those days) and I walked about on the lawn till I found him standing in the moonlight. 'Anything wrong?' I said. 'Can't sleep,' he said. 'Can you tell me why?' I said. Silence for a minute or two. Then he said, 'How can I sleep while our transports are in the Indian Ocean with the Japanese submarines looking for them?' He never went to bed until the transports reached Fremantle.

> Fraser and Green in Thompson and Counihan,
> *On Lips of Living Men* (1962), pp. 70–1

## WINNING THE WAR

*Curtin was also a shrewd political tactician, as the Labor back-bencher Reg Pollard attested when Curtin was chasing votes for a controversial decision in 1943. After the reintroduction of conscription by Menzies in 1939, conscripts were required to serve only within Australia; Curtin wanted to send conscripted men to serve overseas in the 'Southwest Pacific area'.*

I met John Curtin in the corridor one day and he said 'Reg, come in and have a yarn. Sit down, have a cigarette.' He told me what he proposed to do. He pointed out that his trouble very largely was that American troops were conscripts, they were giving their lives to fight for the integrity and future of Australia as well of course as America itself. He said his position was an invidious one under those circumstances. Although he had strenuously opposed conscription in World War I he now proposed to extend the area in which Australian conscripts could serve to some distance north of Australia.

I listened attentively to him and never interrupted, and then I said to him 'Well, Jack, I appreciate and understand your position very well indeed. My position is somewhat different: I voted against conscription in World War I although I served in World War I, and determined that I would never compel any other man to do those things in war which I undertook voluntarily.' I pointed out that I had a relative who was a university student who had enlisted and was rejected because he was in a reserve faculty of study, and this had had a very grave effect upon him, and I said I would never willingly be a party to it.

He listened attentively, he then took me by the arm, led me to the door, the green door that goes out of the Prime Minister's room. As I went out, he put his hand on my shoulder and he said 'Reg, you might be right.' Well, that melted me and eventually accepting the party's decision I cast a vote in favour of the alteration.

Pollard in Hughes, *Mr Prime Minister* (1976), p. 126

## INTERN THE PRESS

*Labor MP Arthur Calwell's lifelong hatred of the press began in the war years, as James Killen recalled.*

As a private member in 1942 he asked the Minister for the Army, Frank Forde, a question concerning the then chairman of directors of the Herald and Weekly Times group of newspapers. 'Will the minister put a censor in each office of the Murdoch press, or will he issue an order prohibiting Sir Keith Murdoch from writing letters calculated to lower public morale, or, better still, will he have him interned?'

Some six years later, as Minister for Information and Minister for Immigration, he told Parliament that 'the proudest day of my life will be that on which I see the editor of the Melbourne *Herald* in the dock charged under that section of the Crimes Act which provides for seven years gaol without the option'.

Killen, *Inside Australian Politics* (1985), p. 69

# Fear of Flying

*Dr H.V. 'Doc' Evatt was terrified of flying, but as External Affairs minister in the Curtin Government he had to do a lot of it. Herbert 'Nugget' Coombs, then his economic adviser, recalled one bad trip in 1942.*

Bad as I felt, I had to take time off to feel sorry for Evatt as we took off from Brisbane. He had a pathological fear of flying and only great resolution enabled him to face the ordeal of going on board. As we roared down the runway I observed streaming past my window a great flame of burning gases. I was too sick to be worried but the Doc was certain we were on fire. He staggered pale-faced up the aisle, to warn the crew of our impending doom. They looked at him with the contemptuous pity of the professional and led him back to his seat where his wife, Mary Alice, wiped his brow with a cologne-soaked handkerchief.

The Doc's fear of flying became a recurring component in the emotional tone of the whole journey. Each embarkation was for him a test of courage for which he had to whip himself into the right state of exaltation. At the best this was wearing for his companions and at its worst humiliating for all involved. When leaving the United States for the London section of the mission we were assembled at the New York airport for a 10pm takeoff and were being given VIP attention. The Doc, normally very abstemious, allowed himself a couple of 'Old Fashioneds', a whisky-based cocktail with a specious air of innocence enhanced by the pink cherry which decorated it, but with the delayed action of a time bomb. By ten o'clock the Doc was ready to face the devil himself, exuding hearty, back-slapping bravado. Unfortunately, departure was long delayed and as the night wore on the Doc's veneer of insouciance, and the patience of those with him, wore transparently thin. There was little admiration or even pity among us for the agonised effort which finally took him aboard.

The plane was an early Boeing Clipper – set up like a Pullman railway carriage with rows of bunks closed off with green baize curtains. At the earliest possible moment I dived into one of the bunks and was almost instantly asleep. At some time in the night I was rudely shaken by the Doc whose urgent voice was saying, 'Nugget, wake up, we're in a fog, we're lost.' Angrily I asked, 'What the hell can I do about it?' and rolled over into sleep again to wake in the soft sunshine of an Irish morning as we came in to land at Limerick. The unfortunate Doc had spent the night pacing up and down between the bunks plaguing the crew for information about our progress. No doubt, one had retaliated.

Coombs, *Trial Balance* (1981), pp. 36–7

## Asylum and Detention

*John Curtin's Government contained a number of new boys. Former Labor MP Fred Daly remembered one who got into trouble.*

Max Falstein, one of the youngest members of Parliament, was an interesting character. Young and impetuous, he was never out of trouble. His comments were always blunt and to the point. His description of Parliament is one that stands out: 'This must be the only asylum in the world where the inmates are in charge.'

Falstein had enlisted in the RAAF and after one of his many conflicts with authority was sentenced to a term of detention. Arriving in Canberra for the session, Labor members found attached to their letter boxes in the party room urgent telegrams from him requesting that representations be made immediately on his behalf to the Minister for Air. Bert Lazzarini (NSW) was the Acting Minister at the time and we took it in turns to present the telegrams to him while he was having lunch. Lazzarini became so exasperated he roared, 'If I get any more of these I'll keep him in for life.'

Daly, *From Curtin to Hawke* (1984), p. 22

## Drawing the Line

*Fred Daly also related the definitive version of one of the most famous Billy Hughes stories.*

In 1944, Curtin presided at a big dinner to mark the fiftieth anniversary of Billy Hughes' election to Parliament – New South Wales and Commonwealth. The four best after-dinner speakers that I have ever heard were present on that occasion: Curtin, Menzies, Fadden and Billy Hughes. This was the occasion when Curtin, in the course of his speech, said, 'Billy, you are the "googly bowler" of Australian politics, but why is it that you have been in almost every party in Australia except the Country Party?' Billy replied, 'Good God, man, you have to draw the line somewhere.'

Daly, *From Curtin to Hawke* (1984), p. 32

## The Arrival of Chif

*Ben Chifley, later prime minister himself, emerged quickly as Curtin's chief lieutenant. He was marked for the job early.*

During the evening of October 3 [1942], after the vote had gone against the Government, Chifley dropped into Curtin's room to discuss some matter of the moment. There he found his leader deep in conversation with ex-prime minister Scullin whose advice and support Curtin so much valued in moments of crisis. Scullin looked up as the door opened and asked: 'Ah, Ben, how is your health standing up?' 'Never better,' answered Chifley laconically. 'That's good!' said Scullin, 'It's got to be; I've got you down on my list for five portfolios already.'

Crisp, *Ben Chifley* (1963), p. 139

# Pure Bloody Politics

*Chifley won a ballot for leadership of the Labor Party after Curtin died in office in July 1945. As prime minister Chifley usually found political solutions without making enemies in the process.*

There is, for instance, the story of his yielding to Pollard's persistent urging that he should revise his decision relating to a major wool-marketing issue. (He used to refer jocularly to his three ministerial colleagues, R.T. Pollard, N. Lemmon and W.J. Scully as the Cabinet's 'Farmers' Union'.) He finally agreed that Pollard should come with his advisers and that he would have his Treasury men present for a complete reassessment. Chifley sat behind his office desk sucking his pipe while the issues were argued back and forth. Finally he saw the opportunity for a compromise and quietly announced: 'I think we'll do this and this and this.' Silence suggested general approval and an old Treasury hand who had a reputation for playing the courtier chimed in: 'That sounds logical, Mr Prime Minister, that sounds logical.' Chifley took his pipe from his mouth, turned round to the speaker and remarked with the faintest grin: 'Logical be buggered – it's pure bloody politics, that's what it is.'

Crisp, *Ben Chifley* (1963) p. 240 (note)

# Wagging School

*Chifley also had a knack of keeping away from controversial areas.*

Chifley, for his part, set his face resolutely against the Commonwealth's moving into direct responsibility for primary and secondary schooling. One of his most senior advisers tried to persuade him that after the war the Commonwealth would have to give direct aid. 'No,' said Chifley, 'I'd like to keep out of education – it has special difficulties for us: it's mixed up with religion, aid to denominational schools, and all that. Besides [almost as a relieved afterthought], the constitution leaves education as a

State function.' 'But,' objected the adviser, 'you're already subsidising preschool centres and the universities directly.'

'Ah,' concluded Chifley, with a broad grin, 'that's different – they're for kids *before* they've got souls and *after* they've lost 'em.'

Crisp, Ben Chifley (1963), p. 195 (note)

## A CHIFFORISM

*Government adviser Nugget Coombs christened Chifley's little aphorisms 'Chifforisms'. One was at the expense of Indian Prime Minister Jawaharlal Nehru, during a trip to India in 1946.*

However, at one point Nehru remarked half-musingly, 'I suppose it would be valuable to have somebody whom you knew would support you when you were right.' At this point Chif took his pipe from his mouth, leant towards Nehru and said, 'Even more valuable if you happened to be wrong!'

While Nehru obviously thought such a contingency too improbable to contemplate he enjoyed the quip.

Coombs, Trial Balance (1981), p. 65

## CITY OF JOY

*Chifley never lost his zeal for reform. On the same trip to India he and Coombs visited Calcutta.*

We walked the streets of Calcutta with their wandering cattle, lacklustre beggars, and derelict humanity in all stages of malnutrition and disease, with the horror and shame which is the usual first response to these sights. 'How would you like to be Director of Post-War Reconstruction here?' Chif asked me. 'Well', I replied, 'I couldn't make it worse.' 'When I look at all this', said Ben, 'and think of the untold millions of wealth which have flowed out of this country to Europe, it makes my blood boil.' He paused for a moment and then added, with a slightly twisted grin, 'And I'm getting too old to have my blood boil.'

Coombs, *Trial Balance* (1981), p. 66

## Making a Deal

*Chifley was at his best when dealing directly with his fellow politicians. Coombs told how he cut through stalled negotiations with the United States in 1946 by going straight to the Secretary of State.*

Our stay in Washington was to be brief and I could see a deadlock developing which would have been very disappointing to the Prime Minister. We reported the outcome of the conversations to Chif whose mouth set in a hard line. 'They can have their cultural fund', he said, 'but that is the end of it.'

He picked up the phone and asked to speak to Dean Acheson and a conversation on these lines followed:

> CHIFLEY  'Mr Secretary, you know our officials have been talking about the Lend Lease settlement. They tell me that there is a difference between us about the amount that is due to you. You make it $US32 million and we make it $US22 million.
> 
> 'I know this is a matter of high policy and I wouldn't want you to think I am bargaining, but I am in a hurry to leave for Japan and I wonder whether we couldn't do a quick deal and settle it.
> ACHESON  'What sort of deal have you in mind?'
> CHIFLEY  'Suppose we split the difference and call it $US27 million in complete and final settlement.'
> ACHESON  (after a short pause) 'Done, Mr Prime Minister.'
> CHIFLEY  'It's a deal.'

Within half an hour Acheson was back on the phone saying his officers had been anxious to talk about civil aviation and trade policy matters. Chifley replied that we were at all times happy to talk about such matters, but not in the context of the Lend Lease Agreement.

Coombs, *Trial Balance* (1981), pp. 86–7

## ANOTHER AUSTRALIAN GG

*Chifley's appointment of William McKell, a former Labor premier of New South Wales, as Governor-General in 1947 provoked an outcry from the conservatives. Chifley had no hesitation in justifying it.*

MR CHIFLEY    Sir Isaac Isaacs had long been dissociated from politics, and he occupied a high position as Chief Justice of the High Court, but the same violent opposition was offered to his appointment as is offered today to the appointment of Mr McKell. I, as leader of the Government, accept full responsibility for the nomination of Mr McKell, and I offer no apologies for having made it. I am completely confident that as time goes on I shall have no reason to regret my action. I recommended his appointment as a distinguished Australian who had retained the confidence of the people of his own State in the political field for his administrative capacity over a considerable period. Mr McKell will bring to the position a ripe experience of affairs, and a knowledge of administration in Australia. He will bring with him also a full appreciation of the aspirations and ideals of the Australian people. Let me remind honourable members that a South African, a man who was also a politician, was appointed Governor-General on the recommendation of a government with which Field Marshal Smuts was associated. Speaking later on the subject, Field Marshal Smuts declared that the appointment of a citizen of South Africa as Governor-General in no way weakened the ties linking that dominion to the Mother Country. I maintain that the position is the same in Australia. Any Australian citizen of sufficient ability, reputation and integrity of character is entitled to occupy the position of Governor-General.

Australia, House of Representatives 1947, *Debates*, vol. 190, p. 27

# Boilers for Spooks

*The Australian Security Intelligence Organisation (ASIO) had very ordinary beginnings.*

In February 1949, an adviser to the Labor Prime Minister, Ben Chifley, found him chuckling to himself in his office in Parliament House, Canberra. 'I've just traded three boilers with Tom Playford for two judges,' Chifley explained. To start a development project in his state, Playford, conservative Premier of South Australia and a tough horse-trader, wanted three large steam boilers from an Australian government munitions plant that had been run down after the war. Chifley required the temporary services of one judge for a Royal Commission; the intended role of the second judge was to be more significant. On 24 February 1949, Chifley formally concluded this arrangement in a letter to Playford requesting the services for twelve months of Mr Justice Reed of the South Australian Supreme Court, to found a permanent Australian security service. In justifying his choice, Chifley stated: 'In order to carry the fullest public confidence I am convinced ... that the new service should be organised under the leadership of a man of high standing and wide experience of affairs.' Justice Reed was accordingly released by Playford and began the formation of the Australian Security Intelligence Organisation.

Whitlam and Stubbs, *Nest of Traitors* (1974), p. 13

# The Secret State

*From the first, ASIO's operations were secret. Chifley and Doc Evatt adopted the technique which later became known as 'neither confirm nor deny'.*

MR CHIFLEY   Where evidence is available that any person in the Public Service is suspected of engaging in subversive activities, the necessary action will be taken to deal with them.
MR RYAN   What is the action that is taken?
MR CHIFLEY   I do not propose to deal in detail with the

operation of the security organisation. That organisation has now been placed under the direction of Mr Justice Reed, of South Australia, who is a reputable and highly qualified gentleman. It is not the practice in this, or any other country, to discuss in the Parliament the methods employed by an organisation of that kind. Therefore, I do not propose to deal with such details here. The work of the security organisation is entrusted to highly qualified men who can be considered to be completely impartial. Should any matter arise which I believe should be reported to the Parliament, I shall take that course.

Australia, House of Representatives 1949, *Debates*, vol. 202, p. 273

MR HARRISON   I direct the attention of the Attorney-General to reports that extreme disquiet is being caused in the Commonwealth Public Service by the activities of the new security service. It is alleged by senior officers that many dossiers compiled by that service are unreliable and highly libellous, and that some of those that have been shown to heads of departments are based mainly on hearsay and uncorroborated evidence. Are these complaints based on fact? If so, will the right honourable gentleman take action to remedy them?

DR EVATT   Last week, or earlier, I indicated the general authority and nature of the security service, of which Mr Justice Reed is Director-General. Following his appointment to that position a reorganisation was effected with the closest cooperation between the British security authorities and the Australian Government. In order to protect our internal security, one result of the new arrangement is to give to the Director General of Security a charter as ample as that possessed by the corresponding authority in Great Britain. Therefore, it is not possible that documents of the kind mentioned by the honourable member would be shown to heads of departments. Such documents are not shown even to ministers. To all intents and purposes the Director-General of Security is free from ministerial direction. That arrangement is essential in order to maintain maximum internal security which, I have no doubt, all honourable members wish to have preserved.

In principle, everything is left to the discretion, good sense and sense of justice of Mr Justice Reed, who for many years has been a distinguished justice of the Supreme Court of South Australia. The honourable member may rest assured that if particulars of any alleged injustice are brought to the notice of Mr Justice Reed – which I undertake to do if they are supplied to me – he will deal with them on the basis of justice, always remembering that the supreme consideration is the security of the country.

Australia, House of Representatives 1949, *Debates*, vol. 204, pp. 347–8

## New Australians

*As immigration minister for the Labor Government Arthur Calwell became famous for barring a Chinese family from entry to Australia with the phrase: 'Two Wongs don't make a White'. But he could be more sensitive, as the Melbourne* Argus *reported in 1949.*

The terms 'Balts', 'Displaced Persons', and 'DP's', had been banned from official communications, Mr Calwell, Minister for Immigration, said today.

Immigration authorities were beginning a campaign to outlaw the terms as applied to immigrants reaching Australia under the agreement with the International Refugee Organisation.

Mr Calwell suggested that all new immigrants should be called 'new Australians', 'newcomers', or 'new settlers'.

In time the expressions 'Balts' and 'DP's' might eventually assume the unpleasant undertones of words such as 'Dago' and 'Reffo', he said.

'No matter how these words are used, they have an unpleasant ring. If they become embedded in the Australian vocabulary, they could easily come to be used disparagingly,' Mr Calwell declared.

'I appeal to Australians to outlaw these expressions. These people have come from Europe to join their destiny with ours in the development of a country they have willingly adopted.

'Today just on 50,000 new settlers have reached Australia

under agreement with the IRO. They were innocent victims of war, displaced from their homes and homelands, and now, as Australia is the land of resettlement for them, they are no longer displaced persons. They are newcomers, new settlers, or, preferably, new Australians.'

*Argus*, Melbourne, 11 August 1949.

## A Spot of Red-baiting

*As early as 1946 Doc Evatt was showing some signs of what was to be called his larrikin strain. Dr John Burton, head of the External Affairs Department, gave an example.*

One of the worst examples of this, perhaps, was the Paris Peace Conference in 1946. Again the [Australian] delegation was well prepared for this conference. It had attached a great deal of importance to the conference of the satellite powers being a success. Attempts were made to draft up proposals which would cover the requirements of Europe in the future. He agreed with all these when they were put to him, and we looked forward to this conference because it looked as though, after all the years of war, something constructive could be done. But this larrikin strain came out. It wasn't introduced by him initially. He had with him Mr Beasley, who was known for his violent anti-Communist viewpoints, and within a day or so of this conference we had the spectacle of Mr Beasley making a speech in answer to Mr Gromyko, when he said, 'We know who you are, we call you "Commies" in Australia.' And this set the tone of the conference, which got worse and worse. Dr Evatt did nothing to pull Mr Beasley back, on the contrary seemed to be encouraging him … thinking that this was the kind of thing which would go down well in Australia. It was not the normal means of conducting peace conferences, and those around him could have no influence at all on him in circumstances such as this. He finally left the conference earlier than was required, and it was to everyone's benefit.

Burton in Whitlam and Stubbs, *Nest of Traitors* (1974), p. 34

## The China Syndrome

*At other times the larrikin in Evatt melded with the political cynic. Burton again:*

He was always very keen on the recognition of China – he thought it was the proper thing to do and in some circumstances pressed for it. But then he was faced with an election in 1949. The United Kingdom government, having recognised China, sent out a senior official to persuade the Australian government to follow suit. And to make this possible, to make it clear that a well-considered decision was being taken, all officers from the whole of Southeast Asia were recalled for a conference to Canberra.

They duly met and discussed the matter, and unanimously agreed there should be immediate recognition. No one had any doubts about it whatsoever. Sir Keith Officer was there. He was perhaps the most senior member of the permanent diplomatic service. After the deliberations, Dr Evatt walked in and said: 'Well, Sir Keith, what do you think?' And Sir Keith said: 'We are quite unanimous, there is no doubt in our minds at all, there should be recognition of China.' And Doc Evatt's response was: 'Keith, you're a Red!' ... And Evatt walked out.

And Australia didn't recognise China. Everyone in that room knew that he'd wanted to, but this was being politically realist in the extreme – it didn't make any difference to the election, of course, and everyone knew it wouldn't.

Burton in Whitlam and Stubbs, *Nest of Traitors* (1974), p. 35.

## Just 42 Little Words

*The key to the 1949 election was Chifley's decision, made back in 1947, to nationalise the private banks. At the time it was a bombshell.*

As the ministers left the Cabinet room and were walking along the lobby, Chifley was, as usual, accosted by some pressmen with a request for any news of Cabinet decisions. He casually remarked as he went on his way to lunch: 'Oh, Don [Rodgers, his press secretary] may have a little piece in there that'll interest you.'

Rodgers handed them a 42-word announcement by Chifley: 'Cabinet today authorised the Attorney-General (Dr Evatt) and myself to prepare legislation for submission to the Federal Parliamentary Labor Party for the nationalisation of banking, other than State banks, with proper protection for the shareholders, depositors, borrowers and staffs of private banks.' It was said that one of the senior gallery correspondents, on reading those 42 words, involuntarily bit right through the stem of his pipe so that it feet clattering to the floor. Within days that small clatter over bank nationalisation had grown to a nationwide furore.

Crisp, Ben Chifley (1963), p. 328

## A Spot of Overtime

*The banks' campaign against the legislation was unremitting. Fred Daly recalled some stormy meetings in 1949.*

I remember going to meetings with [Labor MP] Les Haylen in small halls which were crowded to capacity. These meetings appeared to be peaceful but bank clerks were there in force, paid to attend to protest and disrupt proceedings.

At a meeting in a small hall in Normanhurst, Sydney, I was constantly interrupted by a rowdy crowd. I said to an interjector, 'You're a bank officer and you're being paid time and a half to come here and interject.' He replied, 'That's a deliberate lie, I get double time.'

At another rowdy meeting in Dulwich Hill with Les Haylen, a bank clerk in the audience demanded to know why Daly was not in the Army. 'Will you stand up,' said Haylen. A big, awkward, ugly-looking individual rose in his place, the only one on his feet. Haylen said, 'For the same reason as you couldn't win a beauty contest – physically unfit.' The reply nearly caused a riot and just about wrecked the meeting.

Daly, From Curtin to Hawke (1984), p. 60

# An Uneven Fight

*Daly noted that even some of the Labor members were a trifle overawed by the battle they had started.*

Don McLeod (Wannon, Vic.) said a few days later, 'You know, Freddie, I was strolling in Martin Place the other day with those banking institutions looming above and I thought some of them might fall on me. I don't think all the caucus put together had more than a thousand quid between them and we'd taken over all the great banking institutions in Australia.'

Daly, *From Curtin to Hawke* (1984), p. 59

# Battle of the Slogans

*Daly also recorded that the fight in his own electorate in 1949 went over the top.*

One of my supporters pointed out that my literature could easily have referred to the family dog, there were so many references to 'loyal', 'devoted', 'approachable', 'always available', 'servant' and 'protection of your interests'.

It was a no-holds-barred campaign. The Liberal Party was out to regain the seat. [Their candidate] Jacobs erected large signs throughout the electorate reading 'Be healthy, be Liberal, be clean, change Da(i)ly' with the 'i' crossed out. It was rather funny and clever but some of my supporters were very annoyed and retaliated with 'Give us this day our Daly Fred'. It became the battle of the slogans.

Jacobs, who was obviously of Jewish origin, was described as being a Methodist. He ran into trouble with both these sections by leaving the Jewish faith and by joining the Methodists. A very keen supporter of mine became very annoyed with the 'Change Daly' slogan and said if it continued he would put Jacobs' 'swan song' all over the electorate in 6x3 foot letters. I asked, 'What is his "swan song"?' He replied, ADIEU-ADIEU-ADIEU. When Sir Eric Harrison was asked to speak in support of Jacobs he is reported to have expressed surprise that a person of Jewish origin had been selected for the electorate because there were very few Jews in the district. He was told that Jacobs was not Jewish but was a Methodist. Harrison later told me that when he arrived for the campaign meeting Jacobs introduced himself and Harrison said he looked so Jewish that he made Maxie Falstein look like an Irishman.

Daly, *From Curtin to Hawke* (1984), p. 43

## THROWING OFF THE YOLK

*On the other side Arthur Fadden, a veteran of stormy campaigns, also reported problems.*

An interjector shouted, 'If your mob gets in we will have no money to pay tax.'

I retorted, 'My government would not tax decency or it would owe you a rebate.'

During 1949 campaign meetings the same pattern occurred. At Griffith I was the target for an egg, none too fresh, which fortunately missed me but befouled the platform. The audience seemed to appreciate my comment that after this experience I had no desire to live under the Communist 'yolk'. Soon afterwards a friend presented me with a souvenir of the incident, an ornamental Little Red Hen with the inscription: 'Why depend on the commos? Lay your own eggs on your own platform.'

Fadden, *They Called Me Artie* (1969), p. 109

## A LOYAL VOTER

*Some of Chifley's supporters, even in the bush, resisted the banks' efforts.*

Chifley was amused by the story of the efforts of an Opposition organiser to win the vote of the wife of one of these pastoralist friends in 1949. She was a free-speaking woman and the dialogue went as follows after the organiser stated his business:

'It's no use, I'm going to vote for Ben!'
'But that's silly, Mrs——, he's a socialist.'
'I'm still going to vote for him.'
'But he'd take your property under socialism.'
'I don't care a bugger — I'd take McPhillamy's [the choicest property in the district].'

After the lady had enumerated Chifley's good points, the canvasser changed his tack to what he thought might be a shrewd one in the circumstances:

'His wife doesn't help him much,' he resumed.

'Well, he's only the first bloody man in the land — she couldn't help him much further, could she?'

The canvasser moved on to the next property on his itinerary.

Crisp, Ben Chifley (1963), p. 118 (note)

## No Publicity, Please

*Meanwhile Robert Menzies, as Leader of the Opposition, was already cultivating the aloof style. His press secretary Charles Meeking produced this parody just before the Liberals won the 1949 election.*

ANY DAY 1944–47

C.J.M. (brightly)   Good morning! May I suggest a press conference?
R.G.M.   You may, but I won't have one.
C.J.M. (wistfully)   The boys would like one.
R.G.M..   Curse the boys.
C.J.M. (doggedly)   Well, then, what about a written statement on a burning topic?
R.G.M..   There are no burning topics.
C.J.M. (perspiringly)   It would be good if you could consent to be photographed while shaving! The Sydney readers …
R.G.M..   'Out, damned spot.'
C.J.M. (faintly)   Well, what can I arrange?
R.G.M..   To close the door behind you!
C.J.M. (despairingly)   Hell, what a job!

Hazlehurst, Menzies Observed (1979), p. 302

# The Art of Small Talk

*Menzies had difficulty making light conversation, and even Arthur Fadden couldn't help him. Jim Killen recalled the following story.*

In the old Parliament House Sir Robert Menzies invariably left the building through the office of the staff of the Minister for Supply, Howard Beale. The staff office door opened out onto a small porch with steps leading to the road.

On Howard Beale's staff were Reg Harris, who had served with distinction as a war correspondent during World War II, and Frank Henchlewood, a well-known and highly regarded civil servant.

One evening Artie Fadden returned from dinner with the Prime Minister following him through the staff office. Artie stopped to speak with Reg and Frank, passing some generalities and asking Frank to convey a message to a mutual friend in Sydney. Menzies listened outside the office to the conversation. When Artie joined him he said: 'You talk to people so easily. It is a great gift.' Artie replied: 'Bob, let me get together for dinner some of the fellows on the Government side who you look upon as being a bit hard to get on with. I think you will see them in a different light.' The dinner was arranged, and a convivial gathering looked promising. A lively discussion started as to who would buy the dinner wine.

> SENATOR  It's not every day we have the Prime Minister dining with us. I would like to buy the wine.
> MP  I have known the Prime Minister longer than anybody present. I would like to buy the wine.
> MP  No, I should buy the wine. I had a win recently on the stock exchange.
>
> Menzies listened to the discussion with great interest and total silence until one MP, for whom he had slender regard, said: 'No, I am the person who should buy the wine. My son today announced his engagement to be married.'
> MENZIES  Since when has marriage been an institution in your family?

It took all of Artie's touch to smooth things over.

Killen, Killen in Company (1989), pp. 49–50

## Silence is Golden

*Not all politicians under Menzies were big talkers.*

The former ALP prime minister the late Ben Chifley used to say 'More men have talked their way out of Parliament than ever talked their way into it.' The experience of Mr William Jack, former Liberal Member of the House of Representatives for North Sydney, would seem to justify this observation. Known as 'The Silent One', Mr Jack was in Parliament from 1949 to 1966. During that time he asked eight questions and made seven speeches. One of the speeches was 'I move that the question be put.' His majority consistently improved and he retired in 1966 undefeated.

Reid, *The Gorton Experiment* (1971), p. 85 (note)

## An Informal Dinner

*After Chifley was defeated, he recalled some of the highlights of his career. Former Labor MP Clyde Cameron liked the one about the royal invitation that got turned down.*

Chifley resumed his story about declining an invitation to dine with the King when he was in London for a Commonwealth prime ministers' conference. But the real reason for his reluctance to dine at the palace was that he did not have the dinner suit that was *de rigueur* for such occasions. The official secretary at the other end of the phone was apparently stunned by his refusal of an invitation from the King. It was just not done.

A bit later, Lord Gowrie, who had got to know Chifley when he was Governor-General during the war, phoned to ask whether he could come and see him. Gowrie soon arrived and said that Chifley's refusal to accept the invitation had caused 'a real tailspin at the palace'. Chifley explained that he did not have a dinner suit. Gowrie offered to hire one for him but Chifley replied, 'No you won't. I've never sat in somebody else's clothes in my life. I wouldn't go anywhere in a hired suit. No, no tell them I'm busy.' Gowrie reluctantly went away but phoned back a bit later to say that the King had been told of the problem and he had decided to attend the banquet in a lounge suit. And that was the way it turned out. Never before had the King worn anything but a dinner suit to a formal banquet. However, they neglected to tell the other prime ministers, so the only ones who turned up in lounge suits were the King and Ben Chifley.

Cameron and Connell, *The Confessions of Clyde Cameron* (1990), p. 75

## CAUCUS ROUGHHOUSE

*The 1949 Parliament had some rough and ready characters, especially on the Labor side. Clyde Cameron recalled that Reg Pollard was at his worst after a few drinks.*

In fact he got so drunk one night that he, Rowley James and a few others, lurched into the caucus room and finished up having an argument. Rowley James grabbed one of the pictures from the wall and hit Reggie Pollard on the head. His head went through the frame and broke the glass which cut the tip of his nose. If ever you are in Canberra, and able to look at the picture in the caucus room of a group of members of parliament drawn by some cartoonist, look closely at the middle of the picture and you can see it has been torn and pasted together again.

Rowley James (the father of Bert, who later became the Labor Member for Newcastle) was a big, rough, tough bloke with a neck like a bull. He had been a coalminer and had huge shoulders, but he was so upset by the sight of the blood pouring from Pollard's nose, he said, 'Oh, Reggie, I'm sorry, mate. Go on, hit me as hard as you like.' So Reg closed his fist, threw one right from the floor and missed completely.

Rowley said, 'Go on, Reg, old boy, have another go,' so Reg did and he hit him on the neck somewhere.

Rowley said, 'Ah hah, that wouldn't hurt a flea, go on, old man, you can hit me again, go on hit me.' Reggie did hit him again, but this time he connected and hit him right on the chin. Rowley roared like a bull.

'You bastard,' he shouted and went for him. Reggie ran out of the caucus room, all the way to the Kurrajong Hotel, with Rowley chasing after him. They were both drunk. When Reg woke up next morning he found that his false teeth were missing and there was a great to-do. As soon as he had finished his breakfast, he headed back to the caucus room to see if he could find them. He found the bottom half of his dentures on the side of the footpath and, a little further along, the top half.

Cameron and Connell, *The Confessions of Clyde Cameron* (1990), pp. 68–9

## A Powerful Interjection

*Cameron noted that Rowley James could be just as embarrassing in the chamber as in the caucus room.*

Poor old Rowley had been in a bad car accident in the forties, and he had to use a walking stick. Frequently, after he had had his normal helping of Bundaberg rum, he would come into the chamber to sleep it off. Every now and again, usually once or twice a day, you would see him lift his buttocks off the seat and pass wind. He did not believe in half-measures! They were not, as we would say in the shearing sheds, 'soup coolers' (ones that you could smell but not hear) – they were like rockets. On this particular day, his release was frightening! He dispatched a real rocket which ricocheted back and forth across the chamber and seemed to finish up in a heap right in front of the chief parliamentary reporter, William John Campbell. Eddie [Ward] jumped to his feet and said, 'Excuse me. Did Mr Campbell get Mr James' interjection?' Rowley, of course, did not give a damn. If he felt like passing wind, he did, and that was it!

Cameron and Connell, *The Confessions of Clyde Cameron* (1990), p. 70

## Good Mourning All

*Another prominent Labor man was the stuttering Pat Kennelly. Fred Daly heard this story from a colleague.*

The late Pat Kennelly was a legendary figure in the Labor Party. One of the best stories attributed to him is told by a parliamentary colleague. Kennelly went to the funeral of a member of Parliament. It was a big funeral and many mourners accompanied the grieving family to the cemetery. Kennelly said, 'It w-w-w-a-as a v-v-very s-s-sa-ad occasion. H-h-his w-w-wi-wife and f-f-f-family w-w- were there. There was not a d-d-dry eye in the ce-ce-cemetery. E-e-everyone w-w-was in t-t-t-tears. As I w-w-w-watched them f-f-f-file out of th-th-the ce-ce-cemetery I th-th-thought h-h-how s-s-sad. Th-th-three h-h-hundred m-m-mourners with a s-s-single th-th-thought: "Wh-h-ho's g-g-going to w-w-win the s-s-selection?"'

Daly, *The Politician Who Laughed* (1982), p. 74

## A Spot of Moonlighting

*The 1951 election had its moments. Arthur Fadden reported one of them.*

After enquiring nervously how I felt the chairman said, 'You're going to have a hell of a time tonight, Artie. I hope you've got a better case than I think you have.'

I enquired whether he would take the chair himself and when he admitted that he had been cast for that unenviable role I said, 'Well, brace yourself up for a start and see that the fight is under Marquess of Queensberry Rules.'

The packed audience booed and hooted me. At the back of the hall was an exceedingly vocal interjector; though I could not hear what he was shouting, it was obvious that his remarks were not complimentary and that he was performing to the satisfaction of those around him. But despite the hostile atmosphere I appeared to be making some headway. When question time came the vocal one was deafeningly silent so I invited him to ask a question. Goaded by his mates he shouted, 'Why don't you lazy politicians who live off us do a fair day's work?'

There was loud laughter from the hall. I moved to the front of the platform and shouted back, 'Look, my non-musical friend, I work while you're asleep.'

A voice came from the other side of the hall, 'Of course you do. We all know you're a burglar.'

Fadden, *They Called Me Artie* (1969), p. 118

## AMONG MY SOUVENIRS

*Jim Killen remembered that Fadden's knighthood in 1953 led to an unusual celebration.*

When Artie was created a Knight Grand Cross of the Order of St Michael and St George, the Governor-General, Field Marshal Sir William Slim, held a dinner that evening in honour of some of those who had been at the investiture. Sir Arthur Fadden was present, and not surprisingly he was the life of the party. After dinner he spent some time sitting next to the Governor-General on the sofa near the fireplace, swopping yarns.

After the guests had departed, the comptroller of the household noted that one of the silver-covered matchbox covers was missing, and also the butler reported one of the exquisite Belgium lace mats, which was part of the fruit bowl set, was also missing. Furthermore the Governor-General's reading glasses were missing. The personal staff spent at least thirty minutes trying to locate the missing items, but to no avail. Next morning at about 9.15, a large black Commonwealth car was seen driving in the grounds of Government House. The car came to a stop near the official secretary's office. The driver went to the comptroller's of office. The driver was Sir Arthur's personal driver. He removed from his pocket one silver matchbox cover, one exquisite Belgium lace mat and a pair of reading glasses and stated, 'These are returned from Sir Arthur and please tell His Excellency, with humble respect, the world looks so different through his glasses.'

Killen, *Inside Australian Politics* (1985), p. 26

## AND IN THE LEFT-HAND CORNER ...

*By the end of 1951 Menzies' anti-Communist campaign was having an effect on the public and within the Labor Party, where divisions between Left and Right were becoming more bitter. Fred Daly recalled a public clash.*

It came to a head in an explosive scene in the House on 20 November 1951 when there was almost a stand-up fight between the two Victorians, Reg Pollard and John Mullens. Reg Pollard, a short fiery campaigner, was an old-time Labor radical, pugnacious and cheeky. John Mullens, a flowery old Irish orator, extreme Right, and a fanatical anti-Communist, was bitterly opposed to Evatt and Chifley. It happened during question time and followed a question by Mullens regarding Wilfred Burchett and the author Frank Hardy. Pollard got up to speak and Mullens interjected, 'You are defending the Communists.' Pollard, furious, red-faced and threatening, turned and faced Mullens and roared, 'I brand him for what he is, a narrow-minded skunk and a man who is prepared to do ... ' The rest of the sentence was lost in the uproar.

Mullens leapt angrily from his seat several rows back and tried to scramble over the benches to the central table where Pollard was standing. Pat Galvin (Labor, SA) jumped from his seat and grabbed Mullens by the tie and coat lapels to stop him from rushing towards Pollard. Then in a wild scene they finished up alongside the Speaker's chair – Pollard tiny as a cock sparrow and Mullens towering over him.

Daly, *From Curtin to Hawke* (1984), pp. 113–14

## Menzies is Told

*Menzies was no economist, but he had inherited a formidable team from his Labor predecessors.*

A pattern developed: Menzies would call in such luminaries as Roland Wilson, Richard Randall and H.C. 'Nugget' Coombs and lay out his general budgetary plans for the next fiscal period. He would then look expectantly at the troops, one of whom would reply: 'Prime Minister, you have told us what you wish to do. We will now tell you what you are able to do.' And they would, and he would do it.

MacCallum, *How To Be A Megalomaniac* (2002), p. 20

## Counted Out

*When Doc Evatt decided to challenge Menzies' anti-Communist legislation in court, Ben Chifley had to go to great lengths to avoid open warfare within the Labor Party. Clyde Cameron was in caucus that day.*

At the meeting Chifley was asked whether he had given his approval for Evatt to appear. As was the practice in those days, he was in the chair. Chifley explained that he had not given his approval and that he did not know that Evatt was going to appear. However, he went on to say, 'Let me add this. Had he asked for my permission, I would have given it and I would have given it gladly.' Someone then moved that 'This caucus disassociate itself from the action of Dr Evatt in appearing in the High Court in support of the Communist Party.' Chifley interjected that the motion in that form was out of order because Evatt was not appearing for the Communist Party, he was appearing for the Waterside Workers' Federation. The motion was quickly amended, moved and seconded. A debate ensued, and a vote was taken on the voices. Chifley declared the motion lost.

It was not lost and should have been announced as carried. Those in favour of the motion then called for a show of hands and Tom Sheehan, the Whip, did the count. When he had counted the hands against the motion once he went around a second time until he got enough to say the motion was defeated. Protesting, Tom Burke then called for a division.

By this stage caucus was in a state of bedlam. Members were shouting across the room, especially Reggie Pollard and Eddie Ward, calling the Victorians all sorts of things and they were retaliating. The noise rose to a crescendo when Ben Chifley refused to accept the call for a division. He said a division was a reflection on the integrity of Tom Sheehan who had just counted the hands. Tom Burke moved a motion of dissent from his ruling, whereupon Chifley sucked on his pipe, stood up and walked out of the room saying, 'There will be no dissent from my ruling. The meeting stands adjourned.' And that was it! Nobody else could ever have done that and got away with it, but he did.

Cameron and Connell, *The Confessions of Clyde Cameron* (1990), pp. 76–7

## THE DEATH OF CHIFLEY

*Chifley died from a heart attack on the night of 13 June 1951. That evening a banquet was being held in King's Hall to celebrate the fiftieth anniversary of Federation. Again, Clyde Cameron was there.*

Back at the function, people were dancing to the sound of Jim Gussey's dance band which had been brought up from Sydney. They were drinking and celebrating. It was a very happy occasion. The news came through from Don Rodgers who had been principal private secretary to both Curtin and Chifley. He announced to the press gallery, 'The King is dead, long live the King', and then explained that Chifley had died. The band was still playing some minutes after the news raced through King's Hall and the dining room. Wilfrid Kent-Hughes, the Minister for the Interior who was in charge of the function, refused to stop the band. He said, 'This is an important occasion. We can't help it. I'm sorry he's dead, but I'm not going to stop the dancing.'

I went to Menzies and told him of Kent-Hughes' refusal. Menzies had been very distressed by the news and stopping the band was not the sort of thing that he had immediately thought of, but when I spoke to him about it, he instantly and personally went to the band and directed the musicians to stop at once, which they did. There was great sadness that night. Evatt was sobbing like a child. Some people quietly went on drinking, but everyone was very badly shaken. I will never forget Menzies. He really lost control of himself and did not care who saw him.

Cameron and Connell, *The Confessions of Clyde Cameron* (1990), p. 83

## Acting the Fool

*In 1952 Billy Hughes was still around – but only just, Jim Killen claimed.*

A ceremony was held in Canberra to mark the 25th anniversary of the opening of the old Parliament House in 1927. It took the form of a re-enactment, portraying some of the political figures of the day.

William Morris Hughes had sat in the first Commonwealth Parliament when it met in Melbourne, and had been present at the opening in 1927. Understandably Hughes, who was still in the Parliament in 1952, was one of the figures singled out for portrayal. The person selected to play the part of Billy Hughes was very similar in appearance to Hughes. There was one problem. Hughes heartily disliked the person who was to play his part in the re-enactment, and refused point blank to attend the function. Artie Fadden was asked to mediate.

Knocking on W.M. Hughes' door at the Hotel Canberra, Artie got a very weak-voiced 'Come in'. He did, and found Hughes in bed with the sheet pulled up to his eyes.

'What is wrong?' asked Artie.

Hughes made an attempt to dismiss the enquiry.

'Are you sick? Can I get a doctor?' asked Fadden.

'No,' replied Hughes. 'I am beyond all medical reach. Doctors will be of no earthly use.'

Fadden persisted with his attempts to get Hughes out of bed

and dressed. After considerable cajoling Hughes agreed to attend the re-enactment, but emphatically declined to say anything at the ceremony.

In the car on the return to the hotel Artie asked him what he thought of the performance. The question was met with a desultory grunt.

'What did you think of the fellow who took your part?' asked Artie.

'Took my part,' exploded Hughes. 'All I can say is that one of us is a bloody fool.'

Killen, *Killen in Company* (1989), pp. 45–6

## DON'T MENTION THE WAR

*By 1952 the split within the Labor Party was becoming serious. The 'industrial groups', organised to defeat communist control of the trade unions and supported by B.A. Santamaria and the Catholic Church, were making inroads that some did not want to acknowledge, according to Clyde Cameron.*

When Ken Bardolph first proposed that the industrial groups be given an ALP charter in South Australia, I had never heard of Santamaria. His activities were so secret that it was some years before I heard his name and that was true for the rest of the Party. I was the first one ever to mention his name in a caucus meeting. Afterwards, Arthur Calwell came to me and said, 'God Almighty, don't ever dare do that again. Don't ever mention his name!' It was as though I had committed some serious crime! He was frightened of Santamaria and seemed to think that by not mentioning his name he might go away.

Cameron and Connell, *The Confessions of Clyde Cameron* (1990), p. 92

# A Resignation That Wasn't

*Evatt became leader of the Labor Party after Chifley's death, but the Party was never totally comfortable under his leadership. Percy Clarey was one rival, but as Fred Daly told, Evatt outsmarted him.*

Evatt, on one of the many occasions when he was under serious challenge for his leadership, suggested to Clarey that he intended to resign but before doing so would like to have a vote of confidence in him carried. He could then retire with dignity before Clarey took over. The Senate leader, Nick McKenna, was brought into the act and evidently thought it was a good idea. The position of the Party at that time was so desperate that anything in the way of a change could only be for the better.

At the next caucus meeting, Senator McKenna moved a vote of confidence in Dr Evatt. In the course of his speech which, as usual, was flowery, eloquent and legalistic, McKenna said that Dr Evatt had judgement, capacity, energy and enthusiasm. (This was about the time when a person named Lawson had been jailed in New South Wales for raping five models.) As McKenna spoke a voice from down the back of the caucus room interjected, 'So did that chap Lawson.' This almost wrecked the motion.

Clarey seconded the motion and was not short of compliments on Evatt's great capacity. He was in full flight when Dr Evatt rose and said, 'Please, resume your seat Mr Clarey. I am so overcome by the remarks of Senator McKenna and yourself that I would like you to withdraw the motion. I will then resign my position and throw the leadership open and submit my name again for election.' McKenna and Clarey could not do anything but agree. The move caught everyone by surprise. A ballot was held. Clarey could not nominate because he had burnt his boats by seconding the motion and Evatt beat Calwell easily and was safe in the saddle again.

Daly, *From Curtin to Hawke* (1984), p. 89

# The Petrov Affair

*In 1954 Menzies announced that the third secretary of the Soviet Embassy in Canberra, Vladimir Petrov, had defected and in doing so had unmasked a spy ring in Australia. The drama that followed involved claims of bribery, lies and political double-crossing. But the highlight was undoubtedly the 'rescue' of Petrov's wife Evdokia, put on an aircraft in Sydney by Russian staff and taken off by Australian police in Darwin.*

The dramatic rescue of a heroine, enacted in public on a large scale in full technicolour, worthy of being broadcast to the world, set the tone for all that followed. The Soviet Embassy decided to send Mrs Petrov back to Russia. On the day that Petrov received his £5 payment from the Menzies Government for alleged Soviet documents he had written to an official at the Embassy:

> I have put an end to my life because in our environment the leaders, mainly, have proved themselves to be slanderers and liars who invented various stories in order to dishonour the life of honest people … Let them bathe in my blood and enjoy the fact that I am not among the living. But I have honestly done my duty towards my country.
>
> V. Petrov<br>3 April 1954

A large number of New Australians who heartily detested the Russians and all their works had been organised to assemble at the Sydney airport in a state of near hysteria. The events as they were presented to the Australian public, then and afterwards, are well described by Catholic economist Colin Clark:

> The crowd saw two huge couriers from the Soviet Embassy forcibly dragging Mrs Petrov, clearly against her will, to the plane. That such a thing could happen on Australian soil was a revelation to a great many Australian electors who had not hitherto taken any interest in Communism, and undoubtedly told against Communists and those who befriended them in subsequent elections.

Mrs Petrov even lost her shoe in the rush across the tarmac. The press reported that she was crying out, in English, 'Save me! I don't want to go home.' In a statement handed to the commissioners [of the Royal Commission on Espionage 1954–55] Mrs Petrov affirmed:

> I felt that all the Embassy people who escorted me to Mascot were trying to rescue me from the crowd and according to the fact they were all the time trying to keep me in their hands until entering the plane ... At no time after leaving the car until I entered the plane did I appeal to any one in the crowd to assist me.

The dramatic plan to give Mrs Petrov 'her second chance', as Menzies called it, is claimed by [ASIO agent Dr Michael] Bialoguski to be his, but no one would wish to deny the credit as attributed by Colin Clark:

> One of those present at the airport was Mr W.C. Wentworth, the Liberal member of Parliament, who had taken the lead in arousing Australia to the dangers of Communism ... Mr Wentworth promptly telephoned the Prime Minister, who at fist failed to grasp the importance of what was happening, but eventually agreed to radio certain instructions to the captain of the plane.

Mrs Petrov, at Darwin, having been assured that she could stay safely and be reunited with her husband, signified her agreement. There was an even better piece of political theatre in the photograph of the two large couriers being disarmed by even bigger Australian police. A frail woman had been rescued at the last moment from the horrors of the Kremlin. 'Mrs Petrov immediately became the world's sweetheart in the grip of evil.'

Tennant, *Evatt* (1970), pp. 294–5

## THE MOLOTOV LETTER

*In the Royal Commission on Espionage that followed Petrov's defection, Evatt acted as counsel for two of his staff members who had been implicated in the conspiracy. This allowed Menzies to paint Evatt as a friend of the Communists. Evatt's naive admission that he had written to the Soviet Foreign Minister, Molotov, and had received a reply confirming that the Petrov documents were forgeries played into Menzies' hands.*

His speech to the House on 19th October 1955 was reasonable, quiet. During its progress, in his legal manner, he felt it necessary to mention that he had written to Molotov, with whom he had had many disputes in the United Nations. To him, it seemed right that the accused should state his case; it need not be accepted. The reference to Molotov was greeted with howls of joy from the Government side and groans of dismay from his own. The headline 'Evatt Wrote to Molotov' was enough to black out the portion of his speech printed in the press. Mention of the name Evatt to many Australians now evokes only the response, 'Oh yes, he wrote to Molotov.'

Tennant, Evatt (1970), p. 311

## THE MOLOTOV COCKTAIL

*Even after the Labor Party split, the Molotov letter continued to haunt Evatt. It was used by the Liberals in the 1955 House of Representatives election to bury him.*

It was to be a 'Trounce Evatt' or 'Get Evatt' election. Evatt could deal it out and he could take it, but there had never been an election of such virulent slander against him. When he opened the campaign at Hurstville, on 9th November 1955, he spoke of the £100 million made from the excess profit tax. The difference between profit-making and profiteering was very thin. He promised to reduce defence expenditure and to fix the rates of interest on hire purchase. The audience of 1,800 interrupted with yells of 'Molotov!'

The Liberal–Country Party coalition, said Evatt doggedly, had run the country for the benefit of the monopolists and speculators on a colossal scale. And again the audiences screamed 'Molotov!' 'It was a strange experience,' wrote Allan Dalziel later, 'to see in such surroundings this rather pathetic figure of a man being booed and cat-called – a man who had sat as a judge of Australia's High Court, who had presided over the deliberations of the General Assembly of the United Nations.' There were also meetings that were wildly enthusiastic. 'The Doc knows! Leave it to the Doc. There he goes – working himself to death for the workers, and they don't appreciate it – and the best woman in the world at his side.'

Tennant, Evatt (1970), p. 337

## Take Their Names!

*Evatt finally named members of the right wing of the Labor Party as disloyal. One of them, Senator G.R. Cole, retaliated by moving in caucus that all leadership positions be declared vacant. Fred Daly described the extraordinary meeting that followed.*

The motion was debated on 20 October [1954] and defeated by 52 votes to 28. Cole was pathetic and almost inarticulate when speaking to the motion. I had no intention of voting for the motion as I had nothing in common with [Stan] Keon and [John] Mullens who had bitterly opposed Chifley. I had a lot of trouble with them on discussions on the Communist Party Dissolution Bill and referendum votes.

Before the meeting Les Haylen came into my room and said, 'Be certain to vote against this motion because this is going to be a long fight and there will be a lot of bitterness.' Evidently Haylen was aware of what Evatt had in mind.

It was a bitter debate. Feelings ran high and the attacks of Keon, Mullens and [William] Bourke on Evatt were vitriolic and devastating. Insults, interjections and abuse filled the air as emotions and frustrations rose to fever pitch. I doubt if a worse scene has been witnessed in caucus.

The motion was clearly defeated on the voices, but that did not suit Evatt and Ward – they were going for the kill. I will never forget the scene when Eddie Ward, a real hater, called for a division. To everyone's amazement Evatt leaped onto the table, pencil and paper in hand, red-faced and excited, and triumphantly called out, 'Get their names, get their names!' It was Evatt and Ward at their hating best.

Some of his supporters stood on chairs around the room repeating the call 'Take down their names' as members crossed the floor to vote. It was a degrading and disgusting spectacle – twenty-eight members lined up like Japanese war criminals by colleagues with hate, vindictiveness and triumph written all over their faces.

Evatt's action infuriated Senator John Armstrong who was voting against the motion and he said, 'If that's what you intend to do, I'll vote for the motion, put my name down too.' They were my sentiments as well and Stewart, Luchetti and myself crossed over in rebellion against the worst action I have ever seen from a Labor leader. Some good mates of mine were sincerely supporting the motion, as was their right, and I could not stand by and see them humiliated.

As the division proceeded Joe Clark (NSW) was in two minds and stood with one foot in each camp. Dan Minogue said to him, 'Make up your bloody mind and get on one side or the other. You never know where you're going but you'll have to make a bloody decision today.'

It was a tragic episode for the Labor Party and men like Pat Kennelly would no doubt like to forget it. But Evatt and some of his supporters enjoyed their moment of triumph despite the tragedy of the occasion for the Labor Party.

The memory of Evatt on the table still lingers in my memory. A colleague later said that he was so incensed at Evatt's conduct that he was tempted to lift the table from under him. Fortunately he resisted the temptation or there may well have been a riot.

Daly, *From Curtin to Hawke* (1984), pp. 127–8

# Rising from the Depths

*By 1955 the Labor split had resulted in two different federal conferences, both held at the same time in Hobart. Clyde Cameron was part of an improbable encounter between Evatt and 'the Groupers', as the supporters of the industrial groups were known.*

Evatt, who had not been there for Calwell's speech, called in at the conference just as I finished talking to the journalists. He invited me back to Hadley's Hotel to have dinner with Mary Alice and himself. As we were driving toward Hadley's Hotel, I saw a newsboy standing at a street corner selling the first edition of the Melbourne *Herald*. I bought a copy and stuck it under my arm without reading it. We got in the lift to go up to Mary Alice's room but instead of going up, the lift went down and stayed down. We touched all the buttons and nothing happened. Evatt said, 'It seems as though we are stuck,' at which point I pulled the *Herald* from under my arm and read an imaginary headline: 'Dr Evatt an albatross around the Labor Party's neck declares Calwell.'

He said, 'Is that what they said? Is that what they're saying?' He was fumbling around for his reading glasses but could not find them. He said, 'I'm not going to stop in this lift with that filthy bloody rag, if that's what it's saying. Come on, get out, open the door and get out, find out where we are.' So I opened the door and told him it looked as though we were in the cellar because there were stacks of grog and cartons of wine and whisky and other stuff all around us.

He bent down, picked up a bottle of Johnnie Walker from one of the cartons and was holding it up to see the label with the benefit of the light still coming from the lift when the tissue paper wrapped around it broke and the bottle crashed to the ground. It made a great crash because everything was so quiet in the cellar. The noise must have alerted the cellarman, who seemed to be a long way away. We could see the torch coming towards us. As he walked, the torch was swaying with the movement of his body, and when he reached us he demanded, 'Who are you?'

Evatt said, 'Never mind about who I am. Who are you?'

'I'm the cellarman.'

'Oh,' said Evatt. 'Are you employed by Hadley's?'

'Yes.'

'Then you're an agent of Hadley's and under the famous case of Lord Chief Justice Coke, reported in Queens Bench Volume 73 page 302, you will find that a ruling was given by the Privy Council that where a person is incarcerated against his will, the person guilty of the offence is liable to be punished for a criminal offence which could entail as much as ten years' imprisonment. I'm warning you that unless you get me out of this bloody place I am going to sue you and Hadley's for incarceration against my will.'

Evatt was absolutely furious. I think, for a start, he wanted to frighten the cellarman into cooperating because he had begun by being rather aggressive. He did not know who Evatt was, and he certainly did not know me. He must have thought that here were a couple of burglars who had broken into the cellar and were about to steal the hotel's stock of whisky. But Evatt soon tamed him by threatening to have him imprisoned for a long term for wrongful a imprisonment. So the poor devil told us to go up the stairs to a trapdoor that would let us into the centre of the island bar in the saloon. He told us that if it was locked we should knock to get the barman's attention.

Evatt turned and told me to get up and open the trapdoor. I could not budge it. It was either locked or the barman was standing on it, so Evatt tried it himself. He climbed up the stairs, gave it a bang, pushed up through the trapdoor and found himself standing in the island bar alongside the barman and surrounded by Gair, Keon, Mullens and all the Groupers! They had obviously been angrily condemning Evatt, and the rest of us who had gone to our conference, and were pretty loud-mouthed by now. But the vision of Evatt's body emerging from the cellar caused them to stop instantly. There was not a word out of them! They believed in miracles. One of them had just come back from Lourdes, and here was living proof of another miracle. They had been talking about Evatt and here was the devil incarnate moving up from the bowels of the earth to be among them. They just could not believe their eyes! Evatt was so … I don't want to say dopey, but I cannot think of a better word … that he did not notice the consternation he had caused. He just moved out from the island bar with me following him. There was no sound or any comment at all, they were just spellbound!

Cameron and Connell, *The Confessions of Clyde Cameron* (1990), pp. 146 ff

## THE MAN IN THE WHITE COAT

*One of the most zealous anti-Communists in the Liberal Party was William Charles Wentworth, great-grandson of the famous 'Native Son'. Like his ancestor he lacked restraint. Fred Daly remembered a time when his rhetoric was interrupted.*

Late one night Bill Wentworth was in full blast on unity tickets when the door opened and in came a man dressed in dark trousers and short white jacket. He stood in the passageway alongside Wentworth and beckoned to him with his head that it was time to go. Wentworth did not know what to do. I whispered to Pat Galvin that the waiter would get the sack. Then I recognised him as Leslie Haylen. He and [Eddie] Ward had agreed to borrow two white jackets from the waiters and come in, one on each side of Wentworth, and pretend to take him back to hospital. Ward 'chickened out' but Haylen went ahead. It was a perfect piece of dumb acting – but he was suspended by the Speaker for not taking his seat when ordered to do so: he had nowhere to sit, he was in a passage.

Daly, *From Curtin to Hawke* (1984), p. 91

## THE WAR HERO

*Daly also recalled one of Wentworth's famous wartime exploits.*

The story told many times in the House was that Captain Wentworth, as he was then, decided to try out some of his own ideas during an army manoeuvre on Cronulla Beach in 1942. He landed a small group, carefully simulated a broken Japanese accent and rang the fire brigade and told them to go to Sylvania to attend a fire. He then sent the police to Oyster Bill's at Tom Ugly's Point because a crowd of soldiers were said to be wrecking the place. He reported an enemy force landing and when the emergency service arrived he bailed them up with bayonets. He arrested the colonel in his pyjamas at battalion headquarters and captured the headquarters. He then gave orders over the switchboard adding to the confusion. Then he blew up the wireless station, blocked the railway line to stop reinforcements, short circuited the signals system and put all trains out of order for thirty-six hours.

He and his companions then commandeered five Bren gun carriers and drove to the Ordnance Depot at Liverpool. They got past the single sentry and Captain Wentworth put up a sticker 'Destroyed by W.C. Wentworth, Captain'.

Daly, *From Curtin to Hawke* (1984), p. 91

## The Privilege of Jail

*In 1955 Frank Browne and Raymond Fitzpatrick, publishers of a minor scandal sheet, were called before Parliament on a charge of abusing parliamentary privilege. Daly reported a greater scandal than anything they had printed.*

Browne, the author of a news sheet titled *Things I Hear*, had over a period attacked practically every member of Parliament, particularly Calwell, Evatt and Menzies. He hardly had a friend.

Cabinet met and decided that Browne and Fitzpatrick would be sentenced to three months jail, taking the sentence out of the control of the House.

Browne and Fitzpatrick were called before the bar of the House on the morning of Friday 11 June 1955. It was a dramatic scene: galleries crowded with diplomats, the press and the public, and Speaker Cameron, severe and bewigged, a living picture of the famous Hanging Judge Jeffreys. He was enjoying every minute of his fleeting hour of glory.

Fitzpatrick, a successful businessman but not very well-educated, asked if his solicitor could speak for him. This was refused and he nervously apologised to the House. Browne, an experienced political campaigner who had once stood as a candidate against Dr Evatt, made full use of the parliamentary broadcast. He knew the sentence had been decided so he gave the proceedings the works. He tellingly shattered the confidence of many people in the supposed democratic procedures of parliament.

Frank Green, revered Clerk of the House, was greatly distressed by the proceedings which he believed degraded Parliament. He said later, 'When Browne finished speaking he had left beyond doubt with the Australian people the impression that no politician's parents had married for generations.'

Prime Minister Menzies got up and moved motions declaring the two men guilty and committed them to police custody for three months. Instead of opposing it, Evatt moved that they be not 'imprisoned' but 'fined': a distinction without a difference. They were jailed on a vote of 55 to 11.

Daly, *From Curtin to Hawke* (1984), p. 138

## SEEING IN BLACK AND WHITE

*One of the reasons Australia did not have television until 1956 was the resistance of Menzies to the idea.*

Indeed, the media as a class were among his pet hates. In later years he was to tell Richard Nixon: 'In all my life I have treated the press with marked contempt and remarkable success.' (Nixon commented later: 'No one would ever forget Robert Menzies. I learned a lot from him.')

MacCallum, *Mungo: The Man Who Laughs* (2001), p. 42

## And for My Next Trick ...

*During the 1956 Suez crisis Robert Menzies went to Cairo as a mediator. He had a remarkable dinner conversation with President Nasser, as Nasser's friend, the newspaper editor Mohammed Hassanein Heikal, later recalled.*

The President gave a dinner for the mission on September 5 at the Manial Palace, which before the revolution had been the palace of King Farouk's uncle, Crown Prince Mohammed Ali. It is surrounded by a marvellous group of old trees, and at dinner Menzies talked ecstatically about these trees, saying how beautiful they were. He exercised all his charm and amused the President.

Menzies asked Nasser: 'Have you ever met Churchill?' Nasser replied: 'No, but I admired him.'

'Have you ever heard him talking?' asked Menzies, and again Nasser said: 'No.'

'Do you know,' said Menzies, 'I have the reputation for being the best imitator of Churchill.'

And throughout the dinner Menzies kept whispering in Nasser's ear and everyone thought that they were talking important business about Suez when in fact Menzies was imitating Churchill's speech. He also imitated Bernard Shaw and General Jan Smuts. He was not talking seriously, but he set himself out to charm Nasser, and the President, indeed, found him very likable.

Heikal in Hazelhurst, *Menzies Observed* (1979), p. 349

## Which Side is He On?

*But according to Heikal the formal talks over the Suez crisis were less amiable after Nasser rejected the idea of an international administration for the canal.*

Menzies leaned forward over the desk, his thick eyebrows bristling, and growled: 'Mr President, your refusal of an international administration will be the beginning of trouble.'

Nasser immediately closed the files on the desk in front of

him and said: 'You are threatening me. Very well, I am finished. There will be no more discussions. It is all over.'

Menzies grew red. The Ethiopian Foreign Minister tried to calm the situation. He said that Mr Menzies had expressed himself badly but it was not meant as a threat. Speaking for his country, an African country, he had not come to threaten, and he had not come to impose a solution on Egypt that Egypt would not like. The Swedish Foreign Minister also tried to ease the atmosphere, and Loy Henderson too argued that what Menzies had said was not meant as a threat. Menzies himself, by now terribly embarrassed, apologised: 'I'm sorry, I did not mean to convey a threat to you.'

But the President would not be mollified. He was angry: 'To tell me that my refusal to accept an international administration will be the beginning of real trouble is a threat and I will not negotiate under threat.'

That was the end for the Menzies mission. It was an abject failure. It was doomed anyway, doomed by its originator Dulles who, at a press conference in Washington on August 28, had told the world that 'the Suez Canal is not a primary concern to the United States'. He thus rendered Menzies powerless and President Eisenhower added to Menzies' discomfiture at another press conference on September 4, soon after Menzies had arrived in Cairo. 'We are committed', said Eisenhower, 'to a peaceful settlement of this dispute, nothing else.' When Nasser heard of this, he said: 'That man puzzles me; which side is he on?'

Heikal in Hazelhurst, *Menzies Observed* (1979), pp. 350–1

## A Memorable Debut

*Doug Anthony became a formidable politician and a deputy prime minister, but when he arrived in Canberra in 1957 he was still a bit naïve.*

Legend has it that the young Doug Anthony took years to live down the phrase he used to introduce himself to his peers: 'I'm a country member.' The only possible reply was: 'Of course we'll remember. How could we ever forget?'

MacCallum, *How To Be A Megalomaniac* (2002), p. 36

## A Mutual Problem

*Fred Daly recalled an encounter Menzies had with Archie Cameron, which showed that he did not always have it his own way at home, either.*

It is on record that Menzies once said to Cameron, 'Archie, I do not suffer fools gladly.' Cameron replied, 'It might be news to you to know that bloody fools have a lot of trouble putting up with you too.'

Daly, *From Curtin to Hawke* (1984), p. 95

## Calm and Weighty Words

*The 1958 election campaign saw the Catholic Archbishop of Melbourne, Daniel Mannix, take the most vigorous anti-Labor stand to date. On the eve of the poll he issued this statement:*

Amid the turmoil of the election one thing seems clear.

Every Communist and every Communist sympathiser in Australia wants a victory for the Evatt Party.

That is alarming.

It should be a significant warning for every Catholic and for every decent Australian.

Hitherto I have not deemed it necessary to sound a note of warning. The Communists have long been falsely suggesting that Cardinal Gilroy stands for a comparatively neutral benevolence.

Of course the Cardinal ignored their malevolent use of his name.

But now that the Evatt Party, forgetting all about sectarianism, is trying to shelter under his name in nationwide advertisements and in pamphlets distributed outside Catholic churches to congregations on Sundays, I deem it timely to recall the official attitude of the Church and all the Catholic Bishops of Australia.

Writing at a time when the menace of Communism was not as pressing as it is now, and writing, not in the presence and heat of election time, but in the calm, restrained atmosphere of a national pastoral letter, the Cardinal wrote, and all the Bishops signed the following words:

'At the moment there is one outstanding issue for the nation and the Church.

'It is the immediate Communist threat to the security of the people and to the freedom of religion in Australia.'

The Cardinal, with the Bishops, went on almost prophetically to say:

'It is very regrettable that highly placed public men, including Catholics, seem to have closed their eyes to the great issues involved in the present upheaval.

'They do not appear to realise that they are forwarding the interests of Communism.'

It seems to me timely to recall these calm and weighty words.

It is needless to add that the Democratic Labor Party, Protestant and Catholic alike, at heroic cost to themselves, have stood, and stand consistently for the principles espoused in that Pastoral letter.

Can the same be said of others?

*Daily Telegraph*, Sydney, 21 November 1958.

## A Bad Miss

*Arthur Calwell succeeded Evatt as leader of the Labor Party after Labor's defeat in the 1958 election. Gough Whitlam narrowly beat Eddie Ward for the deputy's job, but Fred Daly noted the two remained enemies.*

Whitlam was a prime target of Ward's animosity. He swung a punch at Whitlam after a dispute at an executive meeting but only succeeded in barking his knuckles on a chair. On another occasion,

Ward did his block and chased Whitlam down the corridor and swung a punch at him. [Les] Haylen saw Ward swing a punch at Whitlam and as he did so lose his spectacles. Whitlam disappeared into his room and Ward, like a blind man, was on all fours on the floor groping around for his spectacles. It was a ludicrous scene. Some time later during a period of ill-health, Ward was asked when did he realise his health was slipping. He replied, 'The day that I missed Whitlam.'

Daly, *From Curtin to Hawke* (1984), p. 155

## A Narrow Win

*The 1961 election resulted in a one-seat victory to the Liberal–Country Party coalition. The last seat decided was won, on Communist preferences, by Jim Killen, who later wrote:*

Kevin O'Donohue, the chief of staff of the *Courier-Mail*, rang. O'Donohue, an agreeable and experienced journalist with Labor leanings, was well known to me.

'You have been hard to get, but then it's not surprising,' he said. 'I'm trying to write a story away from the straight politics. Can you help me?'

'I will if I can,' I told him.

'Now, I know you have heard from the PM. What did he say?'

'Oh, cut it out, Kevin. It was just a personal call to say congratulations.'

'He must have said more than that. Come on, give an old friend a break.'

I protested reluctance. O'Donohue persisted. Finally I said to him, 'He simply said: "Killen, you are magnificent."' Neither Menzies nor I lived it down. Menzies never raised the incident with me, nor I with him. For my part, I certainly did not intend to cause him any embarrassment or hurt. The fact that neither Menzies nor any member of his staff called me during the closing days of the Moreton count was somewhat embarrassing, as I felt an obligation to protect him from the public bewilderment which unquestionably would have appeared if I had replied to questions about the Prime Minister's interest in the outcome: 'Oh, I don't know. I haven't heard from him.'

Killen, *Inside Australian Politics* (1985), p. 51

## Justice was Done

*Don Chipp was a new boy in 1961, and soon faced a dilemma over a bill imposing capital punishment, which he opposed on ethical grounds. He recalled:*

I sought an appointment with Menzies, expecting him to live up to his reputation of being a ruthless autocrat and to demand that I toe the Party line. I told Menzies I could not support the Bill and gave him my reasons. I was surprised when he said that he admired a stand on principle and gave me authority to vote as I pleased.

However, Menzies' release for me to exercise a free vote led me to a second dilemma. It is a fine point for students of politics to debate. We had a majority of one and I was the only Liberal who was not prepared to support the capital punishment clause in the Bill. On the other hand it was Labor Party policy to oppose capital punishment. On matters of policy, every Labor member must vote with the Party or suffer immediate expulsion. On gaining pre-selection, every Labor candidate signs a pledge to this effect.

But at least five members of the Labor Party had already stated they strongly favoured capital punishment. If given a free vote they would have voted with the Government but, as this permission had not been given, they would vote with their Party against the Bill.

One of these members was the ex-policeman from Hunter, NSW, Bert James. The question was: if I voted with the Opposition, the clause would have been defeated – thus producing a distorted vote – because in fact the majority of the members of the Parliament were in favour of capital punishment, namely all the Liberals except myself, and five Labor Party members. I therefore decided to abstain and informed my Whip.

Bert James was obviously going through similar agonies. He wanted to vote for the clause but had to vote against it at Party direction. When the division bells were ringing (they rang for two minutes) I walked into King's Hall and saw Bert hiding behind a pillar – a difficult task for him. He was smoking a cigarette, and looking carefully at his watch. With perfect timing, after the bells had been ringing one minute and fifty seconds, Bert mobilised his seventeen-stone body into a mad rush for the doors of the chamber, arriving there as they closed on him, preventing him from voting. The clause was carried by one vote! Justice was done?

Chipp and Larkin, Don Chipp (1978), p. 40

## I DID BUT SEE HER

*Queen Elizabeth's second tour of Australia was, if anything, even more of a success than her first – especially for Menzies.*

In 1962 the Queen and the Duke of Edinburgh returned to Australia nine years after their first visit and were again welcomed by large and demonstrative crowds. Even the staunchest republicans must have been pleased with the practical repercussions of the royal tour, as large-scale clean-ups and beautification programmes everywhere preceded the arrival of the royal couple. For the Prime Minister, Mr Menzies, the royal visit was one of the high points of his career. At the official welcome he asked the Queen to 'remember that every man, woman and child who sees you will remember it with joy – remember it in the words of that 17th Century poet who wrote these lines, "I did but see her passing by, and yet I'll love her till I die."' The Queen later conferred on him her personal honour of the Most Noble Order of the Thistle, thus admitting him to a select group of only sixteen people outside the royal family; this was the highest honour conferred by the monarch on any Australian. The Queen's visit was warmly welcomed by the press generally, and especially by women's periodicals, as well as by the very large number of British immigrants.

Crowley, Modern Australia in Documents, vol. ii (1973), p. 437

# The Faceless Men

*During the 1963 election campaign one photograph
cost the ALP dearly, Fred Daly recalled.*

The establishment of the North West Cape base in Western Australia by the United States caused bitter and lengthy discussions in caucus and the House. As a compromise caucus foolishly moved to refer it to the federal executive for decision and direction. It created a situation that cost Labor dearly.

While the matter was actually under discussion in Parliament, a special federal ALP conference discussed it at the Hotel Kingston, Canberra. [Arthur] Calwell and [Gough] Whitlam, who were not delegates, were photographed waiting outside the hotel under the lamp light for a decision so that they could take action in Parliament. This photograph made the front page of newspapers throughout Australia. The non-Labor parties immediately described it as the powerful 'faceless men' of the ALP federal executive instructing Labor leaders how to vote in Parliament.

Daly, *From Curtin to Hawke* (1984), p. 62

# Enter Honest John

*John Howard was one young Liberal who had no
scruples about exploiting the situation.*

Howard was Tom Hughes' campaign manager in 1963 when he stood against a sitting ALP member, Les Haylen, in Parkes. The campaign was hard-fought. Howard produced pamphlets which referred to 'Left-Wing Les', and the 'Minister for Peking'. Hughes won.

Barnett, *John Howard Prime Minister* (1997), p. 13

## Keeping Australia White

*Canberra in the early sixties was a pretty bleak place, without the facilities for rest and recreation of some other capitals.*

Hardened foreign affairs officials still shudder at the memory of a visit from an Asian delegation in the early '60s, who demanded a spot of relaxation at the end of a hard day's negotiating. After all, they said reasonably, they had provided any number of willing women during a visit to their homeland by Australian officials; surely it was time for a return presentation. The young bureaucrat in charge of showing them around panicked; he could think of nowhere in Canberra that could be trusted with the job. As the Asians grew steadily more impatient he rang hotels and their doormen and made inquiries from passing taxi drivers; still he drew a blank. Finally, an unsavoury-looking barman gave him an address, not in Canberra but in nearby Queanbeyan. Gleefully he piled his charges into a fleet of cabs and hurtled to the destination, to be greeted by an effusive madam. Certainly, she said, for the right price she could accommodate his eight gentlemen. But as they eagerly dismounted from the taxis her face changed. Sorry, said the madam: no coloureds.

MacCallum, *How To Be A Megalomaniac* (2002), p. 189–90

## Renal Colic or Alc'olic?

*The Senate was generally a quiet chamber, but there was a curious incident there in 1964. Daly again.*

One of the funniest episodes in the history of the Senate occurred in the early sixties on a Bill substantially increasing sales tax on motor cars. Labor defeated the legislation with the support of some Liberal senators but the Bill was recommitted. A Labor senator discovered that a colleague had taken ill with a stomach complaint and was lying asleep in his room. He rushed out, woke the sleeping senator, pushed him into the chamber but somehow in the rush he ended up on the wrong side and voted for the sales tax instead of against it. Half asleep and dazed the senator refused his Labor colleagues' frantic signs to join them and waving them away voted with the Government.

The senator faced disciplinary action as it was a serious mistake. A Labor senator who was a doctor diagnosed his complaint as colic and ordered the senator to hospital for three days. The ambulance was called, a stretcher secured, and he was carried to the waiting vehicle with the doctor walking beside him. Pat Kennelly remarked that the only trimmings missing were the funeral directors from St Kilda Road, Melbourne, in top hats. The senator was saved and no action was taken against him.

Daly, *From Curtin to Hawke* (1984), pp. 170–1

## Whitlam in Hot Water

*Whitlam's quick temper was a source of worry to his colleagues. In 1965 it got him into trouble during a row with the External Affairs minister Paul Hasluck.*

After scornfully mentioning that Hasluck never spoke on repatriation matters, Whitlam said: 'If the Minister for External Affairs is prepared to deny his parents in voting against justice for Salvation Army personnel who have served with the Forces, then I suppose we need not worry about persons with less propriety and pride voting against all the principles which they so loudly espouse during the daytime, and on sacred occasions.' As Whitlam sat down, Hasluck leaned across the table and said quietly: 'You are one of the filthiest objects ever to come into this chamber.'

There followed what Hansard coyly dismissed as an 'incident'. Whitlam took up a glass of water and hurled the contents into Hasluck's face. For several seconds a stunned Hasluck sat quite still. Then, with considerable dignity, he took out his handkerchief and slowly wiped his face and clothing. There was uproar. The chairman of committees shouted for order, but it was some time before order was restored. Whitlam was instructed to apologise and did so, but demanded that Hasluck withdraw 'the unparliamentary and provocative terms which he used and which were heard by several of my colleagues'. He said of Hasluck's comment: 'It was too indecent. I will not repeat it.' Hasluck, in his apology, said: 'The remark was made in a personal and direct way. It was not part of the proceedings of the Parliament.'

During the rest of the debate Whitlam had to endure Government members shouting 'wetty Whitlam' at him across the chamber. 'Waterboy' was another nickname with which he was instantly tagged. When he next spoke a day later he was subjected to more ridicule. He had uttered only seven words when a NSW Liberal, Les Irwin, leaped to his feet and said: 'I take a point of order, Mr Speaker. May the glasses be removed from the table.' Whitlam made the mistake of mentioning Canute, and Don Chipp from Victoria interjected: 'The honorable member has water on the brain.' Mr E'thel Meernaa Hasluck, the ninety-three-year-old father of the minister who had received the drenching, had the last word. He told reporters in Perth: 'I'll excuse Mr Whitlam on the grounds of his ignorance. I don't know Mr Whitlam, but I believe he's an educated man – although he's done some very stupid things.'

Oakes, *Whitlam PM* (1973), pp. 115–16

## An Easy Choice

Many years ago, when parliament was still housed in the unhygienic but user-friendly premises fruther down the hill, Labor's wily veteran Pat Kenneally noticed a newcomer gazing around King's Hall in some bewilderment. Although the new member was not of his own political persuasion, Kenneally took pity on him and decided to offer him a little wise advice. 'Son,' said Kenneally, draping a paternal arm over the short, stout man's shoulders, 'look over there. There are two doors leading out of this hall. The one in the middle goes to the library. The one to the right goes to the bar. Be careful which one you choose; your whole career in this place depends on it.' 'Gee, thanks,' gasped Senator Vince Gair, and disappeared through the door on the right with a zeal that nearly tore it from its hinges.

But in all fairness it must be said that Gair also made good use of the library. He could frequently be found after lunch in one of its comfortable leather chairs, eyes closed in contemplation, breathing slow but regular.

MacCallum, *How To Be A Megalomaniac* (2002), p. 121

## Perfect Position

*On the lighter side was the interminable debate over which of the three possible sites should be used for the new Parliament House.*

The debate was spirited and members were not restricted by a Party view so everyone spoke their mind. However one member despite repeated attempts simply could not get the call. He tried all day to catch the Speaker's eye and finally gave up in disgust. As he stormed out of the House he shouted at the Speaker 'You can shove it up your arse!'

Immediately Jim Cope, the Parliament's wit and later to be Speaker himself jumped to his feet. 'Mr Speaker, I ask that Parliament consider the fourth site suggested by the Honourable Member.'

Cohen, *The Life of the Party* (1987), p. 68

## One Shot in the War

*The Menzies Government had committed Australian troops to the Vietnam War. When Harold Holt succeeded Menzies in 1966 it was still a popular decision. Arthur Calwell's campaign against it nearly ended in tragedy.*

Calwell was sitting in the passenger seat of his car after he had delivered one of these speeches at the Mosman Town Hall in Sydney on the night of 21 June 1966, when a disturbed youth named Peter Raymond Kocan fired a shot at him at close range. The shot shattered the car window, spraying Calwell's face with broken glass, but he was not seriously injured. There was no swelling of public sympathy for the old, embattled leader. Opposition to the Vietnam commitment was confined at that time to academics, the political Left and a relatively small proportion of potential conscripts; pop singers and cricket stars were photographed happily shouldering their rifles. Kocan recovered, won several literary awards and later had two of his works set as prescribed reading on the syllabus of the New South Wales education system.

Stubbs, Hayden (1989), p. 69

## ALL THE WAY WITH LBJ

*Harold Holt became prime minister on Menzies' retirement in 1966. His visit to the United States in the same year produced a warm and flattering speech, and a slogan which was to haunt him for the rest of his life. Holt concluded thus:*

The outcome of this struggle is critical for the hopes that you and we share for a better and more secure way of life for the free people of Asia.

But it does not take a war to bring Americans and Australians close together.

We like each other. Friendships form quickly between us.

We have many mutually beneficial links. Our trade with each other, the investment that you make with us with your capital ...

You know that in Australia you have an understanding friend.

I am here, sir, not asking for anything – an experience which I am sure you value at times when it is not so frequent as it might be.

You have in us not merely an understanding friend but one staunch in the belief of the need for our presence with you in Vietnam.

We are not there because of our friendship, we are there because, like you, we believe it is right to be there and, like you, we shall stay there as long as seems necessary to achieve the purposes of the South Vietnamese Government and the purposes that we join in formulating and progressing together.

And so, sir, in the lonelier and perhaps even more disheartening moments which come to any national leader, I hope there will be a corner of your mind and heart which takes cheer from the fact that you have an admiring friend, a staunch friend that will be all the way with LBJ.

*Australian*, 1 July 1966.

## A Little Foreign Aid

*Harold Holt invited President Lyndon Baines Johnson to visit Australia just before the 1966 election. Fred Daly recorded the enthusiasm.*

LBJ campaigned blatantly for the return of the Holt Government and assured the Australian people that the United States would always be on Australia's side. It is said that he told Holt, 'You make any arrangements you like for me, I'll even kiss the mothers and nurse the babies. You work out the details, I'll do the rest.' New South Wales Premier, Robert Askin, was so enthusiastic that when demonstrators sought to stop LBJ's progress he shouted, 'Run over the b——s.'

Daly, *From Curtin to Hawke*, p. 176

## A Straight Line

*Arthur Calwell resigned the Labor leadership after the 1966 election defeat, and promptly picked up an honour, as he told Jim Killen.*

When Arthur was appointed a Privy Councillor in 1967 he was delighted. He described the ceremony of admission to membership of the Privy Council that was conducted at Government House in Canberra. 'Look, if ever you are appointed remember you do not turn your back on the Sovereign. You walk backwards to your place.' 'How did you manage that, Arthur?' I asked. 'I picked out a seam in the carpet,' he replied. 'Bill McMahon also performed very well.' And then with a look of utter impishness he added, 'Who would have thought it possible for Billy McMahon to walk backwards in a straight line?' It was said without the slightest trace of malice: it was a typical Calwellian indulgence in absurdity.

Killen, Inside Australian Politics (1985), p. 70

## A GIFT FOR LANGUAGE

*Retirement from the leadership did not mellow Calwell, as Clyde Cameron found out.*

If you fell foul of Calwell you found out that he had a marvellous vocabulary. I remember his words on one occasion, after he had resigned from the leadership and we were looking for a safe seat for Jim Cairns who had lost his old seat in the redistribution. I suggested to some of my Victorian contacts that Arthur should resign and make way for Jim. A few days later he met me in the corridor of Parliament House and said, 'Clyde, I heard you're saying that I ought to step down in favour of Jim Cairns?' I agreed that I had done so and he exploded, 'You sneaky little cunt. You've always been a sneaky little cunt, haven't you? A man ought to piss on you. At least that would make you smell like a man!' I burst out laughing because to me it was so funny and so clever. It may have been quite effective on someone who did not have my sense of humour, but the fact that I am recounting it now, and smiling as I do so, indicates that it had absolutely no impact upon me at all, nor did it deter me from continuing to advocate the very course to which he objected. In the end, we found a seat for Jim Cairns somewhere else but that was not because we were concerned about Arthur's feelings on the matter.

Cameron and Connell, The Confessions of Clyde Cameron (1990), p. 182

# Missing Believed Drowned

*Harold Holt disappeared while swimming near Portsea on 17 December 1967. The scramble to succeed him shocked the then junior minister Don Chipp.*

On that fatal Sunday afternoon I was attending a life-saving carnival at Black Rock in my electorate. My wife came down in a distressed condition and told me that Harold Holt was missing – believed drowned. I went home and had many telephone conversations with fellow Liberals who were shocked and genuinely grieved at the tragedy. There were two well known Liberals in particular who had been very close to Holt who needed to be actually comforted, one of whom was near hysteria. He was crying, declaring his love for Harold Holt and stating he would never recover from his grief.

Later in the afternoon Channel 7 in Melbourne asked me to appear on the 7pm news to pay a tribute to the missing Prime Minister. I was a very junior minister – number twenty-five in a pecking order of twenty-seven. I said that surely there would be more senior ministers or officials who would be available, but I was wrong. The grab for the coveted prize of prime minister had already begun. Votes were being marshalled, contenders were already on the phone. The numbers men, the power brokers, had put the word out that Harold Holt had been on a downer and it was not advisable to be associated with him, even though he was dead. HSV7 found no one else willing to appear. The telephone sniveller of the early afternoon had been able to contain his grief, contemplate standing for leader and decide that in the circumstances it would be better if he didn't appear. What a bastard of a thing to do.

Chipp and Larkin, *Don Chipp* (1978), p. 62

# The Arts are Red

*John Gorton became prime minister in January 1968, following Country Party leader John McEwen's brief tenure while the Liberals decided on a replacement for Holt. Gorton appointed Nugget Coombs to head the Arts Council in 1968. Coombs said they had an understanding, as when Coombs recommended a grant to a trade-union children's arts programme.*

GORTON  'You know that union is run by a bunch of Comms?'
COOMBS  'Yes, but it's a good programme and doesn't seem to have any ideological slant.'
GORTON  'The DLP will probably give us hell about it in the Senate.'
COOMBS  'You can blame the Council and point out that it's only in dictatorship countries that the Arts are subject to political censorship.'
GORTON  'Okay, so long as you don't expect me to defend you!'

Coombs, *Trial Balance* (1981), p. 246

# A Kind Word

*Gorton reshaped the ministry, and Jim Killen ended up in the Navy portfolio.*

During my first visit to HMAS *Melbourne* while being shown over the engine room I spoke with a stoker. I was dressed in overalls and we exchanged names. 'And what do you do?' he asked. 'Well', I replied, 'as a matter of fact I happen to be the minister.' Without batting an eyelid he looked at me and said, 'Smart bastard'. It was one of the kindest things ever said about me, and there were many times when I wished the summation was correct.

Killen, *Inside Australian Politics* (1985), p. 152

# A Casual Visit

*By the end of 1968 Gorton's casual behaviour was starting to alarm some of his colleagues. A speech on the adjournment debate by Labor's Bert James did not help.*

The matters raised by James were not new. In late October 1968, President Johnson had informed Gorton that highly secret negotiations were under way with Hanoi and that he hoped to be able to announce cessation of the bombing before the Presidential election polling day. Returning to Parliament House after a theatre party, Gorton held an impromptu press conference with two or three journalists still in the building after midnight and revealed Johnson's secret. Johnson made known his understandable rage. On 1 November, just too late, as it turned out, to prevent Richard Nixon narrowly defeating Hubert Humphrey for the Presidency, Johnson announced the bombing halt. That night, Gorton was guest of honour at the parliamentary press gallery annual dinner. The American Ambassador, William Crook, asked Gorton to call in at the Embassy after the dinner to discuss Johnson's announcement. By this gesture, Crook intended to smooth over any ruffled feelings lingering from Gorton's October indiscretion. Despite repeated messages inquiring when the Prime Minister might be expected at the Embassy, Gorton dallied on at the dinner until about 1.30am. He finally arrived in the company of a young woman journalist and stayed until about 3am. Versions of this incident circulated around the Canberra gossip circuit for several months. The matter became public property only because of the publicity given to James' speech.

Oakes and Solomon, *The Making of an Australian Prime Minister* (1973), p. 145

# Behaving Himself

*Gorton's continued insistence on doing things his way brought a strong reaction from Vince Gair, something of a larrikin himself.*

When told by Gorton at a parliamentary party given by Senate Government leader, Ken Anderson, in March, 1969, that Gorton proposed leaving for an official visit to the United States on the following Saturday, Vincent Gair, leader of the Democratic Labor Party, farewelled Gorton with a trite, usually meaningless Australian adieu. 'Good luck,' said Gair. 'Behave yourself.' From this emerged a clash which epitomised the differing beliefs on how a prime minister should approach the 'grey' area where a prime minister's public and private lives impinge each on the other. Gorton gave Gair a verbal blast. 'John Grey Gorton will bloody well behave precisely as John Grey Gorton bloody well decides he wants to behave,' Gorton said.

Gair, a squat little man, a former premier of Queensland, very tough, with an elephant-like memory, put the other side of the coin with brutal candour. 'Personally, I couldn't care less if John Grey Gorton jumps into the Yarra and drowns himself,' said Gair. 'But John Grey Gorton happens also to be Prime Minister of Australia. I do care how John Gorton conducts himself as Prime Minister of Australia.'

Reid, *The Gorton Experiment* (1971), pp. 10–11

## An Understanding

*During the 1969 election campaign Gough Whitlam took aim at what were seen as Gorton's weaknesses.*

'I'm rather disappointed in the Prime Minister. Before this campaign began we had a distinct understanding – that he wouldn't tell any lies about me, if I didn't tell the truth about him.'

Whitlam did not shrink from imposing on his opponents the ultimate humiliation – quoting their own words for laughs. Gorton's convoluted style of speech made him particularly vulnerable. When Gorton delivered himself of the following opinion, Whitlam was quick to quote it.

'On the other hand, the AMA agrees with us, or, I believe, will agree with us, that it is its policy, and it will be its policy to inform patients who ask what the common fee is and what our own fee is so that a patient will know whether he is going to be operated on, if that's what it is, on the basis of the common fee or not.'

Whitlam continued. 'I enjoy quoting the man word for word. I wish we all had the opportunity of being educated at Geelong Grammar – there is nothing like a Liberal education.'

Cohen, *The Life of the Party* (1987), pp. 24–5

## KEPT IN THE DARK

*Gorton's supporters formed a rather strange group, Fred Daly recalled.*

'The Mushroom Club was a group of Gorton followers who had dinner when Parliament was sitting. Gorton attended as guest of honour and was known as the Chief Spore. The new Customs Minister, Mr Chipp, the new Attorney-General, Mr Hughes, the new Army minister, Mr Peacock, and the new Navy minister, Mr Killen, had been members of the Mushroom Club. Their motto is "Keep them in the dark and feed them bull," Mr Erwin said. But the Mushroom Club is finished now. It is all in the ministry.' It was later reported that Club members wore a tie studded with small mushrooms. The Chief Spore, Mr Gorton, as Club President, wore a tie with a single large mushroom. The Club met regularly once a month in Parliament House.

Daly, *From Curtin to Hawke* (1984), p. 185

## A DIFFERENT STRATEGY

*W.C. Wentworth was Minister for Social Sciences and Aboriginal Affairs. Killen recalled his performance in the 1970 budget Cabinet.*

Gorton's Cabinet met without junior ministers unless they were invited specially to attend. It was the same with budget Cabinet meetings and on general philosophic and economic discussions. Once the broad decisions had been taken junior ministers would be summoned and informed as to what Cabinet had decided upon. Questions could be asked, but the prospects of securing any change were virtually nil. Frequently in the years ahead I would feel sorry for a junior minister who made a suggestion regarding the overall budget strategy being told, in effect, that the suggestion held no merit, when several Cabinet ministers had advanced precisely the same suggestion. William Charles Wentworth was not to be frustrated. He compiled his own budget, dealing with every department, his fertile and vigorous mind extrapolating figures and ideas from wherever he could get them. He entered the Cabinet room clutching a great pile of papers and put them down in front of him. John Gorton eyed him suspiciously, and his eyes seldom were taken away from Wentworth's bundle of papers as Leslie Bury, the Treasurer, gave an outline of the Budget proposals.

When the Treasurer had concluded his remarks Gorton asked for questions or brief observations. Wentworth did not wait to be asked a second time. He told the rather startled Cabinet that he had prepared somewhat different proposals and he would like to explain them to all in the room. It was as much as John Gorton could do to keep him quiet. Eventually Bill Wentworth was silenced, but not before he commented, 'This is not the first Government which I have said was wrong. You'll come to see my point of view.' For those of us who knew Bill Wentworth it was a characteristic and somewhat hilarious display of his zeal, his indefatigable energy and, above all, his determination not to be readily silenced.

Killen, Inside Australian Politics (1985), p. 161

## Keeping to the Tape

*The Labor Party went through a long reform process in 1970, culminating in a week-long federal executive meeting in Melbourne. Clyde Cameron was there.*

There were four tape recorders and two or three operators in the room, to allow recording to proceed without fuss. For the first three or four hours, the debate was fairly stilted, but when you take into account that we sat for eight days altogether, I can tell you that before very long every person in the room became oblivious of the fact that he was being recorded. When you listen to the tapes you can hear comments like, 'Pull your head in, you mug', 'Go and get stuffed,' and 'Oh, for Christ's sake, shut up, you silly bastard.'

Cameron and Connell, *The Confessions of Clyde Cameron* (1990), p. 276

## Censored

*As Minister for Customs in 1970, Don Chipp was in charge of censorship. He recalled that at the time the rules were fairly archaic.*

When I became minister, about one out of every two *Playboy* magazines was banned. I discovered the reason was that a senior public servant in the department was meticulously applying a guideline which had been laid down years before. This was that no publication could be admitted into Australia which contained a photograph showing pubic hair. Each month this senior official reached for a magnifying glass in his top right-hand drawer and applied the acid test. If any of the offending fabric appeared in his lens, that issue was banned from Australia! That guideline was removed and this once excellent publication has since been freely admitted into Australia – except, of course, Queensland which still maintains its own Censorship Board. This could explain why Queenslanders are reportedly less sexually active than the rest of us. My mischievous staff nicknamed the public servant 'PH' after that incident, and it stuck with the poor devil until his retirement.

Such was the public interest in censorship that any trivial incident concerning it became a big story. An unfortunate, over-enthusiastic, young Customs officer once confiscated a book from a returning passenger when he noticed the title *Fun in Bed*. Having been challenged, he was forced to return it – it was a book of games for sick children!

Chipp and Larkin, *Don Chipp* (1978), pp. 104–5

# A Double Header

*Whitlam was not one for censorship of any kind,
as Mungo MacCallum found out.*

And there was the odd joke, unpublishable at the time but always good for a bit of hit later on. The nicest one I can remember was during the 1970 half-Senate election campaign (than which there was nothing duller; in those dim, far off days we really thought that the Senate didn't matter terribly much. *Eheu fugaces*, as the Romans used to say before their own senate fell to pieces). Anyway, there were we in a BAC 1-11 halfway over Bass Strait in the company of Her Majesty's Leader of the Loyal Opposition, The Hon E.G. Whitlam, QC, MP, who was visiting Tasmania for the second time during the brief campaign, to everyone's distaste including his own.

There was much whingeing on board the plane at the prospect of another night alone on the apple isle (about which Whitlam, on his previous visit, had said in a fortunately abortive television interview: 'There's really nothing we can do about Tasmania, is there: I mean, the whole place is fucked'). So, on this occasion Whitlam took it upon himself to cheer up the troops with the immortal line: 'Well there's one thing about Tasmania. With all that in-breeding around, there's always the chance of picking up a bit of double-headed fellatio.' Let us state immediately that nothing could have been further from Whitlam's puritanical, if prurient mind; but it saved an otherwise impossible trip.

MacCallum, *Mungo on the Zoo Plane* (1979), pp. 6-7

# A Flight to Remember

*Prime Minister Gorton's 1970 campaign also had its moments.*

On one memorable occasion he left Canberra by VIP aircraft to address a dinner meeting in Melbourne. It had been a long hard day in parliament, and naturally he used the trip to unwind with a few drinks. Arriving at the Sheraton he found himself among frinds, so a few pre-dinner drinks were in order; then there were the wines and a glass or two of port, and of course it would have been impolite to refuse a palate-cleanser or several later. Eventually they wheeled him back to Tullamarine and poured him onto the plane which was to take him back to Canberra. Sensibly he decided to take a refreshing nap, but when he was woken by the thrumming of the engines some time later he felt decidedly queasy; so much so that he leaned into the aisle and threw up. A stewardess came to clear up the debris, and Jolly John thought he had better make the best of it. 'Well,' he said, switching on all his charm, 'I suppose you're surpised that an old RAAF man like me still gets airsick occasionally?' To which the stewardess replied: 'Well, yes, sir, I am actually, because the plane hasn't taken off yet.' She dined out on it for weeks.

MacCallum, *Mungo: The Man Who Laughs* (2001), p. 196

## An Offer She Could Refuse

*Bob Hawke had a formidable reputation both as a drinker and a womaniser, but occasionally found the two didn't mix.*

There was a celebrated occasion in 1971 on which he appeared, somewhat tired and emotional, on the doorstep of a Sydney socialite whose Labor sympathies were well known – indeed notorious. 'How would you like,' slurred the then president of the ACTU, ostentatiously depositing an overnight bag at her feet, 'to be the mistress of the next prime minister of Australia?' To her great credit, his intended victim did not miss a beat. 'Oh,' she replied, 'I don't really think that Margaret Whitlam would like that,' and closed the door firmly.

MacCallum, *How To Be A Megalomaniac* (2002), pp. 187–8

# The Wrong Punch

*The Queenslanders remained less open-minded,
as Bill Hayden discovered.*

In one of the early debates at the Queensland Labor Party's annual policy-making Labor in Politics Convention at the Chevron Hotel in Surfers Paradise in January 1971, Hayden argued forcefully for a ban on professional boxing. In a later debate he pressed, equally emotionally, for the de-criminalisation of sexual relations between consenting adult homosexuals. 'Delegate Hayden seems confused,' rasped the voice of Jack Egerton, the fat, florid president of the party who had control of the microphone at the top table. 'He's bitterly opposed to a bloke getting a punch in the nose; but he doesn't seem to mind him getting a punch in the bum.' After the laughter subsided, Hayden would not back down and he succeeded in forcing a vote on the issue and having a division called. Egerton narrowly carried the day after he had called for those supporting his point of view to go to one side of the hall and the 'poofters' to the other.

Stubbs, *Hayden* (1989), p. 98

# Billy Moves In

*William McMahon finally achieved his lifetime ambition to become prime minister with the defeat of his despised rival, John Gorton, through a no-confidence vote in the Liberal party room in March 1971. Mungo MacCallum fantasised about the move into the Lodge.*

Billy McMahon arrived at the Lodge this week with his lovely lady wife, and they stood, transported (by Commonwealth car) at the gates, drinking in the beauty of it all.

'Look at it,' Billy breathed. 'A little home of our own.'

'Oh, darling,' said Sonia, looking down at him affectionately, 'it's just what you've always wanted. But who is that strange-looking man who appears to be setting a bear trap in the middle of the drive? Does he come with our unpretentious little acre and a half residence, like the rest of the servants?'

Billy looked, and scowled. 'No,' he said. 'That appears to be the previous tenant. He does not come, he goes.'

The previous tenant walked up to them, and smiled in a friendly, if dishevelled fashion. 'Welcome, and be seen to be being welcome to the Lodge, if that's where we are,' he said. 'I've just been getting things in order for you.'

'That's very nice of you,' Billy said. 'But why the bear trap? Are there many wild animals round the garden?'

The previous tenant nodded. 'Indeed,' he said. 'By an amazing coincidence only this week the thought came to me, why not make the Lodge into a typical animal sanctuary? So I did. Lions. Tigers. Wolves. Rats. Tiger snakes. Hyenas. Vultures. I'm sure', he added happily, 'you'll feel very much at home.'

Sonia nodded. 'How thoughtful,' she murmured. Billy went on scowling.

'And what,' he asked, looking at a series of saplings bent into bows, with cunningly concealed lassos and spring traps attached, 'what is that?'

The previous tenant smiled condescendingly: 'Oh, that's a new form of gardening. We're trying to train them into lovely patterns for you. It's the very latest thing.' He leant over to Sonia confidentially. 'I got the idea', he murmured, 'from your old friend Leslie Walford himself.'

'Ravishing,' Sonia gasped.

'When you have quite finished,' Billy shouted up at them, 'perhaps the previous tenant could explain just why there are what appear to be a series of land mines buried across the approaches to the front door? Landscape gardening?'

The previous tenant looked scandalised. 'Surely,' he said, 'you don't expect me to reveal the top secret security arrangements I have made with the full cognisance and agreement of my new department?'

Billy started to speak, but was cut off by a delightful cry from Sonia. 'Look', she said, 'at all the pretty fish in the swimming pool. Was that your idea too?'

The previous tenant nodded happily. 'I put them there only this morning,' he said. 'A very rare South American variety. You'll find them very approachable when you go for a swim. As will your husband.'

But Billy was now through the door, examining the floor boards. 'These boards appear to have been almost sawn through,' he remarked acidly.

'Oh yes,' said the previous tenant. 'To allow for expansion on a hot day. So much safer, I always feel.'

Sonia had opened the cocktail cabinet. 'A new brand?' she asked, holding up one of the bottles. 'I've never seen whisky marked with a skull and crossbones on the bottle before.'

The previous tenant winked at her. 'Try some of it on your husband before you go to bed,' he suggested. 'It'll do wonders for him.'

Billy was already looking at the bedroom, which appeared to have a two and a half ton anvil balanced on top of the door. But the previous tenant forestalled him. 'An elegant sort of door stop, don't you think?' he remarked. 'All the best people have them.'

'Lovely,' said Sonia. 'As is this intriguing looking box under the bed, which ticks. A new sort of alarm clock?' 'Exactly,' said the previous tenant. 'Very efficient. Well,' he added, looking at his watch, 'I mustn't detain you good people any longer, I'll just collect a few personal belongings,' he went on, removing the circuit breakers, the burglar alarms, the fire extinguishers and half the foundations, 'and I'll be on my way.'

'What a nice man,' said Sonia, as the previous tenant drove away to his suburban home in the Commonwealth car, to which he had thoughtlessly retained a set of keys. But the neighbours in the suburban home weren't so sure.

'Well,' said one of them to his wife as the previous tenant pulled up, 'there goes the neighbourhood. You know how it is. You get one of them in the street, and that's it. Down go the property values …'

MacCallum, *Mungo's Canberra* (1977), pp. 63 ff

# A Felicitous Note

*McMahon cleansed his ministry of Gorton supporters,
of whom Jim Killen was one.*

I was glad to lend my support to [Tom] Hughes. At about 11.30am on 18 March [1971] I was notified that the Prime Minister wanted to see me. I went to his office immediately. 'Good morning, Prime Minister,' I said. He sat at his desk with his hands resting on the top. The moisture from his hands was clearly visible on the desk. He cleared his throat and began to speak. 'I can't leave you ... I can't leave you with the Navy.' 'I am sorry, Prime Minister,' I said, looking him straight in the eye, 'that is the case. I was enjoying the Navy very much. Why can't I stay?' 'You can't ask me that question,' he said with distinct irritation. 'I am doing the decent thing and telling you personally rather than you read about it in the papers.' 'But I have been reading about it for the last week,' I snapped. It was clear that McMahon was uncomfortable. Whenever he tried to portray himself as a dominating character it had almost the opposite effect. He cleared his throat again. I thought I may as well make the most of his discomfiture. 'Very well, Prime Minister, is there anything else you would like me to do?' His voice quavered. 'No, no. I want you right out – right out.' 'Tell me, Prime Minister, why is that?' I asked. 'I told you before you can't ask that question.' 'I thought I would indulge myself in the luxury of asking it,' I said. 'Well, you can ask it, but I am not going to answer it.' 'Very well, Prime Minister, on that felicitous note, good morning.'

I was joined for lunch by my eldest daughter, Diana, who commented, 'I think in the long run it will be for the best.'

Killen, *Inside Australian Politics* (1985), p. 175

# Noose Talk from Bolte

*Victoria's Liberal Premier Henry Bolte was responsible for the last hanging in Australia, that of Ronald Ryan. He was also contemptuous of Gorton. Both issues surfaced at the 1971 Premiers' Conference. Mungo MacCallum wrote:*

Henry (the hangman) Bolte had a splendid couple of days in Canberra for the Premiers' Conference. Although displaying some displeasure at the amount he wrung out of McMahon (for whom he made no attempt at all to conceal his contempt) he had time for a few drinks (till 5am on both Wednesday and Thursday mornings) and made a strong bid for the swinging vote.

As he has frequently said before, Henry reckons one way to win an election is to hang someone and, although he is retiring, he has not, as it were, come to the end of his rope. Indeed, in his happy conversations with the press into the small hours, he confirmed the fact that he is eager to bring on one last hanging before he goes. And he already has victims in mind.

On both nights, Henry entertained the crowds with his reminiscences of [Robert Peter] Tait and Ryan; and many an appreciative chuckle resounded through the bar of the Hotel Canberra as he explained how he had moved some of his less bloodthirsty judges out of the way, or humiliated those weak-kneed humanitarians who failed to share his glee at the final solution.

The grand old man of legalised murder was in good form, and took particular delight in baiting the press for about five hours straight. It was all the press's fault, he said: 'The more the papers tried to save Ryan, the tighter the noose went round his neck.'

And in similar vein: 'I've never felt any qualms about Ryan – never any. The press tried to stop it, but they only made it more certain because you can't make the press the Government.'

He regards Tait as a near miss, with some regret: 'Tait should have gone,' he said. 'When it was all over they sent him back to Pentridge and said he was sane.'

And he was optimistic about the future. Mentioning a case currently running and momentarily lapsing into contempt of court (a lapse which we unfortunately cannot share) he indicated that his mind was running ahead to a prospect that 'would almost be worth staying around for'. There was much more of the same, shouted around a crowded bar, but who was more surprised and hurt than Henry when he found out next day that some of his choicer *bons mots* had been repeated around Parliament House, and were not being well received at all?

Next night, in the same bar, he instituted a witch hunt. It was all off the record, he growled, and he'd never give the press a background briefing again. He seemed particularly upset to think that it could even have been one of 'his own team' (his quaint way of describing the Victorian parliamentary press gallery) who might have been talking about him.

At that stage none other than Ainsley Gotto [private secretary to John Gorton] entered. Henry threw a couple of wild accusations around about where Ainsley had got hold of reports about the previous night and the two of them, quite unbending, went for each other in one of Canberra's more spectacular confrontations. Ainsley did her well-known imitation of a mother lioness and told Henry he'd always been anti-Gorton, and that was dreadful. Henry took the offensive with the splendid party stopper: 'You can't win an argument against a drunk, a fool or a woman. And you, Ainsley' (pause for effect) 'are a woman.' An impartial observer scored it slightly Ainsley's way, before the proceedings broke up in disorder and Henry announced he was going to sleep in that morning.

MacCallum, *Mungo's Canberra* (1977), pp. 69–70

## Getting into Office

*McMahon's definition of politics was a simple one.*

During question time in the House of Representatives one morning in February, 1972, William McMahon found himself and his Government coming under fire over a series of price rises in basic commodities such as steel. After the third Labor Party question on the subject, McMahon complained that 'it should not be made a political football – this is a matter which concerns the welfare of the Australian people and is fundamental to our growth and employment prospects'. A South Australian Labor back-bencher, Chris Hurford, interjected, reasonably enough, 'What is politics about?' McMahon turned with the self-satisfied expression he adopts when he is about to put someone down, and replied, 'Politics is trying to get into office!' The off-the-cuff retort was not a bad summing up of McMahon's approach to his profession.

Oakes and Solomon, *The Making of an Australian Prime Minister* (1973), p. 64

## A Few Familiar Words

*McMahon quickly showed that he had a style of his own, even if it may not have been an improvement on his predecessor's. His trip to the United States in 1971 was an example.*

So here is our Prime Minister at the climax of his momentous trip, having dinner at the White House. And everybody is there – former ambassador Clare Boothe Luce, Washington Redskins football team coach George Allen – just everybody. Our man has already confirmed, with fulsome gratitude, that the ANZUS treaty is still valid; which is just as well because he has been telling the electorate that for nearly twenty years. Triumphantly, he comes down the White House stairs with his wife, whose legs and ignorance of both foreign and local affairs have already been given more space in the American press than the Prime Minister himself.

The band plays 'Fascination', and the President of the United States tells our prime minister that he understands that that was the tune playing when he proposed to his wife. Gratefully, our Prime Minister confirms that is not only correct, but he sang it to her at least ten times. The guests gawk at Sonia's armpit-to-ankle slits and are entertained by our Prime Minister explaining that he had dismissed his predecessor from Cabinet because of his public performances, but that his predecessor was proving a bigger nuisance outside the Cabinet than in. Possibly he has just heard the rousing ovation the Melbourne Cup crowd gave his predecessor earlier in the day.

They sit and eat. The President of the United States asks our Prime Minister how he pronounces his name (McMann?) and introduces him. Our Prime Minister rises. It is his big moment. He has thrown away his notes because he feels that only by an off-the-cuff speech (which is to prove one of the longest ever heard in the White House) can he express the depth of his obsequious gratitude.

He is about to tell the President how humble he feels and how proud the President must feel. Before he does, he wants to coin some memorable phrase. So he says, in ringing tones: 'I take as my text a few familiar words that there comes a time in the life of a man in the flood of time that taken at the flood heads on to fortune.'

Mungo MacCallum, Mungos's Canberra (1977), pp. 74–5

## BILLY GOES RURAL

*McMahon never really got on with the Country Party, and in particular with its leader, 'Black Jack' McEwen, who had originally vetoed him as prime minister. His attempts at reconciliation were not always successful either. Mungo MacCallum recalled that*

his troubles with the Country Party had really started the week before, when he was invited to attend their final piss-up on Thursday evening. He was running rather late, and was less than amused as he rushed out of Parliament House to find that his beloved prime ministerial car was not in sight. Scarcely pausing for breath, he leapt into the nearest ministerial car, which happened to be Ian Sinclair's, and demanded to be driven to Country Party headquarters. The driver said it was all right with him, but why? McMahon replied testily that he was going to the CP party, and the driver replied that the party was upstairs in Parliament House. McMahon leapt out of the car, and rushed upstairs, to where Doug Anthony was addressing the meeting and saying how sad it was that Charles Barnes and Sir Charles Adermann and Sir Winton Turnbull (who?)

were retiring at the end of the session. Another guest, [DLP leader] Senator Vincent Gair, was occasionally making jolly interjections, typical of which was: 'Aargh, none of you bastards would be here, if it wasn't for the DLP. None of you. Aargh … '

Ian Sinclair suggested that, nice as it was to see Gair relaxing after a hard day, he might stop, to which Gair replied: 'Aargh, none of you bastards … ' After he had been ejected his loyal deputy, Frank McManus, poured a little oil on the waters by suggesting that it had been a hard day, and that Vince hadn't meant it, and it should in no way hinder the increasingly close ties between the parties and so on.

McMahon thought he should make a little speech. Only the other day, he confided, he had had a problem, and when he had asked Sonia what he should do about it, she had suggested he should ring John McEwen. And that was very, very good advice, because John McEwen had always been very, very helpful … At this stage a voice from the back of the room said: 'I'm still waiting for the phone call, Billy.' The Prime Minister had apparently overlooked the fact that Sir John McEwen was among those present.

MacCallum, *Mungos's Canberra* (1977), p. 90

## The 'It's Time' Machine

*For the 1972 election campaign Labor borrowed the slogan 'It's time for a change' from New Zealand, and then shortened it to 'It's Time'. It was devastatingly effective, as the Liberals discovered. Labor's secretary, Mick Young, believed it was the most powerful slogan since Federation.*

A problem which sometimes occurs with slogans is that they can be reversed or replied to, negating their effect. But the best the Liberals could do with 'It's time' was to produce the reply 'Not yet'. Negative advertising is ineffective advertising. Young disposed of the Liberal comeback with the comment: 'That's what the Liberals always say. If you suggest abolishing the means test, they say yes – but not yet. They say "Not yet" to everything.'

Oakes and Solomon, *The Making of an Australian Prime Minister* (1973), p. 96

## NOT YET

*Labor's Barry Cohen remembered Killen never
forgave McMahon for sacking him.*

On one occasion, Billy was holding forth at the despatch box when he declared dramatically, 'I am my own worst enemy!' From the backbench came the rich, resonant voice of Killen. 'Not while I'm alive!'

Cohen, *The Life of the Party* (1987), p. 67

## STRIVE TO BE FAIR

*McMahon had a bad time from the press throughout
the 1972 campaign.*

McMahon was correct in later complaining that the press were far harder on him than on Gorton. Until 1969 at least, the press campaign against Gorton was largely subterranean, unsupported by the proprietors. For all his lifelong cultivation of proprietors, McMahon's press support was minimal and grudging. His last prop was removed in 1972 when Sir Frank Packer sold the *Daily Telegraph* to Rupert Murdoch. Murdoch had committed his papers to a change of government. He telephoned McMahon in London to tell him of his deal with Packer: 'I can promise, Prime Minister, that we will be as fair to you as you deserve.' In the background, Packer warned: 'If you do that, you'll murder him.'

Freudenberg, *A Certain Grandeur* (1976), p. 22

## THE POLICY SPEECH

*McMahon's all-important policy speech did not come off well.*

To the sound of majestic music the black Bentley drew up in front of Parliament House. William McMahon alighted and swept up the stairs, past a group of pressmen and radio reporters and through the swing doors. The policeman on guard duty saluted. 'Ladies and Gentlemen,' said an announcer, 'to present his policy speech for the forthcoming federal election, here is the Right Honorable William McMahon, Prime Minister of Australia.' It was an impressive filmed opening. But suddenly the action and the music came to an abrupt end, and in its place was a head and shoulders view of a nervous McMahon looking straight into the camera and speaking in a dry, unsteady voice. 'Good evening. Tonight, as Prime Minister and Leader of the Liberal Party, I want to talk to you about the issues on which we will fight this election. Basically it is an election about policies – policies that will directly affect you and your families for many, many years to come ... '

McMahon had been practising the speech for nearly a week. In his Sydney office he had installed a video tape cassette machine, turning it into a do-it-yourself television studio. There he had sat, going through the speech, then playing it back, getting advice from his wife and his staff, and trying again. At times he got fed up with criticism of the way he looked and sounded, and his temper became frayed. Once he commented bitterly that if he couldn't please anyone he might as well record his speech with his head in a toilet bowl.

Oakes and Solomon,<br>
*The Making of an Australian Prime Minister* (1973), pp. 176–7

## Keep the Happy Times

*Whitlam's visit to Liberal headquarters during the 1972 campaign surprised everyone concerned.*

Whitlam had a late, relaxed, and slightly bawdy lunch with [Graham] Freudenberg, [Mick] Young, and some of the press, and strode out in a good mood. Perhaps unfortunately, the restaurant was next door to the Libs headquarters in Ash Street, which he professed never to have seen; and, having studied the stickers on the windows ('Keep the happy times – vote Liberal') thought he should. He led the troops in, and was justifiably surprised at what he saw.

The Libs' headquarters looks like something straight out of Dickens: it's all musty wood, and piles of unfiled paper, and middle-aged ladies. The only concession to modernity is that there are typewriters on the desks instead of quill pens. Whitlam stood there, aghast; one of the ladies at least recognised him, did a double take, and went back to her typewriter.

But there must have been some sort of burglar alarm, because seconds later a very slightly younger lady appeared, fell about a little, and asked him what he wanted. He settled for a copy of the policy speech and a few pamphlets, and left, visibly shaken. On the way up Martin Place a number of people stopped him to wish him luck.

MacCallum, *Mungo on the Zoo Plane* (1979), pp. 39–40

## One For The RSL

*Whitlam was keen to get on with things after winning the 1972 election, and was not prepared to wait for caucus to elect a ministry. He had himself, with fourteen portfolios, and his deputy Lance Barnard, with fifteen, sworn in to cover the whole government.*

The size of the first Whitlam Government enabled it to establish several firsts. One of these occurred a week after the swearing in of Whitlam and Barnard when they both attended a passing-out parade and graduation ceremony at the Royal Military College, Duntroon. Whitlam told a press conference later that day: 'You might be interested in a remark that was made there – that it is the first time the whole Commonwealth ministry has attended such a ceremony and it is the first ministry which is entirely composed of returned servicemen.' But the cosy arrangement ended when the full ministry was sworn in on December 19.

Oakes, *Whitlam PM* (1973), p. 236

## Musical Chairs

*In Opposition for the first time in twenty-three years, the Liberal–
Country Party coalition seemed unable to work out what to do.*

Almost up to Christmas, the Opposition was practically in retirement. While Whitlam and his ministers were grabbing the limelight, the Opposition were arguing whether the deputy-leader should be the Liberal, [Phillip] Lynch, or the Country Party leader, Doug Anthony. Whitlam and Co. sat on the sidelines and giggled. Before Labor chose its Cabinet and while the Liberals were still thinking about having a meeting to choose a leader, Anthony nipped in and grabbed the room in Parliament House allotted to the Opposition deputy-leader. He was, naturally enough, aided and abetted by the Speaker-to-be, Labor's J.F. Cope, who has an impish humour. The Opposition parties then had an unsavoury wrangle on whether Anthony should have the title that went with the room or merely be known as leader of the third party. Lynch at last got the title.

Edwards, *Labor Pains* (1974), p. 23

## Taking Over

*Some of the new ministers were equally at sea, although
Clyde Cameron received one intriguing message.*

The other thing I found intriguing was the telex machine. I had never had one before and I was fascinated by it. The very first message that came through the machine I inherited was addressed to Phil Lynch, who had been the minister for Labour and National Service before I took over. It came from an overseas contact who was apparently unaware that Lynch was no longer in office. The sender was a Soviet agent looking for business contacts. He also asked about entertainment expenses and travelling allowances. The message seemed to relate to negotiations that were already in progress. I sent it over to Phil with a note saying, 'This is obviously meant for you, Phil, because Soviet agents wouldn't be contacting me. Congratulations on being able to keep two fronts going at the same time.' He was terribly upset by this, especially when I referred to it in Parliament by way of interjection a couple of times.

Cameron and Connell, *The Confessions of Clyde Cameron* (1990), pp. 209–10

## WHO NEEDS IT?

*One Labor member who did not make the ministry in 1972, but made no secret of his ambitions, was Paul Keating.*

On one occasion Gough Whitlam approached Keating after a particularly good performance and said: 'That was a good speech. You should go back, comrade, and get yourself an honours degree.' Keating was deeply offended at what he read as a patronising comment. 'What for? Then I'd be like you,' he retorted to a startled Whitlam. It was not to be the only occasion when Keating's response surprised the Labor leader. On a later occasion, when Whitlam was urging Keating for his support on a caucus vote, Keating was unmoved. The clear-eyed young politician told Whitlam: 'You need me more than I'll ever need you.'

Carew, *Keating* (1988), p. 33

## WHEN ONLY THE BEST WILL DO

*Whitlam's sense of what was proper for his position sometimes got the better of his political common sense.*

When he was elected, Whitlam rejected the stately old prime ministerial Bentley (he called it 'archaic'), and took his transport from the car pool. This gave the impression of a permanent demonstration of democratic sentiment, which his PR people did not dispel.

On 4 April [1973], however, it emerged that he had ordered a new prime ministerial chariot – a 135 m.p.h. white Mercedes, luxuriously fitted and suitable for Whitlam's 6 ft. 4 in., the first of its kind to come to Australia and costing, retail, $20,000.

Questioned in Parliament several weeks later, Whitlam said he 'would be happy if every office-bearer in Parliament were to make do with the ordinary Holden or Valiant, but if there is to be any gradation of cars then, quite frankly, I am going to have the best'.

Edwards, *Labor Pains* (1974) p. 107

## An Unhealthy Portfolio

*As Minister for Social Security Bill Hayden had the job of implementing Labor's new health scheme. The opposition from private doctors and health funds was vicious.*

As the *Canberra Times* recorded later, 'as Social Security minister Hayden was subjected by elements in the medical fraternity to one of the most vicious campaigns of denigration any contemporary politician has had to face'. Dallas [Hayden] was telephoned at home at night and told not to expect her husband home; he had gone berserk on an aeroplane and had been forcibly removed in Sydney and taken to a mental hospital. Stories were widely circulated that he had been drummed out of the police force as a crooked and violent copper; that he was a dropout from medical school who was wreaking his revenge on all doctors; that he had been undergoing psychiatric treatment, but as minister had been able to have his records destroyed.

'I defended you,' Jack Egerton told him once after informing him of the latest lot of malicious lies. 'I told them you didn't have enough brains to have a mental breakdown.' 'The personal pressure began to show. By the end of 1973 he looked older and his hair, in part, turned a shade greyer,' Denis Murphy recorded. The odious campaign was not confined to private whispering: *The Australian GP*, the journal of the General Practitioners Society, depicted Hayden in Nazi uniform, and engaged in personal vilification of him.

Stubbs, *Hayden* (1989), p. 109

# A Special Bastard

*Nugget Coombs joined Whitlam's staff and found it a rowdy experience.*

Added to this the Prime Minister occasionally allowed the inevitable 'foul ups' of busy offices or blunders by his colleagues to provoke him into exhibitions of temper at the expense of members of his staff or others involved. To some extent these were calculated pieces of histrionics, part of Whitlam's tendency to act out, in a style exaggerated to the point of mockery, a kind of caricature of himself. The exhibitions were, nonetheless, often painful to those who, in one way or another had provoked them, and I personally found them distressing. Not that I was ever directly a victim. Indeed one of his senior staff having been on the receiving end of a verbal blast commented: 'I notice you don't abuse Nugget the way you do the rest of us.' Whitlam paused a moment and then replied, 'No, he's the sort of bastard who would walk out if I did.'

Coombs, *Trial Balance* (1981), p. 307

# Biting the Bullet

*After the 1972 election the President of the ALP, Jack Egerton, had said: 'To the victors, the spoils.' In spite of themselves Whitlam and his colleagues acted as if they believed this maxim.*

Part of the Labor Government's image problem had stemmed from an extraordinary political insensitivity on the part of some of the new ministers. Two ministers had attracted unfavourable publicity by taking members of their families on flights in RAAF VIP aircraft. Two others had received a bad press when they appointed members of their families to their personal staffs. An impression was created that the members of the new Government were wallowing gleefully in the perks of office. Whitlam himself was not immune from this sort of thing, even when the slump in the Government's support had become obvious. He seriously suggested that his dentist should accompany him on his trip to China, and was rather piqued when a member of his staff pointed out sarcastically that with eight hundred million sets of teeth in China it was likely that the Chinese had competent dentists available for emergencies. He allowed himself to be talked out of the plan, but insisted: 'I still think it's a good idea.'

Oakes, *Whitlam PM* (1973, pp. 244–5

## The Christmas Spirit

*Others in the party helped to puncture Whitlam's ego.
One was Arthur Calwell.*

When Jim Cope, who became Speaker during the Whitlam Government, placed an invitation on the noticeboard for contributions toward the cost of holding a Christmas function, Calwell had scrawled on the notice: 'When I was the leader, I paid for the Christmas party from my own allowance. You might suggest this to my elongated successor.' Keating took the notice off the board. 'I thought I'd keep that one for the history books,' he remembered.

Gordon, *Paul Keating: A Question of Leadership* (1993), p. 53

## The Economists

*Another not afraid to answer back was Clyde Cameron.*

At one economic discussion the Prime Minister turned to Cameron and said: 'What would a fucking ex-shearer know about economics?' 'As much as a classical Greek scholar,' replied Cameron.

Stubbs, *Hayden* (1989), p. 116

# The New Split

*The Democratic Labor Party had sided with the Coalition to keep the Australian Labor Party out of office. But with that battle finally lost the DLP leader Senator Vincent Gair became more independent. Fred Daly's summary:*

Gair was short, tubby, cocky and arrogant, with a wealth of experience behind him in the hard world of Queensland politics. He was a down-to-earth, ruthless old-time campaigner with a memory like a computer for events and personalities. He cared little for the niceties of politics and dealt out insults, taunts and abuse without fear or favour. Billy Snedden, as Leader of the Opposition, was very upset when Gair described him as 'a lightweight who couldn't go two rounds with a revolving door'. He also said that 'he couldn't make an impression on a pincushion'. Snedden, sneeringly referring to a temporary DLP alliance with the Country Party, said, 'Who is churching the old whore now?' It brought a violent reaction from Gair. Gair said more than once that when the Liberal–Country Party wanted him they were all over him like fleas on a blanket.

Daly, *From Curtin to Hawke* (1984), p. 148.

# The Greening of Gair

*In 1974 Whitlam eventually persuaded Gair to accept an ambassadorship to Ireland in what turned out to be a monumental fiasco. Labor did not get the extra senate vacancy it wanted, and Gair clung to his appointment. Jim Killen gave him a little advice.*

'Vince, come and have lunch with me. We will give the gossipers something to talk about.' He agreed. 'Do you know your appointment reminds me of the story that Artie Fadden told me years ago about Sir John Forrest's appointment to the House of Lords,' I said. 'Why, what happened?' asked Gair. 'Hughes as prime minister wanted Forrest out of the way and prevailed on the sovereign to make him a peer.' 'And then what?' asked Gair. I replied, 'He sailed from Fremantle and died at sea. I would travel Aer Lingus or Qantas, Vince.'

Killen, *Inside Australian Politics* (1985), p. 223

## Losing His Grip

*In the end, Gair and the Coalition were the winners.*

The Libs and Country Party people were going round bursting into uncontrollable fits of giggling. Only the DLP remained a bit confused. On Wednesday Barry Cohen (Labor, NSW) ended up at the same dining table as Senator Jack Little (DLP, Vic). Little leant across to him seriously and said, 'You know, I really think Vince is losing his grip.'

Cohen just stared at him. 'Losing his grip?' he finally spluttered. 'Losing his grip? Look, he's going to Dublin on $20,000 a year, and he's left your party ratshit and my party ratshit and ... he's losing his grip?'

MacCallum, *Mungo on the Zoo Plane* (1979), pp. 139–40

## Just Keep Walking

*As a result of the Gair appointment in 1974 the Coalition and DLP combined in the Senate to block supply and force an election. The Opposition leader Bill Snedden decided to rely on the common touch in Adelaide.*

The idea was that Snedden was going to walk, yes actually walk, the four blocks from the building which the Liberal Country League shares with some of Adelaide's most expensive doctors, and then go in just like any other citizen. Or anyway, almost like any other citizen. He would, of course, be accompanied by a crowd of Lib officials, and a dozen young Liberal birds in white t-shirts with the legend 'I'm a Liberal Lover', and if the radio and television people cared to tag along that would be all right too. But basically, he was just going to meet the people.

So, punctually ten minutes late, Snedden and entourage emerged, linked arms in echelon formation and set off at a steady five kilometres an hour down North Terrace, sweeping women and children into the gutter as they went. The trouble was that a man called Rob Bray had also attached himself to the group, as leader; and Rob Bray was wearing a tall Uncle Sam hat, a false paunch, a sign round his neck saying 'Mr Foreign Company', and a large placard on a pole saying 'Billy wants to sell me Australia'. So the happy procession, with Mr Bray and his supporters in front calling out 'Vote Liberal, Vote Multinational', charged its way through the crowd.

Snedden tried to send Bray up, and jostled him a bit, the fixed smile on the Snedden face looking more and more like that of a shark. Snedden's press secretary Geoff Allen pretended to be a reporter and tried to draw Bray off; the Liberal Lovers surrounded Bray and tried to isolate him from Snedden. But nothing worked, and Bray triumphantly led them towards the meeting.

They were nearly there before someone reminded Allen that it was meant to be a meet the people walk, and Allen rushed up to Snedden and told him to meet a person. Snedden wheeled into a side street and tried to meet a person but unfortunately the side street was the headquarters of the Adelaide stock exchange, which Bray pointed out with vigour. Then Snedden tried to meet another person, who was repairing the footpath; the person said 'Piss off, I've got to get to work.'

MacCallum, Mungo on the Zoo Plane (1979), pp. 83–4

## Getting the Cuts

*Snedden did not fare much better with a press conference and another walk in Newcastle.*

At his next morning press conference, in Newcastle, the press took up the proposed $600 million cuts in Government expenditure. Brian Johns of the *Sydney Morning Herald* asked him if he had a 'reasonable idea' of where these cuts would be made. Snedden replied: 'Let me make it clear, it is the order of arrest expenditure increase we are talking about and in giving that the order of it, I forget about how the question came up, but I would agree that yes, it would be in about that order. About $600 million. Now to come to your question, do I have in my mind the areas in which there is a possibility of saving that sort of expenditure increase, yes I do have it.'

QUESTION  Can you tell us what they are?
SNEDDEN  No, I won't.

After this conference Snedden went to the BHP steelworks for a stroll through the factory. This was probably a good bet as Snedden, of working-class stock, could be expected to have a better rapport with the workers than his predecessors. Even if he didn't pick up any votes the action would show concern for them. He came across a labourer holding a running hose and asked, 'Where does the water come from?' The worker looked at his hand, then at the water, then at the hose and after an embarrassing silence, replied: 'From the hose.' The workers sulked and shouted obscenities as he departed.

Blazey and Campbell, *The Political Dice Men* (1974), p. 112

## A REALLY FABULOUS CAMPAIGN

*The 1974 election that Graham Richardson (then a New South Wales Labor organiser) remembers was not the federal campaign, but that for the Northern Territory House of Assembly.*

I arrive in the Northern Territory, 'cause Geoff Cahill has sent me up there 'cause the party needs help. I took Cheryl and Matthew [his baby son] and we stayed in this tiny little room at the Don Hotel, Matthew in a cot next to the bed. Not exactly a fabulous way to stay.

I got up the next day and went out to find the Labor Party. Well they were pretty hard to find. We didn't have a parliamentary leader, and out of our candidates, several of the candidates didn't have tickets in the party. So it was decided that the secretary of the party in the Northern Territory would deliver the policy speeches, 'cause nobody trusted the candidates.

Three of the candidates were complete and total alcoholics; I called a meeting of the candidates after which they went down to the bar and had a few beers and one of them threw another of them through a window.

They had no plans, they had no money, they had no literature, they had no campaign at all – and the election was nearly upon them. There was this big advertising campaign for the Country-Liberal Party, television, they had everything: we had *nothing*. So I said, 'Look, we can't now go out and do pamphlets in every electorate and everything else, you've got no money, no organisation, you've got nothing. So what we should do is, we'll produce a newspaper, the *Northern Territory Times*. We'll put out one edition of this newspaper and it'll put our spiel across, and we'll put it out everywhere. We won't obviously get it into every letter box in the Territory, but we'll go close.'

And so I had to write a bloody newspaper, and I wasn't a journalist. But one of the candidates was old Jim Bowditch, who was former editor of the local territory paper, the *News*, and he was a terrible alcoholic. Christ. So I went on a Sunday morning about 9 o'clock to his home. And he was out on the porch and he'd already knocked off half a flagon. He said, 'D'ya'wannadrink?' I said, 'No thanks.' So I sat there with him while he drank, and by the end of the day we'd written a newspaper, which I didn't get anyone to check, I just authorised it myself. He had mates at the *Kings Cross Whisper*, so they printed it, we sent the bloody stuff to them and they did it and sent it up to the Northern Territory, 'cause we could do it quicker and cheaper that way than getting it done in the Territory.

And by the time election night came around we didn't win a seat. It was a total disaster. I don't think I could be blamed for it, but really, we had candidates who were just so drunk all the time, you couldn't send them anywhere, you couldn't let 'em meet anyone. And basically the Northern Territory just didn't have a Labor Party, y'know, they just didn't exist.

Richardson in Cumming, *Mates* (1991), pp. 164–5

# Not Leading, Bleeding

*After Snedden lost the election for the Liberals, supporters of Malcolm Fraser resurrected one of Snedden's own campaign lines, 'Wherever I go around the country, people know that something is wrong', to devastating effect. By the end of the year his leadership was in desperate straits.*

But Snedden's most memorable and costly exaggeration was made on Friday 15 November [1974] when he addressed a businessmen's lunch in Melbourne and, at the end of a long question period, was asked a hostile question about the Liberal leadership. At the end of his answer, attempting to be light-hearted Snedden replied, 'I'll tell you why I should be leader of the Liberal Party – I'm the best – that's why I should be. I can give leadership to my team and they will all follow me. If I asked them [Liberal parliamentarians] to walk through the valley of death on hot coals they'd do it. Every one of them trusts me. Everyone recognises my political judgment and, if I say something must be this, it will be. That's why I'm leader.' Snedden's comments amused some businessmen at the $50 a head lunch at Chadstone's Matthew Flinders Hotel. But it enraged a number of Liberal parliamentarians. This statement, made less than a fortnight before the November leadership challenge, cut too close to the bone. In it Snedden all too clearly revealed his need to overcompensate for his own inadequacies. The hallmarks of leadership, authority and perspective, were clearly missing. One of the six Liberals who went in a deputation to ask Snedden to resign the same month said of this statement: 'A party leader can only insult the intelligence and sensitivity of his colleagues so much.'

Kelly, *The Unmaking of Gough* (1976), p. 45

# A Vote of Thanks

*The Liberal Leader Bill Snedden certainly had the common touch – perhaps a bit too common after one Queensland fundraiser.*

Snedden had perhaps overindulged slightly in the XXXX, and proceeded thus: 'Well, first I'd like to thank the good ladies of the branch for providing such a scrumptious repast, and old Jack here for fixing up the hall, and Fred for getting us the sound system and his lovely wife for the flowers, and well, I'm sure there are other people I've forgotten, but who gives a fuck.'

MacCallum, How To Be A Megalomaniac (2002), p. 104

## A Political Childhood

*In the tumultuous Whitlam years, family life was no picnic, as Bob Hawke's wife Hazel recalled.*

In 1974, when Susan was sixteen, I withered when she cried out accusingly to me, 'What have you and Dad given us to believe in ... except the Labor Party? And look at the [expletive deleted] mess *that's* in?'

Hazel Hawke, My Own Life (1992), p. 94

## A Right Royal Greeting

*Even royal visits were no longer sacred.*

During the otherwise uneventful royal visit of 1974 Whitlam was entertaining the Queen in Parliament House when a deputation of Aborigines arrived at the front door demanding to talk to him about the lack of progress on land rights. They were met by the President of the Senate, Sir Magnus Cormack, who sternly informed them that they must wait their turn: the Prime Minister was engaged in a private meeting with her majesty. 'Well, fuck the queen,' one of the delegates exploded. Sir Magnus, a royalist of the Menzies school, reeled back in horror. When Whitlam met the Aborigines later he gently informed them that their suggested course of action would be seen as a serious breach of protocol.

MacCallum, Mungo: The Man Who Laughs (2001), p. 259

# Falling on His Mace

*By early 1975 the Whitlam Government was losing control in the House of Representatives. Fred Daly recalled one of the worst days.*

It reached a climax during question time on 27 February 1975 when Dr Jim Forbes (SA), a most unpopular opponent of the Government, accused Clyde Cameron of telling a 'monstrous lie'. Angry argument and crossfire ensued and the Speaker rose and called for order. Cameron angrily said, 'Look, I don't give a damn what you say.' The Speaker called on Cameron to apologise to the Chair but Whitlam said 'No'. The Speaker then named Cameron. In accordance with my usual practice I rose to follow the usual procedure of suggesting to the Speaker that the member concerned might reconsider and apologise before the suspension motion was moved but the Prime Minister waved me back to my seat and said 'No'.

Ian Sinclair, in a splendid piece of quick thinking, moved that Cameron be suspended from the service of the House and put the Government right on the spot. In the division it was defeated 55–50. Whitlam led his members across the floor to vote against the Speaker. Three ministers, Stewart, Everingham and Beazley, and also Gordon Scholes did not vote. A shocked House then saw Speaker Cope rise and say, 'Gentlemen, I hereby tender my resignation as Speaker of the House of Representatives.' Actually it had to go to the Governor-General. He then left the Chair and the Deputy Speaker, Gordon Scholes, took over. His splendid control won him a lot of support for the position of Speaker in the ballot later that day.

As we crossed over to vote the Prime Minister spoke to the Speaker. The Opposition alleged that he said, 'If this is defeated you will have to resign.' Only Cope and the Prime Minister know what was said and it has never been revealed. The Opposition accused him of intimidation and exaggerated the words he was said to have used.

By a strange twist of fate Cope kept a luncheon appointment at the Lodge after his dismissal. Those present were the Prime Minister, Snedden and the Administrator, Sir Roden Cutlet. It had been arranged some weeks previously.

Daly, *From Curtin to Hawke* (1984), p. 207

## A Letter To The *Age*

*Malcolm Fraser won his second leadership challenge against Bill Snedden in March 1975. As new liberal leader he was respected but not much liked, and some felt that his loyalty was also in question. Don Chipp writes:*

One day when the three of us were frontbenchers in Opposition, Peacock found out that a letter had been written to the Melbourne *Age*, under a pseudonym and with a false address, criticising Peacock and myself and praising Malcolm Fraser. Peacock and I were furious and decided to confront him. We arranged to flank him on the front bench of the House and the conversation went something like this:

> PEACOCK (leaning across Fraser, showing Chipp newspaper) Don, have you seen this interesting letter in this morning's *Age*, having a go at both of us and praising Malcolm?
> FRASER (colouring, and showing surprise) Er ... er ... give me a look at that, Andrew.
> PEACOCK (ignoring Fraser) Don, I have checked on the electoral roll and there is no such person at that address.
> CHIPP (also surprised) Well, that means it must be a friend of Malcolm's.
> PEACOCK It might even be Malcolm himself.
> CHIPP Yes, that's more like it.
> FRASER (looking worried) Now, come on chaps, don't be ridiculous.
> PEACOCK All right Fraser, if you want to have a go at me, be man enough to do it to my face, and don't write letters about my curly hair and buckled belts.
> CHIPP Yes, Fraser, if you want to call us trendies, have the guts to do it in the open.
> FRASER Now, come on ... incidentally, would you like to see my draft rural policy?

PEACOCK AND CHIPP (both stunned)   No!
FRASER   What about lunch?

>Chipp and Larkin, *Don Chipp* (1978), pp. 131–2

## HOLDING UP

*Despite the setbacks, Whitlam managed to keep up morale with a series of brisk one-liners. Here are three:*

Gough never missed an opportunity to publicise his government's achievements.
QUESTION   It has been said that you are the best thing the Labor Government has going for it. What would happen to the Government if you fell under a bus tomorrow?
WHITLAM   With the improvements my Government has initiated in urban transport, this is unlikely to happen.

>Cohen, *The Life of the Party* (1987), p. 47

Gough at a banquet given by the Lord Mayor of London in December 1974: 'I'm told, my Lord Mayor, cricket is not the game in which you excel, nor is it the one in which I do. You were a rowing blue, I'm told, and I was some such myself. It is, of course, an extraordinarily apt sport for men in public life, because you can face one way while going the other.'

>Cohen, *After the Party* (1988), p. 48

Without claiming the comparison, I accept Premier Wran's compliment: 'It was said of Caesar Augustus that he found a Rome of brick and left it of marble. It can be said of Gough Whitlam that he found Sydney, Melbourne and Brisbane unsewered and left them fully flushed.'

>Freudenberg in Kramer et al. (eds), *The Greats* (1986), p. 254

# SHUFFLING THE PACK

*Eventually Whitlam decided to try and reinvigorate his government with a major ministerial reshuffle in 1975. Even this had its problems.*

During the week Whitlam contacted those ministers involved in the reshuffle to inform them of their new portfolios. But there was one minister he did not formally notify until late Thursday afternoon, the day before the swearing-in at Government House. This was Clyde Cameron, who was about to suffer the biggest setback in his political career. For three days Cameron had been reading in the newspapers that Whitlam intended to shift him from the Labour portfolio but he made no effort to contact the Prime Minister about these reports, waiting instead for Whitlam to speak to him. At 4.30pm on Thursday Whitlam's office rang Cameron's office to say the Prime Minister wanted to see the minister. Subsequently Cameron rang Whitlam's office to speak to the Prime Minister but was not put through to Whitlam. Eventually a senior staff member from Cameron's office called back to say the minister would be in his office if Whitlam wanted to see him.

Finally Whitlam was forced to walk from his office around to Cameron's, located in the new wing. It was the first time Whitlam had been to this office and the Prime Minister was uncertain which door to enter. Cameron's press secretary John Stubbs was suddenly startled to find the table and papers stacked against the door, which he never used, moving towards him along with a simultaneous banging on the door. Stubbs cleared the doorway to let Whitlam in and the Prime Minister then walked into Cameron's adjoining office where he stunned Cameron by telling him he would be appointed Minister for Science and Consumer Affairs. Cameron, like Cairns four days before him, refused to accept Whitlam's decision which meant a crushing blow to his political power and reputation. He told Whitlam during a bitter thirty minute meeting that he would think about the job overnight and see the Prime Minister before the swearing in on Friday. When Whitlam's office released a statement later that night outlining the shape of the new ministry, Cameron branded it as untrue. 'Senator J. McClelland is not the Minister for Labour,' he declared. 'That position is still held by me.'

But once again, like Cairns before him, Cameron had only the choice of accepting the demotion or resigning from the ministry. Always a realistic politician he took the former course, suffered his humiliation and privately resolved that this was something he should never forget. But Cameron did come close to refusing the job. On the Friday morning when he arrived at his office he called his staff in and told them he would not accept the new portfolio and a number of them started clearing out the office in preparation for departure. Cameron finally changed his mind after a number of ministers came to see him.

Kelly, *The Unmaking of Gough* (1976), pp. 188–9

## HERE COMES THE JUDGE

*Whitlam also appointed his controversial Attorney-General, Lionel Murphy, to the High Court, against the wishes of the Chief Justice, Sir Garfield Barwick. Bill Hayden caught the aftermath.*

Hayden had been made aware of the animosity between Murphy and Barwick some weeks earlier when Barwick had telephoned him to complain about Murphy's appointment. Hayden arrived late at Cabinet as a result of the phone call and when asked by Whitlam what had delayed him, replied: 'I've had Garfield Barwick haranguing me for almost an hour over what a mess we've made of the High Court.' Whitlam snapped back: 'Yes, but did you tell him how much we'd improved Cabinet?'

Stubbs, *Hayden* (1989), p. 141

# A Dramatic Gesture

*As Labor's troubles mounted during 1975, Whitlam was
still looking for a way to crash through them.*

One of the most spectacular expressions of Whitlam's vision, which represented a continuing nightmare to Treasury, was given form in a plan to buy a major shipping company, with the whole scheme culminating in a scene Hayden later privately described with a sort of fascinated detachment: 'He had a great idea he was going to buy the Furness Whitney shipping company. He had Frank Crean in, and he was opposed to it, so he had me in. He had the support of the transport minister Charlie Jones; he and Gough just loved ships, planes and trains; they were still big boys at heart. I ran through a list of reasons straight off the cuff why I thought it would be unwise, not least of which was that we would have to get legislation through a hostile Senate, and then there were potential industrial problems … a whole range of things. And, lo and behold, I found Frank Crean had said almost exactly the same things. He had been briefed by Treasury, I hadn't. Gough was still trying to get the numbers on side, so I got dumped a little bit later because I wasn't on side. However, I was sitting there one day and got called up with a big team of people and Peter Abeles was there, and all of the Treasury fellows were there: and when I say all, their style was always to have six people, or, for something really big, up to ten or a dozen people even, to try and duress you if they could. They were terrified of Gough's harebrained schemes, and rightly so. We were all sitting there and, all of a sudden, Gough said something like: "Jesus Christ, you Treasury people lack imagination: you lack creativeness. What I want is ideas. What I want is the dramatic gesture: like Disraeli buying the Suez Canal!"'

Hayden said it was the only time he had seen the faces of the whole Treasury group fall apart: 'You could hear the clunk as all their jaws simultaneously hit the floor: the louder thumps were from people like myself who fell out of our chairs.'

Stubbs, *Hayden* (1989), p. 137

# Basso Profondo

*When Whitlam's deputy Lance Barnard retired it
meant a by-election in his Tasmanian seat of Bass.
Graham Richardson learned how unpopular Labor was.*

'I went down to Tasmania for the Bass by-election the following year [1975]. That was really bad. The [Brian] Harradine machine was just coming apart, he'd just been booted out of the party.' [Harradine had been a member of the ALP federal executive, but after leaving the party was elected to the Senate as an Independent in December 1975, a seat he has held ever since.]

'The old Right machine was just, *just* unravelling. And Launceston was one of the hard areas of the Left and I was given a pretty hard time by some. I was abused, and called a Grouper and all sorts of ... I was told to get fucked by everyone in sight, basically [he laughs ruefully]. But I mean the party organisation down there was dreadful, it was basically nonexistent, so I gave up trying to organise anything with them, that was basically impossible. So I spent most of my time, in that by-election, just door-knocking and doing menial tasks.

'I'll never forget the day of the by-election. I was standing in a polling booth across the road from my hotel, where some of Whitlam's campaign staff and the national campaign people were staying: the more important people were staying in a better hotel, I wasn't in a good one; I think it was called the Hotel Cornwall. I was there standing in the polling booth right across the road from it. Pissing down rain, freezing cold, I mean, no umbrella, *nothing*, just *dripping* cold, miserable. And up comes the big white chariot out the front and it was David Combe and Richard Whitington and a whole team who'd taken off for lunch. [Combe, the national secretary, and Whitington, a member of Whitlam's staff, were running the Bass campaign.] Heading off for a rest from politics. Fuck me. I was handing out how to votes in an election where we were as popular as pork chops in a synagogue.

'And then I moved from that polling booth to another one on the outskirts of town where I was the only Labor Party worker. Hanging out, freezing cold. The whole day I never got a sandwich, cup of tea, or a thank you. And then a Liberal lady, who was delivering goodies to their workers, took pity on this poor, frozen, dripping figure, and she gave me a hot cup of coffee and an apricot tart. I was very grateful, I think I would have voted Liberal if they'd given me a vote that day.

'And then I went and scrutineered until about half past nine; I came out; there was no lift for me, the street was in darkness, I had to find a public phone, to ring up a taxi. Yes, I did wonder why I worked for the Labor Party then, I was pretty pissed off with the world that night, especially because the result was so horrible, so excruciatingly painful – because I knew then, that we [the Whitlam Government] were finished. There was no way we were going to win an election. And that the end result would be pretty frightening.'

Richardson in Cumming, *Mates* (1991), pp. 165–6

## GIVING UP THE DRINK

*Labor's federal executive meeting to discuss the Bass disaster at least provided some light relief, courtesy of Bob Hawke.*

A few days before the executive meeting Bob Hawke had declared on television he would give up drink if he became prime minister. Whitlam was unable to resist replying to this and when he arrived outside John Curtin House in Canberra on 31 July [1975] he stood on the footpath and waited for reporters to interview him, an uncharacteristic habit. The following exchange occurred between Whitlam and Peter Harvey of Channel 9:

HARVEY    Prime Minister, what are your hopes for this executive meeting?

WHITLAM    Oh, you must realise Peter I'm very worried this morning. In my usual style I have a terrible hangover and I realise, of course, that to hold my position I've just got to undertake a very rigorous program of social drinking ...

HARVEY    Prime Minister, you don't expect any criticism from the State branches about this problem?

WHITLAM   Oh I expect a wide ranging, frank exchange of views. You know, where we all come clean about our failures.
HARVEY   Do you think they may demand that you …
WHITLAM   I mean this will be like an Alcoholics Anonymous meeting I expect.
HARVEY   Well, indeed yes. You don't think that they'll be demanding that you drink more?
WHITLAM   I fear so. They will. That's what I expect. I was in training. I've got a terrible hangover … that's why I'm giving this curbside interview … breaking the habits of a lifetime … pity the ABC missed out.

Kelly, The Unmaking of Gough (1976), p. 201

## A Shrinking Giant

*The final straw for the Whitlam Government was the so-called loans affair. In 1975 the Government had attempted to secretly borrow $4 billion for massive development projects. Minerals and energy minister Rex Connor believed that his shadowy contact Tirath Khemlani, a Pakistani international commodities dealer, could still deliver, even after Cabinet revoked his authority to proceed. Graham Freudenberg wrote:*

In the following weeks he lived for, almost literally lived with, his dream, waiting for the message that never came. His young friend and closest caucus colleague, Paul Keating (destined to fill briefly the Cabinet vacancy left by Connor in October), found him morning after morning, in March and April, asleep in his office, unshaven and dishevelled, waiting for the ring and rattle of the telex machine, which would herald Khemlani's message that he had at last delivered the goods. It never came. Connor had learnt how to operate his own machine. Keating pleaded with him, 'For God's sake, Rex, this is no way for a minister to behave.' The strain was telling visibly. Connor's giant frame seemed to shrink. And still he held on in pursuit of his dream.

Freudenberg, A Certain Grandeur (1976), p. 353

# The Peanut Man

*The Opposition flew Khemlani to Canberra to try and provide evidence against Whitlam and Connor, but the exercise backfired. Fred Daly described the fiasco in Parliament.*

I understand that yesterday afternoon a Commonwealth ministerial car was booked by the deputy leader of the Opposition to meet Ansett flight 361, 2.10pm from Sydney, and that of course commenced a drama in Canberra yesterday that has rarely been equalled. The car was to meet a person named Mr Khemlani. I understand that the gentleman approached the Commonwealth car dressed in a safari suit and wearing dark glasses. He was met by bearded investigators who hustled him into the VIP room while the Commonwealth car backed into the normally restricted luggage area and his eight bulging briefcases were loaded into it.

Mr Khemlani was then pushed into the Commonwealth car along with two sinister bearded staff members and taken on a high speed car chase through the back streets of Fyshwick reaching speeds of 100 kilometres per hour, turning down side streets and doing sudden U-turns before coming to a sudden stop at his destination – a $23 a night room at the Hotel Wellington. Mr Khemlani, still using the car, and the men then disappeared into room 49 – the room adjoining the motel shoeshine box. Lemonade, potato chips and two Sydney afternoon papers were pushed through the breakfast hatch. He stayed locked in his room while the staff members stayed huddled in a corner sifting through his eight suitcases of documents. Later in the afternoon Mr Khemlani was taken on another high speed car chase. This time, as a taxi pulled up at the front of the motel, Mr Khemlani disappeared out the back door and sped off in a late model gold Torana with the manager of the Wellington Hotel at the wheel. That is service. It raced through the peak hour traffic, went one and a half times around State Circle, and reached speeds of up to 120 km along Commonwealth Avenue before swinging around and returning to the hotel. Then Mr Khemlani disappeared.

An hour later his briefcases were lugged into a lift at the $33 a night Lakeside Hotel where Mr Khemlani usually stays. But he was not booked in there last night. Last night Mr Khemlani was locked up with two Opposition front benchers, Mr Bob Ellicott and Mr John Howard, going through suitcases full of documents. As if he were not in enough trouble without being locked up with them! I come back again to the Commonwealth car. Poor Mr Khemlani: he had come all the way from Singapore, at his own cost and without a visa, to clear his name and he had all that excess baggage with him. What must he think of Australia — his life was endangered by high speed car chases in Commonwealth cars; his bags were searched by bearded investigators, and as far as we know they were not false beards; he was booked into a $23 a night room next to a shoe shine box yet his bags were booked into a $33 a night international hotel; he was locked up all afternoon with bearded men and then all night with two members of the Opposition.

MR WHITLAM   And fed with peanuts.

MR DALY   And then fed with peanuts. He must also be wondering why the Opposition would pay out all that money for his bags but was too lousy to pay for a taxi fare for him to go from the airport to the hotel. That brings me back to the original point about the misuse of a Commonwealth car ...

Freudenberg, A Certain Grandeur (1976), pp. 385–6

## A Copper's Instinct

*When Connor was sacked for misleading Parliament in 1975, Fraser used his numbers in the Senate to block supply. Whitlam was certain the Governor-General, Sir John Kerr, would resolve the impasse in his favour. After a conversation with Kerr, Bill Hayden was not so sure.*

'Then Kerr said, and I remember the conversation episodically: "If an election were called now, there is no doubt that, with his back against the wall, Gough is a magnificent fighter — he fights like a lion — he would be back within a term at the most, I would expect." I said: "Jesus Christ, it's not as easy as that; when you go out it's bloody hard to get back, and it usually takes more than one term. We've just had twenty-three years trying to get back." Anyway, that was the conversation. I got very uneasy about that. I had to catch a plane home. Being Treasurer had its distinctly different demands from Social Security, which took me all around Australia – sometimes I would be away from home for two or three weeks on the run during that Medibank debate, which was pretty awful for Dallas, but I had no choice. With Treasury you could get home, but the workload would follow you. I didn't want to miss the plane, so as I left Government House I said to the driver: "Go flat out, I want to see the Prime Minister."

'At Parliament House I hurried to the Prime Minister's office, and in there were Freddie Daly, Gough and the Commonwealth Electoral Officer, and I thought "Oh, oh, what are they up to?" In fact they were sorting out when an election could be held if one were forced on us, and what were the problems – there are always problems like school holidays and so on. I said: "Gough, I've got to talk to you", and he came out of the room. I said: "This was the conversation, this is what Kerr said. I'm telling you now, my copper's instinct tells me that this guy is going to sack you. He's thinking of an early election to sort this thing out." Gough had his spectacles in his hand, and his striped shirt on as I remember, and he drew himself up and boomed: "Comrade, he wouldn't have the guts," and he walked back into the room. And I said, "Okay", and I headed off ... and next week we were out of a job ... not that there was anything Gough could have done to stop it.'

Stubbs, *Hayden* (1989), pp. 142–3

## Goodbye

*Kerr held meetings with Fraser as well as with Whitlam and his ministers. Although Fraser was always certain Whitlam would be sacked, by 11 November 1975 many of his supporters were wavering. On that day Whitlam met Fraser and said he would seek a half-Senate election to break the deadlock.*

Returning to his own party room, Fraser did not report on his meeting with Whitlam. He did not inform his supporters that Whitlam intended to seek a half-Senate election. Instead, he asked for 'support and trust'. And, at a press briefing after the meeting, his deputy, Phillip Lynch, said: 'We believe events will work themselves out ... We believe the present course is sound *for reasons which will become apparent to you later*' [author's italics].

Caucus applauded as Whitlam announced his decision to request an election for half the Senate. Whitlam, confident and ebullient, suggested to [Attorney-General Kep] Enderby that he himself might, after all, attend the Remembrance Day wreath-laying ceremony at the Australian War Memorial where Enderby was to represent Whitlam and the Government. Enderby however insisted on going. At the War Memorial, he escorted the Governor-General and Lady Kerr to and from their car. Kerr spoke not a word. As Enderby farewelled the viceregal couple, only Lady Kerr spoke, with stony finality: 'Goodbye Mr Attorney.'

Freudenberg, *A Certain Grandeur* (1976), p. 391

## A Short Run

*Paul Keating had only been a minister for three weeks when the Labor Government was dismissed by Kerr in November 1975.*

Legend has it that Keating was the first to encounter an enraged Whitlam, returning to Parliament House after the dismissal at Yarralumla on 11 November. 'You're sacked!' Whitlam growled at a shocked Keating. 'What for?' Keating called back, unaware that the entire government had been deposed.

Carew, *Keating* (1988), p. 4

# The Security Blanket

*Having easily won the 1975 election, Fraser decided to reform the process of government. Russell Schneider, press secretary to a senior minister, found this had its problems.*

All ministerial staff were advised of strict penalties for divulging Cabinet details and only two members of any minister's staff were permitted to receive Cabinet material.

These instructions had their absurdities. One tried and trusted Opposition staff member who had been party to details of some of the Opposition's secret plans for the rejection of supply was rudely told that she could not accept Cabinet papers on her minister's behalf. As her minister lived out of town and would have to pick them up from his interstate office before taking the early morning plane to Canberra, he pointed out the difficulties entailed. Fraser had insisted that all ministerial staff be cleared to 'top secret' and then decided the clearance didn't justify their being given access to 'top secret' information. The secretary thus did not have access and the Cabinet Secretariat was unshakeable. A lengthy haggle ensued. Finally [the Department of Prime Minister and Cabinet] discovered a way of overcoming the problem: it arranged for the papers to be vocadexed to the regional Foreign Affairs office, put in an envelope and delivered by safe-hand messenger to the minister's office. On arrival, the safe-hand messenger blithely handed over the vocadex copies to the secretary who had been unable to handle the originals. She then went about indexing the material, more than a little miffed about the fact that so-called 'top secret' papers had passed through half a dozen extra hands, and transmitted over a virtually public line rather than sent direct in the secure bags that had handled some of the Opposition's innermost secrets.

Schneider, *War Without Blood* (1990), p. 41

## Hide and Seek

*Whitlam had offered to resign the Labor leadership in favour of Bill Hayden, but Hayden refused. By the time he was prepared to challenge for the leadership there were doubts, as Laurie Oakes reported in the* Bulletin.

Bill Hayden has a slightly offbeat sense of humour, and there is one joke he likes to play over and over. He will invite someone to his office but when they open the door they find an apparently empty room. Mr Hayden will be hiding either in a cupboard or on hands and knees under his desk. Hiding as a joke is one thing. What worries some of Mr Hayden's colleagues is what they fear may be a tendency to hide on occasions when things are serious.

Kelly, *The Hawke Ascendancy* (1984), p. 38.

## You Tell Him

*Don Chipp found the Fraser style too autocratic, and wrote to tell him so.*

In early January 1977, Fraser telephoned me and asked me to see him about 'the charges in my letter'. In his Melbourne office I was surprised to see Tony Street, Minister for Employment and Industrial Relations, there. Fraser told me that he had shown my letter to several Cabinet ministers.

I was furious that he had shown a personal and confidential letter to others, and told him so. Fraser then replied that he had brought Tony into the discussion *to assure me that he, Fraser, did not dominate the Cabinet.* He then said, 'Tony, you tell Don that.' Tony, with Malcolm towering above him, dutifully complied.

I burst out laughing, but neither Fraser nor Street could understand why. I remember thinking, 'What's the bloody use!'

Chipp and Larkin, *Don Chipp* (1978), p. 176

# Out of the Cake

*Fraser's Government was a serious one, but occasionally his colleagues organised some light relief.*

In these circumstances, it was perhaps a happy thought when Don Cameron (Liberal, Qld) decided to organise a party of Liberal MPs to celebrate their tenth year in the Parliament. It became known as 'Don's Party'. The function was held in the members' dining-room and attended by quite a number of MPs of all ages, some of them getting a bit long in the tooth.

At a certain stage in the proceedings, much to the surprise of those present, a large cake was brought into the dining room and out jumped a very beautiful young woman in a bikini. Bert James (Labor, NSW) later in the House asked the Prime Minister a question: 'Is it a fact that this was the only occasion on which the Fraser Government has given effect to their promise to stimulate the private sector?'

Daly, *From Curtin to Hawke* (1984), p. 279

# Fear and Laughter

*Fraser was an aloof man, known to few. He seldom talked about himself.*

Fraser only described his childhood twice when he was Prime Minister. The first time was in the 1977 campaign:

> What was Mr Fraser's most frightening experience as a child? … Well, he said there was this time when his father took him on a picnic during a flood in the Riverina. He was left on an island in the middle of the flood and his father rowed off. Young Malcolm knew that snakes made for higher ground in a flood and he was terrified snakes would get to him before his father got back.

Then the Prime Minister recalled his funniest boyhood experience:

The sulky got bogged and his father told him to unharness the horse. When the shafts were released from the harness, the sully overbalanced backwards, catapulting his mother into the mud. His father was ready with his camera to photograph the incident.

Edwards in Kelly, *The Hawke Ascendancy* (1984), p. 49

## Lynched

*During the 1977 election Phillip Lynch, then Treasurer, became involved in a land scandal. Jim Killen was present when the Liberals' federal secretary, Tony Eggleton, rang Lynch asking him to resign.*

An ashen-faced Eggleton read from the notes he had taken during the conversation. 'He is very put out,' said Eggleton. 'He is very angry. He has said: "I, too, have bits of paper. I will hold a daily press conference. I will bucket you all. You needn't think you are getting rid of me so easily. It's that Victorian crowd that is trying to get rid of me."'

The effect on the ministers present was devastating. [Robert] Cotton and [Tony] Street shook their heads in disbelief. Most of the others were motionless and stunned. There was further talk as to who could possibly help Lynch understand the plight into which he was thrusting the Government. The names mentioned were Robert Southey, a former federal president of the Liberal Party, Mrs J. Mein, the State president of the Victorian division of the Liberal Party, and Mrs Yvonne McComb, the State president of the Queensland division of the Liberal Party. It was decided the Prime Minister should speak to him.

Malcolm Fraser's conversation with Phillip Lynch could only be described as incredible. We could not hear what Lynch said, but we could hear what Fraser said and we could watch his face and reactions. Malcolm's enquiry as to how he was feeling apparently brought a sharp response. Fraser's face became grim and grey. 'Steady on, Phillip, steady on ... Are you all right, Phillip? Steady on, Phillip. Hold on, Phillip.' He held the phone to his ear for what seemed to be an interminable time without speaking. The silence in the room was desperately uncomfortable. 'Can somebody help him?' Fraser was apparently talking now not to Phillip Lynch but to some other person. It was clear that Lynch had spoken to Fraser in terms of thorough acerbity. Whatever he said, Fraser never let on. He put down the phone and turned to us thoroughly apprehensive and bewildered.

Killen, *Inside Australian Politics* (1985), p. 272

## A Fun Campaign

*Predictable as it was, the 1977 campaign had its moments, as Mungo MacCallum discovered when Fraser went to Melbourne.*

Princes Park was almost empty of a couple of hundred bedraggled men, women, and children determinedly skipping, soccering, tennising, volleyballing, frisbeeing, and painting each other's faces. Fraser got off a bus, fresh from losing a bout of knuckle wrestling with the local Youth minister Brian Dixon, clad in the rather odd combination of a T-shirt and a cravat. Someone immediately painted a large black dot in the middle of his forehead; a wet and bored looking policeman said loudly, 'That's so you'll know where to aim for.' Premier Dick Hamer received a grey nose, and a heckler said, 'What's that on your face, Hamer, mud from the land deals?' A nearby hearty grabbed the heckler by the shirt and snarled at him, 'Why can't you just have fun like the rest of us?'

The royal party, as one of the organisers described it, got onto a dais, and Hamer gave Fraser a cartoon, and Fraser gave Dixon a statue and told everyone to have more fun. An enterprising photographer asked one of Fraser's staff if the Prime Minister would paint 'ALP' on his forehead, as that was obviously what was on his mind at the moment, and was told that of course the Prime Minister wouldn't do anything so silly. Instead, the Prime Minister played European bowls very badly, and got involved in some game that looked like a group grope, and was passed over the heads of a crowd, and hit Dixon for some time with a large rubber phallus, and painted his face green and blue. 'It shows,' one of the staff said bravely, 'that he has a sense of humour.'

He finally left, still painted, for the airport, frightening a number of children in the process, and headed for Launceston, where there was to be a barbecue at the racecourse. He was met at Launceston by a small group of very hostile Aborigines, which must have made him feel that the Tasmanians couldn't even commit genocide properly, and by a 'guard of honor' of nineteen bikies (the other thirty-one promised had failed to turn up). Fraser likes bikies (especially the sort that don't pack-rape democracy) but he likes the bikes better. He found an Italian job that cost $7,500 and said to Tamie, 'Doesn't it make you drool,' and went for a burn round the race track on it. The owner, who apparently had a sense of humour, had switched off the petrol, so there was just enough in the carburettor to get Fraser around behind a clump of trees before the bike stopped.

When Fraser failed to reappear, there was a mild panic among the cops, but eventually he worked it out and rode triumphantly back to eat a hot dog, and leave for Hobart, where the perpetual floating 'Four Corners' team was setting up yet more spontaneous interviews with journalists. The burden of the interviews seemed to be that there wasn't much happening, and that if anything Whitlam and his staff were being bigger shits than Fraser and his staff, and everyone wanted to go home.

MacCallum, *Mungo on the Zoo Plane* (1979), pp. 202–3

## AMONG THE DWARFS

*The fun continued the next day in Hobart. Mungo MacCallum again.*

In the morning Fraser went to inspect the Electrolytic Zinc plant, a factory which manufactures vast amounts of heavy metal pollution to pour into the Derwent river, and as a side effect produces some zinc for export. The start of the inspection was marred by the fact that Fraser and his party went off to one part of the plant, and his police escort, obediently followed by his staff and most of the press, drove off at high speed to another. It then drove at even higher speed to another wrong place, and finally to the right place, just as Fraser was leaving. The two parties came together for the second part of the tour, which consisted of walking several hundred yards past metal plates in a shed apparently devoid of human habitation.

After some time, the manager found a very small token worker. There was some speculation among the press as to whether he was in fact a dwarf. The local Liberal member, Michael Hodgman, came over to the press and said, 'If you call him a dwarf, I'll sue you. That's very defamatory to call him a dwarf. He's small, but he's not a dwarf. And if you say that a dwarf was forced to talk to the Prime Minister, I'll sue.' After a little while he came back to the press and said, 'The trick is that the dwarf's deaf, and doesn't have to listen to what Fraser's saying.' Quite. After walking another kilometre or so, Fraser found a couple more workers. Hodgman said to a reporter, 'You're a bastard, I'll bet you say he talked to a dwarf first, and then a new Australian and then a man with glasses.'

But, after walking rather wistfully past a building labelled 'Power control section', Fraser found a slightly more inhabited area, where there were lots of workers. Fraser appeared fascinated by this sight; work is, after all, something outside his experience. He spoke to many of them, and spent a long time gazing raptly at a number of machines in particular something called an auto stacker, which he and Hodgman spent five minutes observing at work (or possibly play). One reporter said to another, 'I can't believe they're spending all that time talking about auto stacking, can you? His companion thought for a minute. 'Yes,' he replied.

MacCallum, *Mungo on the Zoo Plane* (1979), pp. 203–4

## An Election Strike

*Campaigning could be a lonely business, John Button found.*

Senator John Button, Labor Party leader in the Senate, was to address a lunch-hour meeting at a meatworks outside Sydney during an election campaign. He arrived at noon, the appointed time for the meeting, but much to his surprise the only person in sight was the chairman.

'What's happened to the crowd?' asked Button.

'Well,' said the chairman, 'that's an interesting question.'

He then revealed that the management had refused permission for the meeting to be held. The employees had called a stopwork meeting about 8am to discuss the matter. A resolution was moved to the effect that the meeting would be held at noon as arranged to hear the senator and then as a protest the men would stop work for the day.

'Well,' said Button, 'where are the men?'

'Let me finish,' said the chairman. 'Following the moving of a resolution for a stoppage at noon an amendment was moved that the men go on strike immediately. It was carried and they all went home. The fact is that I'm the only one left in the place, and I've come along as a matter of courtesy to inform you of the position and the reason for your one-man audience.'

Daly, *The Politician Who Laughed* (1982), p. 96

## It Worked

*The National Party leader, Doug Anthony, was a political pragmatist, according to Don Chipp.*

This is illustrated by an incident that occurred on election night 1977.

He came into the tally room in Canberra late in the night and it was clear that the Government had been returned with an overwhelming majority. A woman journalist – a confessed Labor supporter – angry, devastated, and encouraged by the urge which only alcohol can give, approached him and said, 'Anthony, you are a liar!' One could conclude by looking at Anthony's face that he almost enjoyed the taunt. If not, he certainly enjoyed his rejoinder, which was given with the best of his boyish, fresh-faced grins, 'Yes, but it worked, didn't it?'

Chipp and Larkin, *Don Chipp* (1978), p. 142

# This Bloody Party

*Towards the end of his political career, Whitlam showed the strain — even to his personal friend and political enemy Jim Killen, who recalled the following incident.*

When the former minister for Minerals and Energy, Rex Connor, died in 1977 Whitlam was again leading the Opposition. Parliament was sitting and the Labor Party balloted as to who would attend the funeral. Clyde Cameron, who had considerably vexed Whitlam and continued to do so, was not among those selected. I was Minister for Defence and RAAF planes were being used to take mourners to and from Wollongong for the funeral. Cameron came to seek a seat on an aircraft. With all of the authenticity of voice of a Dickensian solicitor reading a will he said, 'But it would have … but it would have been the late Mr Connor's wish that I attend.' 'But Clyde,' I said, 'I understand your party had a vote. What will Gough say to me?' The Dickensian solicitor's voice was replaced with the authentic voice of the shearing shed and he gave me advice as to what Gough's fate should be and stalked out. I sent Gough a note at question time explaining my difficulty and saying I would come to his office when I could. I returned for a few minutes to my own office. The large frame of Whitlam burst through the door. 'This bloody party, comrade, will kill me yet,' he expostulated. 'Well, I'm in a spot,' I said. 'I don't want to upset Clyde on an occasion such as this.' That evoked from Whitlam precisely the same gathering of language which Cameron had applied to him. He paced around the room and began again. 'This party, this bloody party, this bloody morbid party. What can you do with it?' He quietened and looked at me hopefully. 'What do you want to happen when you die?' I asked. He took a deep breath and said, 'I just want you to get up and say: "Let the Senate be his pyre."' He was gone as quickly as he came. Cameron got to Wollongong.

Killen, *Inside Australian Politics* (1985), pp. 209–10

# A Matter of Trust

*After the 1977 election Bill Hayden succeeded Whitlam as Labor leader, but relations with Fraser did not improve.*

Relations between Fraser and the Opposition remained acrimonious throughout Hayden's term as leader. Within weeks of Hayden becoming Opposition leader, Fraser summoned him and his deputy, Lionel Bowen, to his office to inform them of some matters connected with security. Hayden nodded his head occasionally as Fraser spoke, but there was no response at all from Bowen. Eventually Fraser asked Bowen what was wrong with him. Bowen answered: 'I'm listening. It's just that I don't trust you, you bastard.' As they left Hayden congratulated Bowen for being so direct with the Prime Minister.

Stubbs, *Hayden* (1989), p. 186

# The Matador

*Hayden's new team began to show some style of its own.*

Kim Beazley senior first spoke of the matador in Paul Keating. It was during the late 1970s, when the Labor Party was under attack from the Catholic church on the issue of abortion. Beazley remarked that Keating demonstrated a bullfighter's courage and sense of drama one Sunday morning when, after missing his usual mass and arriving at another church in the Bankstown area, he witnessed a tirade against the ALP from the pulpit. The claim was that the Labor Party was in favour of abortion and Keating, whose theatrical skills were usually confined to the Parliament and caucus room, stood up in his pew and said in a loud voice: 'That's not right!' When the priest repeated the charge, Keating repeated the retort. 'I didn't move,' he recalled. 'I stood my ground. It was a highly unusual thing to do. This fellow obviously thought he could make fallacious claims about the Labor Party with the protection of the pulpit. I made sure he didn't. It was about social policy and how the Labor Party was in favour of abortion. It wasn't. It was a free vote matter and a lot of people didn't support it — abortion on demand.'

Gordon, *Paul Keating: A Question of Leadership* (1993), p. 57

## A Good Cigar

*Meanwhile Fraser was starting to have trouble with his ministers. In 1979 a royal commission on electoral matters found Reg Withers had acted improperly, and Fraser acted promptly.*

Around four o'clock an attendant in the Commonwealth Parliament offices entered Withers' office and removed the electric typewriter used to draft versions of Withers' statement; it was needed for Geoffrey Yeend. Withers was called into Fraser's office at six. Lynch was by Fraser's side. Fraser offered Withers a cigar and said: 'The meeting has decided you must go. I am therefore withdrawing your commission tonight.' 'As you like,' Withers said, 'thanks for the cigar.'

Schneider, *War Without Blood* (1990), p. 125

## Menzies Wouldn't Have Done It

*In the process of sacking Withers, Fraser made enemies.*

The origins of the hostility that built up towards Fraser among his senior ministers lay partly in the Prime Minister's streak of self-righteousness. In 1975 Fraser had justified his strike against Whitlam by appeal to moral principle. Yet Fraser's career was littered with the shells of men whom he had destroyed: Gorton, Whitlam, Connor, Snedden. Nobody in politics had displayed such ruthlessness. Fraser's senior colleagues — and Reg Withers and Doug Anthony were among the toughest — had nothing but respect for his tactics. Yet Anthony and Withers were honest about what they did: they lived by that great axiom of politics: 'If you see a head, kick it.' Now they saw Fraser falling victim to some of his own propaganda about principle.

Withers simply dismissed Fraser as a hypocrite when Fraser sacked him from the ministry. Withers told journalists: 'When the man who's carried the biggest knife in this country for the last ten years starts giving you a lecture about propriety, integrity and the need to resign, then he's either making a sick joke or playing you for a mug.' Anthony criticised Fraser to his face arguing that loyalty was more important than morality: 'Menzies and McEwen would never have gone on like this. They would have stood up for their ministers and got their ministers to stand up for them.'

Kelly, *The Hawke Ascendancy* (1984), p. 57

## WEARING IT

*New South Wales Premier Neville Wran was considered to be one of Labor's strong men, but he could not stand up to the Party's State president John Ducker. Graham Richardson remembered.*

And Ducker did have extraordinary authority. There were a couple of examples of it; the best came in '79 when we were having a rule change on the upper house, putting them [members of the upper house] into the lower house caucus: a joint caucus. This was being fiercely resisted by the Left [even though NSW was the only place where this was not already done] and Wran came up with a statement saying he wouldn't support it.

So Ducker and I went up to meet Wran, one Sunday morning in Wran's office. We went in there, this would have been May '79. Ducker said, 'Okay, what's your problem?' and he [Wran] said, 'This is going to create too much upheaval, I just won't wear it.' And Ducker said, 'You won't wear it, eh? I'll tell you what you'll f——ing wear!' And he gave Wran a five minute serve that was just devastating, about what he'd do to him if he wouldn't wear it, and at the end of that he said, 'Not only are you going to wear it, you're going to f——ing move it [at the conference]!' And Wran did.

Richardson in Cumming, *Mates* (1991), p. 225

# A Quiet Little Drink

*Bob Hawke clashed with Bill Hayden at Labor's 1979 federal conference in Adelaide. His behaviour after he believed Hayden had broken a deal on industry policy was remarkable. John Stubbs was there.*

It was an almost classic demonstration of the volatility of Bob Hawke in his drinking days at times when he was under strain and in the spotlight. He had lunch at State Parliament House, some wine, a port or two, a cigar, and then, towards the end of the afternoon back at the conference venue not far away joined a group of people I happened to be with that included Mick Young and Eric Walsh. We were in a round of six or eight, drinking stubbies at a price we considered quite excessive in the foyer of the Festival Centre. Somebody arranged for most of us to have dinner with our wives at Ayers House, then considered Adelaide's most prestigious restaurant. I was instructed that Hawke was not to be made aware of the arrangement.

When the group had faded into the night, Hawke went to an improvised television studio and gave a restrained television interview during which he said only that the deal 'was something that occurred over lunch time. I haven't had time to consider it'. Asked about his political future he said that if delegates thought he could serve the party better in another capacity he would expect them to come to him and express their view, adding, 'and so far they haven't'. Ducker had restrained Hawke from attacking Hayden on the conference floor, and Hawke later said, 'John Ducker saved me.' After the calm interview Ducker embraced Hawke. Then, as the *National Times* story said:

> The ABC, sensing they might be on to a story, brought in some bottles of beer to keep the duo around … but after an hour or so John Ducker, realising Hawke's capacity to exaggerate was leading to overkill, began to play down the incident, telling colleagues, 'It will all be over after a good night's sleep.' But to no avail. Sleep was low on Bob Hawke's priorities.

Hawke had not eaten since his lunch at Parliament House,

and Ducker was not in good health and had to retire early from his role as minder.

Hawke went across North Terrace to the Gateway Inn and found in the expensive Rotunda Bar, among the furry red-and-gold wallpaper, a group of delegates and journalists. Hawke's 'temper warmed when he spotted Hugh McBride, original author of the amendment moved by Bill Hayden, and Simon Crean, also a member of the Victorian delegation.' Both were members of the Centre Unity faction. 'You're all bloody gutless,' he told them. Then he told five or six journalists, some of whom had tape recorders: 'As far as Bill Hayden and I are concerned, Hayden is dead,' and then, louder: 'As far as Bill Hayden and I are concerned, it's finished … he is a lying cunt with a limited future.'

Stubbs, *Hayden* (1989), p. 194

## THE TROIKA

*Hawke was a candidate for Parliament in 1980. His uneasy reconciliation with Hayden led to a campaign based around the trio of Hayden, Hawke, and the popular New South Wales Premier Neville Wran.*

In mid-1980 Hayden and Hawke held their most important talk on the leadership before Hawke's entry into Parliament. They faced each other, declared a truce, and laid the ground for the remarkable ALP troika. The meeting was at John Curtin House in Canberra during a break in a national executive meeting. Hawke told Hayden he wanted to make his position clear. 'I will work my guts out in this campaign to get you elected as prime minister,' he said. 'I will go to the last ounce of my energy to do this. It would be dishonest of me if I didn't say the embers of Adelaide remain in my mind, but I want you to know I can put this away and work for the party and your success.'

Kelly, *The Hawke Ascendancy* (1984), p. 84

## Lost for Words

*All prime ministers have a delicate relationship with their speechwriters, as Bob Hawke noted after being handed the wrong speech at a function.*

I was a little more fortunate than my predecessor, Malcolm Fraser, of whom a story is told which, I am assured, is not apocryphal. Fraser had had a hell of a row with his speechwriter. The Prime Minister had to deliver an address in Melbourne that night and, again, in the rush of events it was put in his hands just before he went on stage. Malcolm read the first two pages and then turned them over to be confronted with a sheet which was blank except for the words: 'Now you are on your own, you bastard.'

Hawke, The Hawke Memoirs (1994), p. 163

## Big Bloke

*Fraser was still not overly popular with some of his own troops.*

In early 1980 Andrew Peacock and his long-standing Country Party friend Peter Nixon were waiting in the anteroom for Cabinet to begin. Peacock had just bought a share in a new horse and was planning to enter him in that year's Melbourne Cup. Nixon, a keen racegoer himself, was naturally interested in the deal. As the discussion continued, Prime Minister Malcolm Fraser wandered by and, overhearing the conversation, joined in.

'What'd you call him?' Fraser asked.

'Big Bloke,' Peacock replied.

'Aha, named him after me,' Fraser said. 'How's he doing?'

'Well, he was a bloody nuisance at first,' Peacock said. 'It was just about impossible to get him to do anything. Then we found the solution and now he's perfect.'

'What did you do?' Fraser enquired seriously.

'I had him gelded,' Peacock replied, laughing at the point he had just scored. Fraser, black-faced, stalked off.

Schneider, The Colt From Kooyong (1990), p. 129

# A Way with Words

*After Labor's narrow loss in 1980, Paul Keating started to emerge as one of Labor's strongmen. He was still loyal to the Right wing in New South Wales, and mercilessly bullied the Left.*

Keating's complaint about the Left, then and later, was its opposition to so many moves that he sees as necessary to 'stop the joint going backwards'. His famous remark about 'Balmain basketweavers' was part of a diatribe against the Left's anti-growth stance, which he derided as an attitude that boiled down to 'wider nature strips, more trees and making wicker baskets in Balmain' – another version is 'wider nature strips, more trees and eat your own shit'. Keating identified Balmain as the home of Left-wing trendies – the former working-class Labor stronghold in inner Sydney had been gentrified in the late 1960s by an influx of academics and young professionals.

Carew, *Keating* (1988), pp. 53–4

# And More Words

*Keating also became a ferocious debater in Parliament.*

The Opposition collected and circulated a list of terms which Keating had used when referring to them in Parliament: harlots, sleazebags, frauds, immoral cheats, cheats, blackguards, pigs, mugs, clowns, boxheads, criminal intellects, criminals, corporate crooks, friends of tax cheats, brain-damaged, loopy crims, stupid foul-mouthed grub, piece of criminal garbage, dullards, stupid, mindless, crazy tenet of the Opposition, alley cat, bunyip aristocracy, clot, fop, gigolo, harebrained hillbilly, malcontent, mealy-mouthed, ninny, rustbucket, scumbag, scum, sucker, thug, dimwits, dummies, a swill, a pigsty, Liberal muck, vile constituency, fools and incompetents, rip-off merchants, perfumed gigolos, gutless spiv, glib rubbish, tripe and drivel, thugs of Australian politics, constitutional vandals, stunned mullets, half-baked crim, insane stupidities, champion liar, ghouls of the National Party and barnyard bullies.

Carew, *Keating* (1988), p. 53

## Too Clever by $69 Million

*Premiers conferences are always tricky occasions, but in 1981 Fraser and Howard were a bit too tricky.*

The premiers exploded with anger at their May conference when Malcolm Fraser and Howard unwisely briefed journalists on an unattributable basis that cabinet had originally agreed to an allocation which was $69 million higher than the level the states subsequently accepted. Sir Charles Court laid the blame on Howard, and called for his resignation.

Howard was spotted by the Nine Network's Peter Harvey walking morosely along a corridor. 'Malcolm and I have been a bit too clever,' Howard told Harvey, who invited him to confide his problems. Harvey listened, decided a second opinion was needed and called on Alan Reid, whose experience in the Press Gallery covered about forty years. They advised Howard to make a clean breast of it. It made sense to Howard who went to Fraser. They decided that the way to follow this advice was for Howard to have a press conference. This he did on 6 May 1981.

The *Sydney Morning Herald*'s Peter Bowers asked on 6 May 1981: 'Mr Howard, why are you, and you alone, taking the blame for this, when just about everybody in this room, including yourself, knows the Prime Minister also briefed on this?' Howard said he had done the initial backgrounding. 'It was an error of judgement on my part and the part of the Prime Minister,' he said. Howard had briefed the *Australian*, and Fraser had briefed the Herald and Weekly Times group, and it was in one of these newspapers, the *West Australian*, that Court had seen the report.

Court, and the Queensland Premier, Sir Joh Bjelke-Petersen, felt they had been made to look foolish, and were unforgiving of Howard.

Barnett, *John Howard Prime Minister* (1997), pp. 142–3

# The Film Star

*In 1982 Hawke was ready for his first challenge to Hayden. Hayden called him on in July.*

That evening Hayden turned his attention to the leadership. He spoke to his three closest colleagues in the Party – John Button, Peter Walsh and John Dawkins. Hayden said he thought Hawke might defeat him but he had to force the showdown. Then Hayden told [Lionel] Bowen. The deputy's view on the Hawke challenge had been summed up in his quip to delegates: 'If we want a film star why not go the whole way and get Jane Fonda.' The next morning Hayden told Left leader Brian Howe so the faction had prior warning. Just before 3pm on 8 July Hayden walked across the conference floor to Hawke and told him of his intention. Then he issued a statement announcing a special caucus meeting eight days hence, 16 July, to settle the leadership.

Kelly, *The Hawke Ascendancy* (1984), p. 210

# An Announcement

*Hayden won narrowly, giving rise to a dual press conference.*

QUESTION  Will you now appoint Mr Hawke to the Electoral Strategy Committee?
HAYDEN  (Laughter) Yes.
HAWKE  What a hell of a way to announce it!
HAYDEN  What a hell of a way to prove you've had to get there.

Kelly, *The Hawke Ascendancy* (1984), p. 241

# A Favour for a Mate

*Graham Richardson, Hawke's numbers man,
also held out an olive branch.*

Soon after Hayden had defeated Hawke in the July challenge a new Morgan Gallup poll showed a sharp increase in his standing as Opposition leader. Graham Richardson sent Hayden a telegram which said: 'Congratulations on the *Bulletin* poll. Your popularity now matches that of the national president [at that time Neville Wran]. We really did you a favour.' Hayden replied: 'I had not quite looked at the matter from this point of view, but I suppose that your motivation was to do me a big favour. However, was it necessary to try to take my balls away in the process?' The sensitive Richardson framed the exchange and displayed it on his office wall.

Stubbs, *Hayden* (1989), p. 230

# A Shakespearian Figure

*With an election looming in 1983, Labor was
moving away from Bill Hayden and towards the proven
popularity of Bob Hawke. Even Hayden's close
friend John Button warned Hayden his time was up.*

Hayden said that Button did not understand him. 'I'm an existentialist,' he said. 'Things happen to you and I'm prepared to accept responsibility for my actions. It's like Coriolanus and Macbeth.' Button confessed he was unfamiliar with Coriolanus but knew Macbeth well. Hayden described Coriolanus as a Whitlam figure; he himself was like Macbeth. Macbeth was involved in crises arising from his ambition but, when he came to fight his final battle with Macduff, he never asked for mercy; he accepted the consequences. Hayden said, 'If I lose the election, I won't be asking anyone for mercy.'

Button at this stage became angry. He said that that was beaut for Hayden, but there were hundreds of thousands of people who wanted a Labor Government. Not many of them were existentialists and if Labor lost they would not be interested in Hayden's views about the quality of mercy.

Kelly, *The Hawke Ascendancy* (1984), pp. 346–7

## THE DROVER'S DOG

*Hayden resigned his position as Opposition leader in 1983 as Fraser was in the process of calling the election. He remained certain that Labor would have won under his leadership.*

Hayden then went on to coin another phrase that has found a lasting place in Australia's political vocabulary. He spoke without pause for reaction or any lightness in his voice: 'I want to say that I am not convinced the Labor Party could not win under my leadership. I believe a drover's dog could lead the Labor Party to victory the way the country is [and the way the opinion polls are showing up for the Labor Party].'

Stubbs, *Hayden* (1989), p. 253

## BACK TO EARTH

*The Labor campaign meeting that followed was almost too euphoric.*

Australia's most popular public figure, Hawke, the man who only a few days before had been widely regarded as a divisive and corrosive force within the Labor Party, was now given the job by his colleagues of bringing the party to power with reconciliation and consensus being advanced as his major redeeming qualities. The meeting became quite carried away with the theme of consensus and reconciliation until brought back to reality by Wran. 'Delegates,' he croaked, 'it's all very well to go on with all this spiritual stuff, but if those greedy bastards out there wanted spiritualism they'd join the [expletive deleted] Hare Krishna.' The meeting quickly decided to place more emphasis on the tax cuts in the policy speech.

Summers, *Gamble For Power* (1983), p. 71

# Hiding Under the Bed

*The 1983 campaign was a series of disasters for
Fraser, but one stood out.*

The turning point of the campaign – the stage at which it became clear that Fraser could never recover – was Tuesday 22 February. Fraser had already attacked the ALP-ACTU accord; now he was trying to nail Labor as the party of economic irresponsibility. The day before, Howard had replied to Labor's costings estimating them at $4,200 million, not $2,750 million – but this attack should have been made by Fraser to get maximum impact. Then at a Melbourne lunchtime rally Fraser screamed into a microphone that people should not assume their savings were safe in the bank. He warned: 'Under Labor it'd be safer under your bed than it would be in the banks. They would be robbing the savings of the people to pay for their mad and extravagant promises.' (Hawke riposted with devastating mockery: 'They can't put them under the bed because that's where the Commies are!')

    The banks were concerned, some of their depositors became anxious and senior Liberals began to retreat from their own leader. Howard rang a senior Fraser aide asking: 'What the fuck is this money under the beds line?' Later on television Howard said that it was a 'colourful' description – but refused to endorse it. The anti-Fraser backbenchers, Senators Kathy Martin and Don Jessop, criticised Fraser. So did [Queensland] Premier Bjelke-Petersen, obviously sensing Fraser's defeat. The newspapers heavily criticised the Prime Minister, and then the Executive Director of the Australian Bankers Association Research Directorate, Ron Cameron, deplored the comments. The latter guaranteed a damaging news story for Fraser.

Kelly, *The Hawke Ascendancy* (1984), p. 407

## The Day I Saw The Light

*One of Hawke's first acts as Prime Minister was to hold a national economic summit. It went better than some cynics expected.*

The sceptics were converted. I recall one of the more sophisticated and articulate of them, the Canberra press corps veteran Mungo McCallum [sic], an immense but often wasted talent, coming up to me and saying, 'Hawkie, I thought it was all bullshit – but it worked.' His excitement excited me.

Hawke, *The Hawke Memoirs* (1994), p. 185

## Back to the Old Days

*As Prime Minister after the 1983 election, Hawke quickly came to rely on Keating for advice on many matters, not just the economy.*

Hawke took the unusual step of inviting Keating to join his mid-year US trip. Before his meeting with President Reagan Hawke said: 'I think I'll tell Reagan that we're friends and that friends have the right to disagree.' But Keating dissented and told Hawke not to say this. 'You're the first Labor Prime Minister to come here since Whitlam. There's lots of bad history. Tell Reagan that we're friends. Don't compromise the message by saying we can disagree.' Hawke took the advice.

Kelly, *The End of Certainty* (1992), p. 71

## The Backslappers

*Gerry Hand, a left-wing minister, told of the closeness between Hawke and Keating in the early days.*

'How are you, Bob?' said Keating as he sauntered into the room.
    'Good, Paul. Now what would you like to drink, boys? A cup of coffee?'

While Hawke was out of the room organising the drinks, Keating began: 'Boys, you'd have been proud of him, here last night. We had the mining industry here and Bob sorted those bastards out. Laid it on the line. No mucking around. Brilliant stuff it was. Really what the Party's all about.'

When Hawke returned, he took a seat next to Keating, placed his hand on the Treasurer's shoulder and said: 'You should have seen Paul yesterday. We had the banks in. Bloody hopeless. I had to get Paul to outline the big picture to them. Did he set them straight! You'd have been proud of the boy.'

Gordon, *Paul Keating: A Question of Leadership* (1993), p. 75

## STONED

*Although Keating and the Treasury secretary John Stone later fell out, they both knew how to work hard and play hard. Tony Cole, later Treasury secretary himself, recalled a 1983 trip to the United States during the America's Cup.*

'What do we do now, Treasurer?' queried Stone, to which Keating replied: 'Let's go to Newport.'

'That's the best decision you've made since you've had the job,' was Stone's comment.

Cole and one of the Treasury officers arranged an aircraft and they left for Newport after about two hours' sleep. The day that followed was long but exhilarating. Keating remembers it as a funny day. The Australians were scattered among different boats – Peta Furnell, a staffer in Keating's office, and Tony Cole were on one boat, Stone and Bob Johnston (Governor of the Reserve Bank of Australia) were on another and the Treasurer was on another with Australia's ambassador to the US, Sir Robert Cotton. Stone was a dashing figure in navy blazer and commodore's cap.

At the end of the day Alan Bond's yacht had won and it was Tony Cole's task to round up the party to fly back to Washington. Stone, a beer container full of champagne in his hand, was insisting: 'There's no way we're leaving tonight; we must participate in the celebrations.' Ambassador Cotton and Bob Johnston left, taking Peta Furnell with them, back to the plane and back to Washington. Cole was instructed to 'stay and look after Stone and Keating'. He remembers arranging overnight accommodation in a friend's rented house.

> In the meantime the champagne was flowing. We went on to Bondy's party later. Stone didn't want to leave but we dragged him away. Keating was ready to go. We still had no way of getting back to Washington and we had to be there the next day, for the President's address and the formal opening of the IMF/World Bank meeting, which we'd come halfway round the world to attend.
>
> Carew, *Keating* (1988), pp. 93–4

## No Need for Chopsticks

*An early highlight for Hawke's prime ministry was the visit of China's premier Zhao.*

There was only one hitch to his productive six-day Australian visit in 1983. We had not yet elected the new Speaker and Bill Snedden, who held that position under the Fraser Government, was therefore seated on Zhao's right at the parliamentary lunch in his honour. I had been speaking with Zhao for some time through his interpreter, sitting opposite, and indicated to Bill that he might like to talk with our guest. He did so for a while and then leant across Zhao and, to my horror, said to me, 'Prime Minister, I think we should congratulate the Premier on his use of the knife and fork.' I watched the eyes of the normally impassive interpreter momentarily widen with shock. She was equal to the occasion, however, and must have covered Bill's faux pas with some innocuous translation. I monopolised Zhao's attention for the rest of the meal.

Hawke, *The Hawke Memoirs* (1994), p. 343

## Out of the Blue

*Keating's ways of persuading other ministers to his viewpoint were unorthodox but effective, according to fellow minister Michael Duffy.*

He came in one day and asked me if I liked those old Second World War movies, particularly the ones with fighter planes. And I said they didn't grab me tremendously, but some of them were all right. We talked about them for a while and then he said if we came to an agreement on this matter, it would come as such a surprise that we'd be like two Spitfires hovering above the clouds. 'The Messerschmitts are down there and we just swoop out of the clouds, go "whack" and they're gone,' Keating said. The Messerschmitts, of course, were the rest of the Cabinet. We were the two Spitfires. Anyway, I was called down to [the Expenditure Review Committee] and ultimately agreed to his savings option. Surprisingly, it got up and as I went to leave the room Paul put his two hands up like two Spitfires and went 'Whooosh' and smiled. No one else in the room had any idea what he was on about.

Gordon, *Paul Keating: A Question of Leadership* (1993), pp. 101–2

## A Man of Culture

*Although Keating paraded his cultural sophistication, he sometimes liked to play the ocker. Barry Cohen, Minister for Arts in 1984, later wrote:*

One of the traditional highlights of the Sydney Festival has been the 'Opera in the Park'. Each year the Australian Opera estimates that a crowd of around 100,000 gathers for this annual spectacular in the Domain. Leaving aside the question of the Opera Company's numeracy, a very large crowd enjoys superb music under the stars.

A special section is roped off for VIPs, so it was there that Rae and I, Bob and Hazel Hawke, Paul and Annita Keating, sat on rugs chatting to Patrick Veitch, Kathleen Norris, Ita Buttrose *et al.* The Opera Company had thoughtfully provided an exquisite hamper for our supper prior to commencement of the evening's entertainment. We were quietly munching on sesame seed chicken, pâté, and sipping the Bollingers, when the voice of Paul Keating quietly broke the silence, 'Hey Bazza, this beats being in Opposition, eh? If we were, we'd be up the back chewin' a Mars Bar.'

Cohen, *The Life of the Party* (1987), p. 147

## THE SONG AND DANCE MAN

*Keating's diversionary tactics sometimes annoyed Hawke, according to Michael Gordon. Kelty is Bill Kelty, secretary of the ACTU.*

During another session at the Lodge [in 1984], Keating and Hawke had been engaged in a heated argument over the implications for wages policy of a devaluation when the arrival of a pot of tea interrupted the debate. Keating then proceeded to chat to those around him about Fred Astaire, saying he had a tape at home of 'the best two dances in the history of the world'. When the serious discussion resumed, Hawke asked: 'Where's Paul?'
KELTY  'He's gone.'
HAWKE  'Gone where?'
KELTY  'Gone home, to get the tape.'
HAWKE  'What tape?'
KELTY  'Fred Astaire and Ginger Rogers.'
  Hawke's exasperation did not ease when Keating returned with the video and proceeded to place it into the Prime Minister's machine, only to have extreme difficulty in making it work. When Hawke proved similarly incapable, deliberations on wages and the currency were delayed another half hour while one of the Lodge staff fumbled with the machine and finally found the two numbers Keating was so intent on showing. They were, in Kelty's assessment, 'quite good', but Hawke was clearly unimpressed. Asked if Keating had done it to break the tension, Kelty said he was not sure. 'I think it just crossed his mind.' At the end of one interview, around midnight one evening in October 1992, I asked Keating what the songs were. He paused, then began to sing: 'Nothing's impossible/You just pick yourself up/Dust yourself down/And start all over again.'

It could have been his theme song. The other number could have been dedicated, sometime later, to the caucus. It was called 'I'm Putting All My Eggs In One Basket'.

Gordon, *Paul Keating: A Question of Leadership* (1993), pp. 128–9

## PM IN TEARS

*Hawke's daughter Rosslyn was a serious drug abuser, a fact which reduced Hawke to tears at a press conference in 1984. His staff were worried.*

Hawke's aide Peter Barron was surprised but not shocked at the tears. He knew that Hawke liked being the emotional focus of attention. Hawke was guilt-ridden about his daughter. Once he had told the public he could cope better with the guilt – he felt better when the whole world knew. It was melodrama as therapy. After the media conference Hawke dropped into Barron's office. 'Sorry, it won't happen again,' he said. 'It had bloody better not,' grumbled Barron. But a few days later Hawke was almost sobbing on the John Laws show.

Kelly, *The End of Certainty* (1992), p. 141.

## A CHOICE OF MENUS

*Hawke remained paralysed through the 1984 election campaign, which Labor won more narrowly than had been expected. He decided to propose a tax summit, for which Keating proposed a plan including a consumption tax. Hawke's advisers opposed it.*

The debate was a contest for Hawke's favour. [Peter] Barron found its elemental nature remarkable. He would persuade Hawke against the package by week's end. But on Sunday Keating would go to the Lodge and talk Hawke back to his side. Barron would find at the start of the next week he had to begin again. Keating saw its funny side; he talked about getting Hawke back 'in the tax cart'. The Keating tax cart became one of the extended metaphors of politics. But it was not the only one. Keating, complaining to the press about Hawke's staff, said, 'They're offering Hawkie caviar, I go up and tell him to bite a shit sandwich.'

Kelly, *The End of Certainty* (1992), p. 159

## BAD COMPANY

*Keating, having lost the tax battle, fell out of favour with the business community.*

John Leard, the prominent conservative businessman with whom Keating had regularly chatted about the economy and who was now a strident critic of the Hawke Government's policies, reminded a group of business people at a Securities Institute lunch in Sydney in December [1985] that it was a little more than twelve months since Keating had been crowned Euromoney's finance minister of the year. 'I wonder whether you know the Treasurer of Mexico won it the year before,' Leard said.

Carew, *Keating* (1988), p. 145

## SORRY, WRONG NUMBER

*John Howard and Peter Reith were close allies, so when Peter Rees, a journalist on the Melbourne* Sun-Pictorial, *rang Howard in 1984, he got a better story than expected.*

What Howard told Rees was that there was a general view that Peacock had earned another go as party Leader, but his own view was that Andrew Peacock had had his chance. 'We don't really know what he stands for,' he informed the startled Rees: 'I don't think Andrew is ever going to be prime minister. He has some fundamental weaknesses. We have been directionless for eighteen months. I am not certain that he won't fall over next year.'

Howard told Rees that there were strong overtones of 1974. This was when Bill Snedden, having failed to win against Whitlam, was challenged for the leadership by Malcolm Fraser and, early in the following year, deposed. The conversation was interrupted, and then resumed, at which point Rees reintroduced himself. This time, Howard heard his name correctly. 'I thought you were Peter Reith,' he said. He asked Rees not to publish what he had said.

Barnett, John Howard Prime Minister (1997), p. 291

## THE BANANA REPUBLIC

*In 1986 Keating warned that Australia's foreign debt had become a real problem, and he used the phrase 'banana republic' to describe the potential economic situation. The money market panicked. Hawke, in Tokyo at the time, was horrified.*

The next day, 15 May, Hawke tried to calm the waters from Tokyo's Imperial Hotel. After a phone call with Keating, Hawke was reassuring: 'This is not a time for panic.' Asked if he believed Australia was heading towards a banana republic he said: 'No. I don't.' Hawke conceded that Keating's remarks, if taken out of context, could be 'rather horrific'.

Kelly, The End of Certainty (1992), p. 213

*Keating, however, refused to back off. Hawke, now in China, decided to reassert his authority, as Geoff Kitney wrote in the* National Times.

Hawke went on to an official dinner. His advisers, with time to reflect on what had happened, concluded that Keating had acted appallingly and that Hawke was in an invidious position. When Hawke returned from the dinner, the decision was taken to direct Deputy Prime Minister Lionel Bowen to set up a meeting of senior ministers in Hawke's Parliament House office on Monday morning, which Hawke would address by phone from Beijing. In an 11.30pm call to Bowen, Hawke told his deputy to take charge of events and to tell ministers to hold their tongues. After speaking to Bowen, Hawke was satisfied that the matter was under control.

But that was not the public perception. The next day, Saturday, saw Hawke go from golf course to sumo wrestling, apparently oblivious of the storm breaking around him ... By Sunday morning, as the prime ministerial party packed and set off for China, his silence had become absolutely peculiar. All requests from the press to get a word from him were refused. He was too busy, was the response. But ... the press applied pressure ... When he reached Beijing, Hawke ... was told by his advisers that correspondents travelling with him were prepared to write highly critical reports about his apparent failure to exercise leadership. The strong advice to Hawke was that details of the phone calls to Bowen should be released, to show both that he had acted decisively and that he, and not Keating, was the leader of the Government. Hawke took the advice.

Carew, *Keating* (1988), pp. 158–9.

*Paul Kelly took up the story back in Australia.*

The Chinese teleprinter operators had a busy night and the newspapers carried banner headlines the next day typified by 'Hawke pushes Keating aside' and 'Hawke moves against Keating'. When the ministers met that morning in Canberra for the phone hook-up Hawke's remarks were hardly necessary. He merely confirmed with the same phrases the reports in the press. Keating sat, newspaper on lap, ticking off the points as Hawke made them. After Hawke had finished Keating angrily accused him of inspiring the newspaper reports.

The ministers saw Keating's temper flaring. 'Be careful, the Chinese will be listening,' they cautioned. 'Fuck the Chinese,' Keating replied. 'Just what's the point of this bullshit, Bob?' Keating demanded. 'Who's that?' Hawke asked. 'Who the fuck do you think it is?' replied Keating. 'We've got problems here and we're trying to solve them. Just what the hell do you think you're playing at.' The Chinese listeners received a graphic insight into ALP politics.

Kelly, *The End of Certainty* (1992), p. 216

# The Start of a Vendetta

*John Howard had deposed Andrew Peacock as leader in 1985. An incident early the next year made Keating and Howard implacable enemies.*

Hawke and Keating were sophisticated and ruthless in keeping the pressure upon Howard. The transformation of Keating, the decisive political figure during Howard's leadership, into an implacable enemy was a milestone. It happened in February 1986 as a result of an aggressive parliamentary strategy Howard had approved involving the chief Liberal 'hit man' Wilson Tuckey. Tuckey raised the name of a woman who was plaintiff in a breach of promise action against Keating 13 years before, and hurled a confusing barb: 'Kristine had a little girl called Paul.' Keating interpreted the comment as falsely implying that he had had an illegitimate child by the woman. He descended into biblical mood – but this was old testament law, not new testament forgiveness.

Keating announced on the stairs of Parliament House his quest for revenge: 'From this day onwards Mr Howard will wear his leadership like a crown of thorns and in the Parliament I will do everything I can to crucify him … to obliterate him from the leadership.' Then he went unto his office, rang Howard and delivered the same threat – just to make the message personal.

Kelly, *The End of Certainty* (1992), p. 247

# Joh for Canberra

*In 1986 an extraordinary campaign was initiated to make Queensland's charismatic but highly eccentric National Party Premier, Sir Johannes Bjelke-Petersen, prime minister. It was led by a group of businessmen, one of whom was Mike Gore.*

In autumn 1986 Gore had his first talk with Bjelke-Petersen about the Canberra push – at least eight months before it become a public issue. Joh talked about destroying Hawke just as he had destroyed Whitlam through his notorious appointment of Albert Patrick Field to the Senate in 1975. Gore told Bjelke-Petersen that through his business links in North America he knew people who could help. He meant the market research company International Strategies, whose subsidiary Decima was run by a Canadian, Alan Gregg. They had been involved in the Reagan campaigns and in the election of Canadian Prime Minister Brian Mulroney. From the start Gore saw the Joh push in marketing terms, just as he was marketing Sanctuary Cove. He never grasped the complex political issues involved.

Gore went to Toronto to meet Gregg, brief him and organise his support. Gregg agreed to come to Australia to meet the messiah. Gore rang Joh from Vancouver and felt a discreet warning about Gregg might be appropriate: 'You should know Joh that he's 33 years old, has hair down to his shoulders, wears a T-shirt under his coat and calls everybody a motherfucker.' But Joh didn't complain.

Kelly, *The End of Certainty* (1992), pp. 292–3

## A Cosmetic Solution

*Mungo MacCallum recalled that some of Queensland's customs – and some of Joh's ministerial backers – were a trifle peculiar themselves.*

But still, it was better than Queensland. Anything is better than Queensland. There is a certain symbolic irony in the fact that, with the advent of daylight saving in the most civilised parts of the country, it takes just a quarter of an hour on the clock to get from Sydney to Brisbane, but two and a quarter hours to get back. And after that quarter of an hour, it all came flooding back. Queensland must be the only place in the Western world where candidates still think it's good campaigning to nail pictures of themselves to trees, with slogans like 'Don't fuss, vote Russ,' on the bottom of them.

('Russ', incidentally, is a man named Russell Hinze, who is seriously spoken of in some quarters as a possible successor to Bjelke-Petersen. He is also the man who recommended 'casteration' [sic] for sex offenders. When asked by a television interviewer whether this might not be a little drastic, and what he would do if he found he had 'casterated' the wrong man, Hinze revealed his deep sense of humanity and knowledge of anatomy with the immortal reply, 'Well, we'd just sew him on a bigger and better one.')

MacCallum, *Mungo on the Zoo Plane* (1979), p. 163

## Let him go

*Russ Hinze was keen to see the back of Joh.*

At [a conference of Joh supporters in 1986] Hinze called Queensland health minister and future premier Mike Ahern to his hotel suite. 'You're not going to believe this son but the old bloke is going federal,' Hinze said. He had a message: 'Let the bastard go. Don't interfere. Don't oppose him for God's sake.' When Ahern kept professing disbelief, Hinze said: 'I'm telling you this is going to happen. There's a lot of money and a lot of support. Some of the biggest people in Australia are backing this. I've had Andrew Peacock in my home talking about it.'

Kelly, *The End of Certainty* (1992), p. 294

## A Troublesome Lunatic

*John Howard and the federal National Party leader Ian Sinclair realised that the Joh push could be a disaster for the federal coalition.*

The 1986 Queensland election therefore had a dual significance. It would determine not just the fate of the State Government but whether Joh had sufficient momentum to launch his bid for national office. A poor State result would have killed the Joh for Canberra push.

Joh, in fact, snatched a win from the jaws of defeat. He was saved by two factors – a furious last-week big spending drive by the Nationals and a blunder by the Liberals, who drove voters to Joh by raising the prospect of a hung parliament. Election night, 1 November, became a triumph for Bjelke-Petersen who entered the Brisbane tally room radiating vindication and alluding to a federal crusade. Watching Joh on television John Howard said to Janette: 'We'll have trouble with this lunatic now.'

Joh gave thanks at Kingaroy's Lutheran church, posed outside for the media and declared of the federal Coalition: 'They will work by the policies I set or I will work against them.' Joh was beyond restraint, a 75-year-old able to indulge himself in federal fantasies from the safety of office, having cleared his own State election hurdle. Joh had nothing to lose; Howard and Sinclair had an election to lose. Joh says: 'The momentum for me was huge. The phone never stopped. I had businessmen from all over promising to fund me. I told them I'd start a bushfire but the grass was drier than I thought. Howard and Sinclair couldn't win. Nobody in his right mind was going to back them.'

Kelly, *The End of Certainty* (1992), pp. 296–7

## THE GIFTS OF THE MAGI

*By the end of the year the Joh-for-PM brigade were confident they would follow through to the end.*

On Christmas Eve 1986 the 'white shoe brigade' – Mike Gore, Brian Ray and Gordon Douglas – made a famous 'Apocalypse Now' journey in Gore's helicopter to Joh's Bethany property. Here was high symbolism; they flew into Bethany to deliver Bjelke-Petersen their final blueprint for the takeover of the Australian Government. It was their Christmas present.

Gore felt the meeting was a triumph, giving Joh the completed strategy which they had bankrolled and which they believed would install their own white knight in the Lodge. Gore told Bjelke-Petersen: 'It's over to you now Joh.' Ray said later: 'We just went to say Happy Christmas!' Gore told Joh he was sure that Peacock would run in tandem with him. Bjelke-Petersen replied, 'Andrew, my goodness, he's a nice boy.'

Kelly, *The End of Certainty* (1992), p. 299

## Upside Down Politics

*Joh's principal campaign was against his own federal colleagues.*

In early February [1987] Bjelke-Petersen began to savage Howard and Sinclair. Their policies were no good; nobody knew what their policies were anyway. Howard's team couldn't be trusted. They weren't firm and strong. If Howard wanted to support him, that was okay. 'I'm not interested in John Howard, for goodsake stop talking about John Howard,' Joh told two million listeners on 'AM'. Joh would have no trendies or wets. He would run candidates against every sitting member who rejected his policies, regardless of party. He left open the question of whether he would give Howard a job after the election. Joh declared, 'I am determined to turn politics upside down in Australia. I am Joh Bjelke-Petersen of Queensland with a lot of experience and I know what I am doing.'

Joh accused Ian Sinclair of 'cuddling up to the Liberals'. He attacked both Howard and Sinclair as losers who 'mucked it up when they were there'. He promised to 'do a General MacArthur' on Howard and Sinclair and explained: 'We will annihilate them'. Sinclair's call for Joh to support the coalition was merely 'stupid'. Australia's problems were simple, there was no need for detail. Reporters struggled to find exactly what he intended but Joh was elusive.

Kelly, *The End of Certainty* (1992), pp. 301–2

## Meeting the Press

*Joh's approach to the media was scarcely more sophisticated.*

Bjelke-Petersen gave some classic radio interviews; witness this exchange from 'AM' on 5 February [1987]:

Q   Sir Joh, how can you expect to stay part of the National Party?
A   I'm not interested in staying part of the National Party.

I'm only interested in doing what the people of Australia deserve.

Q   You might resign from the National Party?
A   I won't resign from the National Party.
Q   But you just said you're not interested in staying part of the National Party.
A   Well, I can't stay ...
Q   So if the National Party in Canberra won't do what you want, will you leave the National Party?
A   Lead it, I'll lead it, not leave it.
Q   No. I said leave it, leave it.
A   No. Don't be stupid ... otherwise I won't talk to you.
Q   When can we meet some of these candidates you were talking about before?
A   Well, they don't grow up like mushrooms.

Kelly, The End of Certainty (1992), pp. 302–3

## A FRIENDLY PHONE CALL

*To add to Howard's problems, his old rival Andrew Peacock was stirring again. Things came to a head after the interception of an extraordinary phone call between Peacock and Victoria's Opposition leader Jeff Kennett.*

The Howard–Peacock issue boiled over during the weekend of 21–22 March 1987 after Peacock's friend, Victorian Liberal leader Jeff Kennett, rose above the Liberal squabble to win a State byelection. That night Peacock and Kennett had a conversation on a car phone. The conversation was tapped by a member of the group People for Equality not Institutionalisation (PENI), and extracts were quoted in the Melbourne *Sun* newspaper on Monday, 23 March 1987.

Kennett began by describing to Peacock his earlier phone call to Howard. Kennett said that he told Howard: 'Tomorrow I'm going to bucket the whole lot of you. Tomorrow, John.' Peacock urged him not to do this. According to Kennett, Howard had said, 'I know where your sympathies lie.' Kennett continued: 'I said, "I couldn't give a fuck. I've got no sympathies any more. You're all a pile of shit. And tomorrow I'm going berserk." Well, he went off his brain and at the end of it I said to him, "Howard you're a cunt, you haven't got my support, you never will have. And I'm not going to rubbish you or the party tomorrow but I feel a lot better having told you, you're a cunt … And the poor little fella didn't know whether he was Arthur or Martha."'

After Peacock praised Kennett for the by-election result, Kennett said: 'I thought I should let you know where I ended up with your little mate.' Peacock replied: 'Well, fuck him. I'm not worried … I almost bloody cried … l was terribly worried. My fuckin' anger yesterday as Margaret knows … The first thing I came in last night I said, "Aah fuckin' cunts!" I said the whole fuckin' thing could upset tomorrow … And she said, "What's Jeffrey done?" I said, "It's not what Jeffrey's done, it's what everyone's fuckin' done to Jeffrey."'

Referring to the next day's State conference Peacock said: 'I've got to sit in a chair about four or five rows back from the front and allow Howard after he's had his tumultuous reception to come down sit next to me and be photographed together smiling. Kennett replied, 'How pathetic.' They rang off. Kennett said, 'See you then. Give my regards to your good lady.'

Confronted with the publication of the Kennett-Peacock exchange on the Monday morning, Howard decided to dismiss Peacock from the shadow Cabinet. He secured the agreement of the other three Liberal [parliamentary] leaders and Sinclair.

Kelly, *The End of Certainty* (1992), p. 319

## Headed for the Stars

*After Labor won the 1987 election, thanks largely to the Joh factor, Keating became impatient to replace Hawke. He reacted savagely to a newspaper column by former Whitlam minister Jim McClelland. McClelland wrote of Keating:*

It will be a pity if such a gifted human being cannot match character with intellect … his performance to date leaves a big question mark over his capacity to be anything more than clever. And that's not enough.

Keating was so incensed at McClelland's column, and at follow-ups in other media, that he rang up his former colleague. McClelland says the call came through early in the morning. Keating was on the line himself, not through a secretary. 'That you, Jim? Paul Keating here,' he began and then launched forth: 'Just because you swallowed a fucking dictionary when you were about fifteen doesn't give you the right to pour a bucket of shit over the rest of us.' Keating the externaliser lets people know what he is thinking. McClelland pointed out that Keating's reaction confirmed his point – there is more to debate than smacking down the opposition. But to Keating the slightest show of dissent equates to being the enemy. McClelland took the chance to chide Keating for his open friendships with business people, for accepting their hospitality. He recalls Keating's reply: 'You know me, Jim. I love stars.'

Carew, *Keating* (1988), p. 212

## SPITTING THE DUMMY

*Cabinet meetings in the Hawke years were generally peaceful affairs, but this was not the case with the 1990 debate over telecommunications. Treasurer Paul Keating was in the middle of it all.*

In one of the most dramatic scenes of the Hawke Government, the debate built to the point where it became obvious that the Treasurer was going to lose the argument. As Robert Ray has recalled, 'Paul was doing a very slow burn as the summing up was done.' What really set Keating off, as the then Treasurer remembers it, was the comment by someone that the Keating model, 'was not going to go down well with Bob Pomeroy from the Centre Left in Adelaide'.

'And I looked at Hawke,' Keating recalls, 'like, here we are, done all these big things over the last few years because they were the right thing to do and we had our eyes on the big picture, and here we are now in the Federal Cabinet, being dictated to by somebody from the Centre Left – *the Centre Left!* – in South Australia.

So I said, "Well, if it gets down to this, if you want to sit here and participate in an economic decision of very diminished quality on the basis of a bit of political gobbledy-gook from a boutique faction and a couple of unions that in the past, you and I, Bob, we would have pushed to one side, then I am wasting my time".'

At this point, Keating suddenly threw his pencil on the table, stood up, and gave his considered estimation: 'This is a fucking second-rate decision by a bunch of fucking second-raters!' before furiously storming out of the room. 'Spit the dummy!' Senator Robert Ray called out after him. Keating kept walking.

Fitzsimons, Beazley (1998), p. 318

## THE KIRRIBILLI HOUSE MEETING

*Keating finally insisted on setting a date for the leadership handover. Hawke agreed to a meeting, with Bill Kelty of the ACTU and the businessman Sir Peter Abeles acting as witnesses. It took place at Kirribilli House in 1988.*

When they met, Hawke got straight to business. He wanted to lead Labor to the fourth election. If it was won, then he would serve a suitable time, stand down and 'hand over to Paul'. Keating, in return, would serve the current term and fight the next election with Hawke. It was considered important for Labor's chances that Hawke and Keating be together. Hawke's resignation pledge was subject only to one proviso: if the story leaked, it was null and void. The pact was understood by both men and both witnesses. The deal had to be kept secret at the coming election since it was recognised that such a transition pact would hurt Labor if revealed. Overall, it provided for a smooth transition of the Labor leadership in the next term. The deal was oral and was not put on paper.

At the conclusion Hawke lectured Keating: 'I want to say to Paul that he can't keep coming late to Cabinet meetings. It doesn't show much respect for the colleagues. Secondly you've got to be more agreeable with the colleagues.'

Kelly, The End of Certainty (1992), p. 454

# What You Get

*Hawke and Keating were reunited for the 1990 election campaign, when Peacock again led the Opposition.*

Hawke and Keating then laughed at the Liberals. The press had reported that morning that a 'central theme' of the Liberal campaign would be the line that 'a vote for Bob Hawke is a vote for Paul Keating'. It was a sound tactic to tap the community antagonism towards Keating and the doubts over whether Hawke would serve another full term – [Tony] Eggleton was keen to exploit the line. But Keating had borrowed a counter from Hawke's press secretary, Barrie Cassidy, and, when asked at his press conference how Labor would respond to the Liberal campaign, he fired: 'It's obvious … a vote for Andrew Peacock is a vote for Andrew Peacock. What you see is what you get … not much.'

Kelly, *The End of Certainty* (1992), p. 558

# Placido Domingo

*But the unity was shattered after Labor won the election by a speech Keating gave to the press gallery's annual dinner. John Hewson was the new Liberal leader.*

Keating said that Australia had much of which to be proud – its standards, decency and compassion. It occupied a continent; it had absorbed people from many other nations. He said most Japanese still lived in 'dogboxes'; Germany's environment was being destroyed by acid rain. The public was hostile towards politicians but it was politicians who changed things. Politics, above all, was about leadership and leadership changed the nature of nations. 'Leadership is not about being popular, it's about being right,' Keating said. He pointed to the great difference between America and Australia. The US had had three great leaders – Washington, Lincoln and Franklin Roosevelt. 'The trouble With Australia is that we've never had such a leader. We've never had one leader, not one, and it shows.' The Labor heroes weren't great leaders; Curtin was a 'trier' and Chifley was a 'plodder'. Australia was 'teetering on the brink' of becoming a great nation. But it needed a leader who could communicate a vision, and not by 'tripping over television cables in shopping centres'.

Winning elections was about leadership. Keating said: 'I got the election date right this year and I got it right in 1987.' (So much for Hawke!) Keating said that he had the right blend of politics and economics. He called himself the 'Placido Domingo of Australian politics' while Hewson was 'the hall attendant at the back of the theatre'. Running Australia was no easy task and the media should grasp the unique position he had established as Treasurer. 'I've got the confidence of the financial markets, I've got the central bank, I've got the support of organised labour and I've got the confidence of the Treasury and the policy-making centres in Canberra.' Keating went on: 'If you can't manage these, then things will fall apart quickly.' He ridiculed the shadow treasurer, Peter Reith. 'Now, I'm not interested in Reithy,' Keating said. 'I'll leave Reithy to you. I'm interested in Hewson but I can't get a run at him because he won't debate me.' Keating said he had already established a 'psychological ascendancy' over Hewson who, he said, had no capacity to lead the nation or to inspire. Hewson was a 'Waverley cemetery headstone'.

Kelly, *The End of Certainty* (1992), pp. 621–2

## Keeping Intact

*Keating's reaction after the speech was a little ingenuous.*

After Keating had finished, a number of journalists suggested to him that his address had been seen as his statement of claim to Bob Hawke's job. He not only disagreed; he seemed genuinely surprised. Buoyed and unburdened, he gave the same response to the *Age*'s Michelle Grattan and the *Telegraph Mirror* correspondent, Amanda Buckley, while dancing to the 'sixties cover versions of the 'Hopeless Romantics' sometime later. But he also hinted that he did not expect to emerge unscathed. 'I'm sure it's breaking a rule of politics to turn up at one of these things twice,' he said at one point. 'Getting in here and getting out with one's arse intact is the key thing, and having done it once, one should never try again.'

Gordon, *Paul Keating: A Question of Leadership* (1993), p. 11

## EAR TO THE GROUND

*Throughout 1991 Keating stepped up the pressure on Hawke to go.*

Keating asked, 'How can you have your ear to the ground and not hear it?' 'Hear what?' asked Hawke. 'Hear that you're finished,' said Keating 'Our primary vote was 39 per cent at the last election. It's got lower at every election. We can't win any more on a falling primary vote and a high share of preferences. We've got to reverse the trend and that means getting the primary vote up. You say you can turn it around but how, how are you going to do it?' Hawke found these questions extraordinary. He shot back: 'You mean I can't, but you can?' Keating answered: 'Maybe I can. Maybe I say to other people that maybe I can. But for you, I say that you can't. I just want you to honour your agreement.'

Kelly, *The End of Certainty* (1992), p. 626

## THE PARIS OPTION

*Under the so-called Kirribilli agreement, Hawke was to have stepped down to make way for Keating. But after the Placido Domingo speech he changed his mind.*

I repeated my own conviction, the belief of others and the evidence of the polls that I had a much better chance of winning for Labor than he and then, looking him straight in the eye, I asked, 'Tell me this, Paul, are you saying that even if you believed I had a better chance of winning the next election than you, I should stand aside for you?' He answered, 'Yes.'

I was horrified that Paul Keating was prepared to place his

own interests above those of a Labor victory. As disturbing as this was, worse was still to come. Keating's 'Paris option' was part of political folklore but it was now given its ugliest formulation. The question arose of what he would do if he didn't get his 'turn' as Prime Minister. I said I thought he should stay but he rejoined, 'We'll be off to Europe. We won't be staying here – this is the arse-end of the world.'

Hawke, The Hawke Memoirs (1999), p. 501

## A Direct Answer

*Eventually even Hawke's closest allies, including Kim Beazley, decided it was time for a change. But it wasn't quite so simple.*

Early the following morning, just before 8 o'clock, Beazley called his political adviser and friend Gary O'Neill into his office to advise him of the meeting the previous night. 'We're all very strong supporters of Bob,' O'Neill remembers his boss explaining, 'but we've nevertheless decided that it's in Bob's best interests to declare publicly that he is leaving some time in the near future, so he can go out gracefully with all of the party behind him. So that's what we're going to do this morning. We're going to go around to Bob and tell him that while he continues to enjoy our total support, we think it's time for him to go.' O'Neill found himself somewhere between bemused and bewildered. At first glance, it didn't seem to him like such a crash-hot idea, and he came straight to the point in reply. 'What are you going to do when he tells you to *piss off?*' O'Neill asked evenly. Beazley paused, O'Neill recalls, for all the world as if this possibility had never occurred to him. 'No, no,' he demurred. 'Bob will understand we're not plotting against him, this is a group of Bob's supporters, there has to be a way found out of this situation because Paul is not going to give up, it is causing an enormous amount of damage within the party, so we are going to tell him.'

'And I said,' O'Neill remembers, 'well, I reckon he will tell you to piss off. So he just looked at me sideways, go up and walked out of the room and went around there.'

Beazley returned over two hours later. 'Well, what happened?' O'Neill asked his oddly silent boss. 'He told us to piss off,' Beazley replied, a little morosely.

Fitzsimons, Beazley (1998) pp. 351–2

## THE END OF HAWKE

*Keating eventually defeated Hawke in a caucus ballot in December 1991. Labor's new secretary Bob Hogg was worn out.*

While Hogg was heartened by Hawke's gracious words in defeat, his private notes record no satisfaction with the outcome. 'As usual in the wash-up you go beyond emotion and exhaustion,' he wrote. 'So there is no emotion, no nothing. Just a great tiredness and awareness that there is one hell of a tough job ahead. What's different? That's the Labor Party.'

Gordon, Paul Keating: A Question of Leadership (1993), p. 184

## HIS DOOR WAS ALWAYS OPEN

*When Don Watson joined Keating's office as a speechwriter at the beginning of 1992 it wasn't quite what he expected.*

You never know who might turn up in the PMO. There was nothing to stop anyone coming in and I never heard of anyone being asked to leave. You would glance through your window and there might be a rock singer with a shaved head strolling down the corridor, or a delegation of red-faced grain growers, an advertising whiz, the Prime Minister of New Zealand or the Dalai Lama; the member for Capricornia or somewhere would suddenly pop his head in and tell you to tell the PM to remember the words of William Tecumseh Sherman before the battle of whatever. I looked up from my desk one night and Courtney Walsh, the formidable West Indian fast bowler, was standing in my doorway. He said something like, 'Where do I find de tall blond girl, man?' 'Down the other end,' I said, 'but she's gone home.'

Watson, *Recollections of a Bleeding Heart* (2002), p. 42

## The Lizard of Oz

*Keating's reception for the Queen annoyed the opposition leader John Hewson, and also the English tabloids.*

But before the crockery was cleared from King's Hall John Hewson shot out of Parliament House to tell the media that Keating had made a political speech and failed to show proper respect. He, John Hewson, had learned respect, but this prime minister plainly had not. John Howard bought in: the reception was 'insultingly low key', he said, and managed to add something to the effect that the 1950s had been a splendid period in Australian history. Next day news arrived from the old country that the tabloids were up in arms: Keating was dubbed the 'Lizard of Oz'. He had compounded his wife's insolence in failing to bend her knee at Sydney airport by putting his arm around the Queen in King's Hall. 'Hands orf Cobber!' they said. There were front-page photos of the offending limb encircling Her Majesty as he introduced her to none other than Bob Menzies' widow, Dame Pattie. It was amazing news, and almost entirely welcome.

Watson, *Recollections of a Bleeding Heart* (2002), p. 116

## Keating's Kokoda Kiss

*A visit to Papua New Guinea in 1992 produced an amazing scene.*

Somewhere on the flight from Moresby to Kokoda, as he talked to David Horner, Keating decided that he should make a gesture which would do justice to these events – an act of some kind which would indelibly mark Kokoda in Australia's collective memory, as perhaps Gettysburg was marked in the American mind by Lincoln. So when he reached the modest memorial at Kokoda, to the utter surprise of everyone around him, including Horner, Keating dropped to his knees and kissed the ground.

The press thought his advisers had put him up to it, but the advisers they came hurrying towards had not even seen it happen. Standing beside him, Professor Horner was said to have thought that the Prime Minister had suffered a heart attack. Even by Keating's standards it was a remarkable act.

Watson, *Recollections of a Bleeding Heart* (2002), p. 183

## FIGHTBACK

*The political antipathy between Keating and Hewson had reached a deeply personal level by the end of 1992.*

Nowhere has the antipathy been more palpable – at least in public – than in the Parliament, particularly when Keating and Hewson face each other across the despatch box. When, for instance, Hewson asked Keating why, if he was so confident in his view of the Opposition's platform [the Fightback Strategy], he was not prepared to call an early election, Keating looked his opponent in the eye and replied: 'The answer is, mate, because I want to do you slowly. There has to be a bit of sport in this for all of us ... I want to see those ashen-faced performances; I want more of them. I want to be encouraged. I want to see you squirm out of this load of rubbish over a couple of months. There will be no easy execution for you ... If you think I am going to put you out of your misery quickly, you can think again.' This from a man who made it a practice to turn off the television if he saw an act of violence on the screen.

Gordon, *Paul Keating: A Question of Leadership* (1993), p. 208

# The Crocodile Smile

*As an election grew closer, the animosity between
Keating and Hewson intensified.*

Hewson challenged Keating to a debate. Keating said he'd be there 'with bells on', and flashed a smile. 'It's a great tactical smile,' I said. 'You may as well be relaxed,' he said and flexed his shoulders loose. 'They don't know what you're thinking when you smile,' I said. 'That's right,' he said, 'they wonder – what's the cunt thinking?' 'That's right,' I said. 'Bad things,' he said, 'that's what I'm thinking. Bad things.'

Watson, Recollections of a Bleeding Heart (2002), p. 268

# I want to win

*Keating resisted the pressure for an early election
from his own party as well.*

When Graham Richardson returned to the scene of Keating's Placido speech to address the annual dinner of the Canberra press gallery of 1992, he recalled an episode of a few days earlier, on 16 November, when Keating was in the Queensland town of Bundaberg. According to Richardson, Keating had contemplated the option of calling an election for 19 December. Richardson's advice, like that of Bob Hogg and others, was that the Government could win if it waited until after the Western Australia election. He said: 'I was asked my opinion and I said, "Look, when you wanted to become leader, I said to you, 'Your job is to bring us out of the wilderness. We can't win. But what you can do is make sure we don't get slaughtered. Make it close, get us into a position where we can win one term in Opposition.' If you have an election on 19 December, you'll achieve all of that. We'll lose by a few: two, four, six, but not many. We'll go real close and everyone will say nice things about you. They'll say this is the bloke who almost got us there."' As Richardson recalls it, Keating's response was an emphatic statement of his approach to politics.

'Stuff that,' the Prime Minister said. 'I want to win.'

Gordon, *Paul Keating: A Question of Leadership* (1993), pp. 229–30

## WITH FRIENDS LIKE THESE

*The 1993 election was especially tough for Kim Beazley, whose seat of Swan was marginal. And he and his adviser Gary O'Neill did not need help with door knocking from the well-meaning Foreign Minister Gareth Evans.*

O'Neill tried to put them off. 'Look, we are very, very busy,' he recalls replying, only to be told that Gareth was already on his way. Some ministers demand of their staff a formal bowing and scraping to precede each new conversation. Beazley was not of their number, and shortly thereafter O'Neill was happy to speak his mind: 'Jesus! Gareth is on his way here to doorknock with you.'

'No, no, I can't I am too busy,' Beazley replied calmly, barely looking up from his reading. When advised that O'Neill had already tried that, and that Gareth was unstoppable, the two gave in. They decided that Beazley would take him just down the road to the evenly poised suburb of Kensington, where the vision of the Foreign Minister on their doorstep just might winkle out a few extra crucial votes from the constituents. Evans duly arrived, and the two Cabinet Ministers went off together, as O'Neill waited back at the office for the next hour. Presently though, he heard the sounds of the Member for Swan returning. 'So Kim waves Gareth goodbye,' O'Neill recounts, 'and he comes back into the office and he is absolutely white, white as a sheet. And I said, "Jesus, what's the matter with you"!?!'

'You wouldn't believe it,' Beazley replied. 'We walked to the first house, knocked on the door, this woman opened it, but before I could get anything out Gareth said to her, "Now give me three good reasons why you wouldn't vote for Kim Beazley"!'

Fitzsimons, *Beazley* (1998), p. 378

# A Fair Question

*Even in 1993 Keating sometimes seemed less than committed to re-election.*

Througout the first year in the Lodge his attitude and behaviour provoked sporadic outbursts of anger and amazement. A week from the 1993 election the former Hawke adviser, Peter Barron, snarled down the phone to me that when it was over Labor people would come after him asking why he had taken the leadership from the most popular prime minister in the country's history if he didn't want it. At the time it seemed a reasonably good question.

Watson, *Recollections of a Bleeding Heart* (2002), p. 61

# A Hundred Per Cent Mabo

*The High Court's Mabo judgement had recognised indigenous ownership of some land areas. The government's legislation in response was fiercely opposed by Hewson's conservatives and passed only after a marathon debate. It was an emotional moment.*

In front of a packed public gallery the Bill passed at 11am on 21 December after the government moved the guillotine. The scenes which followed were probably unprecedented in the parliament's history. As Evans and Kernot embraced, the gallery, full of those big rodeo hats which had become part of the scenery in Parliament House over the past eighteen months, rose and applauded. The happiness was palpable and infections – people *wept* with it. The press joined the applause. The Labor side stood and applauded the gallery. In offices and other places all through the building there was cheering. And, in striking contrast to the demeanor of his Coalition partners, the National Party Senate leader, Ron Boswell, who had opposed the Bill, rose and wished the Aboriginal people well.

Watson, *Recollections of a Bleeding Heart* (2002), p. 453

# Return of the Lizard

*Keating and the Queen had a second encounter at the D-Day jubilee in London in 1994. Don Watson was there.*

At the dinner that night in the Guildhall at Portsmouth the leaders of all the former Allies (except the Russians) were gathered at a long table on the stage. At tables in front of them, Allied veterans were assembled. Some veterans' widows had been invited and seated prominently near the stage. Opposite me a France Libre survivor told the English widow beside him that he wished they had met when they were young. The Scottish widow on my left said my prime minister should not have been so rude to the Queen and should certainly not have touched her, and on several occasions politely removed from her own shoulder the ravaged hand of a Canadian veteran seated on her other side. When the Queen rose and her strange hooting voice cut through the hall, the Frenchman gasped and whispered, 'I never thought I would see this.'

With his fellow leaders, the Prime Minister had visited Buckingham Palace on his arrival in London. They lined up to greet her and when she reached him she asked how things were going in Australia. He was telling her how we were now in our tenth quarter of growth and unemployment was declining, when jets roared overhead. 'That will be those Canadians,' she said, looking up at the ceiling. The Prime Minister refused to be fazed by this distraction. 'I have a clock exactly like that one behind you,' he said. 'Do you?' she replied. 'I do,' he said. 'Wherever did you get it?' she inquired. 'Melbourne', he said.

Watson, *Recollections of Bleeding Heart* (2002) p. 497

# Not a Moment to Lose

*When Bronwyn Bishop began her run to become Liberal leader, Gareth Evans had a good one-liner.*

Bob Hawke's Foreign Minister Gareth Evans was to say of his bete noire, the Liberal Bronwyn Bishop: 'Why do so many people take an instant dislike to Mrs Bishop? Because it saves time.'

MacCallum, *Mungo: The Man Who Laughs* (2001), p. 175

## A Career in Tatters

*After losing the unloseable 1993 election John Hewson lingered on as Liberal leader, but in 1995 was replaced by Alexander Downer. It was a short and accident-prone tenure.*

He issued a statement of Liberal Party directions called *The Things That Matter*. One look at it told us that it might destroy him. It had enough of Fightback to keep the government well fed with opportunities for derision; enough untruths to punch holes in its credibility; and so little of anything else substantial it was almost sunk on the first day when in Tokyo the Prime Minister derided it as Mills and Boon. He said he read it in twenty minutes while eating a plate of sushi. So bad was the document, Downer satirised it himself in a notorious, mind-numbingly foolish speech which included the observation that Liberal policy on domestic violence might be called 'The Things That Batter'. The self-inflicted wound was probably fatal.

Watson, *Recollections of a Bleeding Heart* (2002), p. 511

## Whose Assassination?

*When John Howard replaced Downer as opposition leader, all the old animosity between him and Keating resurfaced, as quickly became apparent.*

The Israeli Prime Minister, Yitzhak Rabin, was assassinated and the Prime Minister flew to Jerusalem for the funeral. Even on this most brief and solemn foray abroad, political trouble accompanied him. Howard had phoned before he left, requesting a seat on the plane. Keating had refused: he rang me, saying that he knew Howard would make capital out of his refusal. But refuse he must. He simply could not bear the prospect of a forty-eight hour journey with his rival; the boredom of it was unthinkable. So Allan Gyngell told Howard's office there was no room on the plane, and the press were told that the Prime Minister alone would represent Australia. As predicted, Howard made great play with the apparent pettiness and partisanship of it and the funeral of Yitzhak Rabin went badly for us.

From Jerusalem the PM reported that the city was wonderful. He had been around the different quarters and followed the Via Dolorosa. 'You know you can see where Christ walked on the way to the Crucifixion,' he said. I wished I had gone. 'But I think that little bastard's done us some damage,' he said. 'Ignore him,' I said, not wanting politics to spoil any miracles the Holy Land might work. 'I'm not going to ignore him,' he said. 'I'm going to drive an axe into his chest and lever his ribs apart,' he said.

Watson, *Recollections of a Bleeding Heart* (2002) p. 650

## ACCENTUATE THE NEGATIVE

*Howard's 1996 campaign relied heavily on the accumulated resentment of Keating:*

Political consultant Malcolm McGregor captured this phenomenon by re-tooling a joke American comedian Mort Sahl told about Ronald Reagan's landslide presidential defeat of Jimmy Carter: 'John Howard only won in a landslide because he was running against Paul Keating. If he had run unopposed, he would have lost.'

Richard McGregor in Waldren (ed), *Future Tense* (1999), p167

## A GOOD PLACE TO SQUAT

*When John Howard finally became prime minister, it wasn't The Lodge he and his family were after.*

It was at this moment in his career that John Howard announced casually that rather than move to Canberra he planned to take over Kirribilli House, the Sydney harbourside mansion previously available to prime ministers only when it was not being used by visiting VIPs. The ostensible reason? As a good family man he wanted to be near his son during his last year at school. Six years later the Howard family was scattered across the face of the earth, although still funded by taxpayers for everything from parking fees to conducted tours of Paris. But John and (especially) Janette were still esconced at Kirribilli, and it would have taken several tonnes of high explosive to remove them.

MacCallum, How To Be A Megalomaniac (2002), p. 217

## DODGING BULLETS

*When a madman killed 45 people in a gun massacre at Port Arthur, Howard surprised everyone by backing a national ban on many types of firearms.*

The ban applied to all self-loading rifles and shotguns, from the semi-automatic and pump action shotguns, used by clay-pigeon shooters and duck-hunters, to the rifles used by pig shooters, and by rifle clubs in their field and service competitions. Howard took a keen interest in military history, but he had never gone hunting, or fired a rifle, and had no empathy with the owners of close to 50,000 firearms which were handed in over the following year, about half of whom, statistically, would have voted for the Liberal or National parties on 2 March, and who were suddenly equated with a mass murderer.

Howard addressed a rally of protesting Victorian gun owners in Sale, wearing, on the advice of the security services, a bullet-proof vest. It was a measure of the hysteria which had been whipped up about gun ownership, and it angered sporting shooters and rifle club members.

Barnett, John Howard Prime Minister (1997), p. 750

## A Clapped Out Black Panther

*From the start Howard was obsessed by immigration and its potential as an electoral weapon.*

Even as prime minister, with the office's manifold responsibilities, Howard jumped on seemingly trivial issues where foreigners were supposedly threatening our borders. Take his stridency over the Australian visit of Lorenzo Ervin, a pardoned former plane hijacker correctly described by one newspaper as a 'clapped-out Black Panther'. Howard recalled Ruddock home from a state visit to Belgrade to sort out a kerfuffle over Erwin's low-key speaking tour, which apparently made him a menace to national security.

Richard McGregor in Waldren (ed), *Future Tense* (1999), p. 169

## How Time Flies ...

*The 1998 election saw many changes. One, the veteran National Party warhorse, Ian Sinclair, was a reluctant victim.*

Having finally decided to resign from his seat of New England he changed his mind at the last minute, and fronted to his party branch to demand reinstatement. After hearing him out, the chairman asked him politely what he had done for the electorate recently. 'Well,' replied Sinclair, 'I got you the New England Highway' – and indeed he did; in an extraordinary exercise in pork barrelling Sinclair, as minister for transport, had designated the New England, rather than the much more trafficked Pacific, as the main route between Sydney and Brisbane and consequently the recipient of Commonwealth funding. The chairman nodded. 'But Ian,' he said gently, 'that was 30 years ago' – and indeed it was. Even for the patient squatters of the northern tablelands, 30 years is a long time between drinks. Sinclair's bid failed.

MacCallum, *How To Be A Megalomaniac* (2002), p. 78

# A Khaki Election

*In the wake of the September 11 attacks in America and the Tampa furore, the 2001 election was a tense affair. Howard and his colleagues pushed the security issue to the limits.*

Security was all pervasive, even invasive. Not once, not twice but three times, the audience for the Liberal Party launch was checked. Bags were searched. Metal objects were removed. Everyone had to pass through the kinds of devices found in airports all over the world. Security guards in their para-police, para-military uniforms waved wands with determination but no discrimination at the City Recital Hall on the morning of Sunday, October 28.

Outside Angel Place, once a charming quarter of oyster bars, bespoke tailors and cafes for illicit assignations but now just another unlovely inner-city cavern, the police presence was strong. Federal agents muttered odd incantations into their sleeves and looked anxiously at the arrivals. They need not have bothered. This was an invitation-only affair. Journalists covering the launch had to register well in advance, and produce photo identification to pick up passes. In the wake of September 11, the detail of Australian Federal Police guarding the Prime Minister had been increased.

On that pleasant Sunday morning they were out in force, boosted by a large contingent of their New South Wales colleagues. Security outside, security inside and security, from the Tampa in August and September 11 in America, dominating Australian domestic politics in this 2001 election campaign.

Peter Charlton & David Solomon in Solomon (ed), *Howard's Race* (2002), p. 1

# Embedded with the Diggers

*The election campaign was full of images of Howard and his ministers in military postures, some distinctly dubious.*

That day was the day after the Americans began their bombing campaign in Afghanistan. Under the circumstances, a picture of the Defence Minister sitting behind the controls of a helicopter was irresistable. Deputy Prime Minister John Anderson joined in the fun. In this period he was photographed sighting – but not firing – a Steyr rifle on the army's range at Majura, not far from Duntroon in Canberra. The Prime Minister even managed a visit to Lavarack Barracks in Townsville, in the electorate held by Liberal Peter Lindsay with what was then a wafer thin margin. Lindsay had somehow managed to convince local journalists that the battalion he was visiting – Second Battalion, the Royal Australian Regiment – was known as Howard's Own. When travelling journalists put the nickname to the Diggers of 2RAR, they were politely bemused. The non-existent sobriquet was another example of how the Liberals draped themselves in khaki for the campaign.

Peter Charlton in Solomon (ed), *Howard's Race* (2002), p. 119

## THE TERROR OF THE BOAT PEOPLE

*Throughout the campaign Howard sought to link the war on terrorism with his rejection of boat people, even if the link was tenuous in the extreme.*

As Tom Allard of the *SMH* reported after the election, 'It was past deadline for most newspapers so *The Courier-Mail*'s political editor Dennis Atkins had his laptop computer open and was showing his fellow reporters the front page splash the Brisbane paper was running the next morning. The article, based on a wide-ranging one-on-one interview, began: "Australia had no way to be certain terrorists, or people with terrorist links, were not among the asylum seekers trying to enter the country by boat from Indonesia, Prime Minister John Howard said."' The article went on to say that Howard had linked terrorism and Australia's border protection stance for the first time. It paraphrased him comparing the current situation with the end of World War II, when Nazi war criminals had slipped into Australia. As the Prime Minister passed by, Atkins showed the story to him. 'Good,' Howard said. 'Excellent!'

Peter Charlton in Solomon (ed), *Howard's Race* (2002), pp. 127–8

# We Will Decide

*While Howard's tactics appalled what he called the 'elite', the opinion polls showed massive approval. Kim Beazley offered little opposition. In the end, the disapproval of many prominent Australians may even have worked in Howard's favour.*

The *Age*'s Fairfax stablemate brought together those 'former senior liberal politicians and … former senior public servants' in a page eight report on November 8. Under small photographs of each, the *SMH* reported their remarks.

MALCOLM FRASER, FORMER PRIME MINISTER   'When policy falls heavily on the poor, the destitute, those seeking to flee hunger, brutality and tyranny, then that policy is wrong. It is inhumane. The destitute have been made pawns in a harsh political contest.'

DR JOHN YU, CHANCELLOR, UNIVERSITY OF NEW SOUTH WALES   'most strikingly, this loss of communal caring is seen in the lack of humanity and the heartless, xenophobic extremes used to exclude those seeking to escape … the hopelessness of Afghanistan and Iraq.'

JOHN MENADUE, FORMER HEAD OF THE IMMIGRATION DEPARTMENT AND PRIME MINISTER'S DEPARTMENT   'This is not strong leadership, to attack vulnerable, outcast, weak people. It is cowardice, it is not courage and it is not strong leadership.'

IAN GEORGE, ANGLICAN ARCHBISHOP OF ADELAIDE   'The bipartisan policy is … failing lamentably. It's destroying our international reputation, brutalising the Australian people's attitudes and making us a less compassionate people.'

FRED CHANEY, FORMER LIBERAL MINISTER   'What the political leadership in Australia is doing – and I say that across the board – it's not government or opposition – I think what both are doing is esssentially appealing to the worst in our natures.'

MARGARET REYNOLDS, FORMER LABOR SENATOR   'Obviously I would have preferred Kim Beazley to have stuck to his original position rather than roll over. And that would be the view of many people in both the Labor and Liberal parties.'

IAN MACPHEE, FORMER LIBERAL MINISTER   '[Howard's] total lack of vision, history, geography and cultural sensitivity is evident to all who are capable of independent assessment. Howard is a throwback we must throw out.'

JOHN HEWSON, FORMER COALITION LEADER 'Ironically, Howard ... has never had a genuine passion for policy. He has, however, successfully manipulated prejudice to his personal political advantage. I guess, to many, that is what makes him a good politician.'

JULIE BISHOP, LIBERAL MEMBER FOR CURTIN 'If another boat were to sink with hundreds of people, that would be unthinkable. We need a new approach ... It is vital there is an agreement with Indonesia.'

RICHARD WOOLCOTT, DIPLOMAT AND FORMER SECRETARY OF THE DEPARTMENT OF FOREIGN AFFAIRS AND TRADE 'We are witnessing in Australia a tragic recurrence of those old barbarisms: racism, religious intolerance and jingoism.'

NEVILLE WRAN, FORMER NEW SOUTH WALES PREMIER 'The race card has been introduced into this election. It's a card and an introduction which we and our children will live to regret.'

PETER CARNLEY, ANGLICAN PRIMATE 'there will have to be a rethink because the number of island states around the Pacific that are prepared to take refugees is not infinite and it's going to run out unless we start placing them in the Antarctic.'

TIM COSTELLO, PRESIDENT OF THE BAPTIST UNION 'I don't remember a time when there has been an election with such a clear moral issue but treated by the major parties with such clear amoral electioneering ... really we have had an election in a moral vacuum.'

TOM UREN, FORMER LABOR MINISTER 'Both parties rejected the churches' position because of political expediency. It's a terribly sad outcome and will take generations to overcome.'

The following day, the *SMH* published a letter from a John Crutchley of Springwood, on the foothills of the Blue Mountains: 'Thank you, *Herald* ... You made up the mind of this swinging voter. The 14 photographs published on Thursday's front page have convinced me to vote for John Howard.'

That says it all, really.

Solomon (ed), *Howard's Race* (2002), pp. 234–6

# Sources and Acknowledgements

The editor and publisher thank copyright holders for granting permission to reproduce copyright material.

*Argus* 1949.
Australia, House of Representatives 1947. *Parliamentary Debates* (Hansard). Vol. 190. © Commonwealth.
Australia, House of Representatives 1949. *Parliamentary Debates* (Hansard). Vol. 204. © Commonwealth.
*Australian* 1966.
Baker, Donald W. *Days of Wrath.* Melbourne University Press, Melbourne, 1985.
Barnett, David with Goward, Pru. *John Howard Prime Minister.* Viking, Melbourne, 1997.
Belloc, Hilaire. *Cautionary Tales For Children.* Thomas Nelson, Edinburgh, 1940.
Blazey, Peter & Campbell, Andrew. *The Political Dice Men.* Outback Press, Melbourne 1974.
Blewett, Neal. *A Cabinet Diary.* Wakefield Press, 1999.
*Braidwood and Araluen Express* 1901.
Broadbent, James & Hughes, Joy. *The Age of Macquarie.* Melbourne University Press, Melbourne, 1992.
*Bulletin* 1893.

Cameron, Clyde & Connell, Daniel. *The Confessions of Clyde Cameron*. ABC Books, Sydney, 1990.
Carew, Edna. *Keating*. Allen & Unwin, Sydney, 1988.
Chipp, Don & Larkin, John. *Don Chipp: The Third Man*. Rigby, Melbourne, in association with Beckett Green, Adelaide, 1978.
Clark, C.M.H. *A History of Australia* Vols. i–vi. Melbourne University Press, Melbourne.
> *From the Earliest Times to the Age of Macquarie*. Vol. i. 1963;
> *New South Wales and Van Diemen's Land, 1822–1838*. Vol. ii. 1968;
> *The Beginning of an Australian Civilisation, 1824–1851*. Vol. iii. 1973;
> *The Earth Abideth for Ever*. 1851–1888. Vol. iv. 1978;
> *The People Make Laws, 1888–1915*. Vol. v. 1981;
> *'The old dead tree and the young green tree', 1916–1935*. Vol. vi. 1987.

Cohen, Barry. *After the Party*. Penguin Books Australia, Melbourne, 1988.
Cohen, Barry. *The Life of the Party*. Penguin Books Australia, Melbourne, 1987.
Coombs, Herbert Cole. *Trial Balance*. Macmillan, South Melbourne, 1981.
Crisp, Leslie Finlay. *Ben Chifley: A Biography*. Longman, Melbourne, 1963.
Crisp, Leslie Finlay. *Federation Fathers*. Melbourne University Press, Melbourne, 1990.
Crowley, Francis K. *Modern Australia in Documents*. Vols. i & ii. Wren, Melbourne, 1973.
Cumming, Fia. *Mates: Five Champions of the Labor Right*. Allen & Unwin, Sydney, 1991.
*Daily Telegraph* 1931, 1958.
Daly, Fred. *From Curtin to Hawke*. South Melbourne, Sun Books, 1984.
Daly, Fred. *The Politician Who Laughed*. Hutchinson, Melbourne, 1982.
Deakin, Alfred. *Federated Australia*. Melbourne University Press, Melbourne, 1968.
Denning, Warren. *Caucus Crisis: The Rise and Fall of the Scullin Government*. Cumberland Argus, Parramatta, 1937; reprinted by Hale & Iremonger, Sydney, 1982.
Edwards, Cecil. *Labor Pains*. Hill of Content, Melbourne, 1974.

Ellis, M.H. in the *Bulletin*, 22 March 1961.

Evatt, Herbert Vere. *Rum Rebellion: A Study of the Overthrow of Governor Bligh.* Angus & Robertson, a division of HarperCollins Publishers, Sydney, 1938.

Fadden, Arthur. *They Called Me Artie: The Memoirs of Sir Arthur Fadden.* Jacaranda Wiley, Milton, 1969.

Fitzsimons, Peter. *Beazley.* HarperCollins Publishers, Sydney, 2002.

Freudenberg, Graham. *A Certain Grandeur: Gough Whitlam in Politics.* Macmillan, Melbourne, 1976.

Gordon, Michael. *Paul Keating: A Question of Leadership.* University of Queensland Press, St Lucia, 1993.

Hawke, Bob. *The Hawke Memoirs.* William Heinemann, Sydney, 1994.

Hawke, Hazel. *My Own Life.* Text Publishing, Melbourne, 1992.

Hazlehurst, Cameron. *Menzies Observed.* Allen & Unwin, Sydney, 1979.

*Historical Records of New South Wales (1892–1901).* Vol. vi. Facsimile edition published by Lansdowne, Slattery & Co., Sydney, 1978–1990.

Holman, Ada. *Memoirs of a Premier's Wife.* Angus & Robertson, a division of HarperCollins Publishers, Sydney, 1948.

Horne, Donald. *In Search of Billy Hughes.* Macmillan, Melbourne, 1979.

Hughes, Colin A. *Mr Prime Minister: Australian Prime Ministers, 1901–1972.* Oxford University Press, Melbourne, 1976.

Hughes, Robert. *The Fatal Shore.* HarperCollins, Sydney, 1987; reprinted by Pan Macmillan, Sydney, 1988.

Hughes, William Morris. *Crusts and Crusades.* Angus & Robertson, Sydney, 1947.

Hughes, William Morris. *Policies and Potentates.* Angus & Robertson, Sydney, 1950.

Kelly, Paul. *The End of Certainty.* Allen & Unwin, Sydney, 1992.

Kelly, Paul. *The Hawke Ascendancy.* Angus & Robertson, a division of HarperCollins Publishers, Sydney, 1984.

Kelly, Paul. *The Unmaking of Gough.* Angus & Robertson, a division of HarperCollins Publishers, Sydney, 1976.

Killen, James. *Inside Australian Politics.* Methuen, Sydney, 1985; reprinted by Reed Books, Melbourne, 1989.

Killen, James. *Killen in Company*. Allen & Unwin, Sydney, 1989.
Kramer, L. et al. (eds). *The Greats: The 50 Men and Women Who Most Helped to Shape Modern Australia*. Angus & Robertson, a division of HarperCollins Publishers, in conjunction with the *Bulletin* and Channel 9, Sydney, 1986.
La Nauze, John Andrew. *Alfred Deakin*. Melbourne University Press, Melbourne, 1965; reprinted by Angus & Robertson, a division of HarperCollins Publishers, Sydney, 1979.
*Labor Call* 1931.
*Labor Daily* 1930.
Lang, John Thomas. *The Turbulent Years*. Alpha Books, Sydney, 1970.
MacCallum, Mungo. *How To Be A Megalomaniac*. Duffy & Snellgrove, Sydney, 2002.
MacCallum, Mungo. *Mungo on the Zoo Plane: Elections 1972–1977*. University of Queensland Press, St Lucia, 1979.
MacCallum, Mungo. *Mungo's Canberra*. University of Queensland Press, St Lucia, 1977.
MacCallum, Mungo. *Mungo: The Man Who Laughs*. Duffy & Snellgrove, Sydney, 2001.
Martin, Alan William. *Henry Parkes*. Melbourne University Press, Melbourne, 1980.
Martin, Alan William. *Robert Menzies: A Life*. Melbourne University Press, Melbourne, 1993.
Oakes, Laurence. *Whitlam PM: A Biography*. Angus & Robertson, a division of HarperCollins Publishers, Sydney, 1973.
Oakes, Laurence & Solomon, D. *The Making of an Australian Prime Minister*. Cheshire, Melbourne, 1973.
*Register* 1914.
Reid, Alan. *The Gorton Experiment*. Shakespeare Head, Sydney, 1971.
Ross, Lloyd. *John Curtin for Labor and for Australia*. Australian National University Press, Canberra, 1971.
Schneider, Russell. *The Colt From Kooyong: Andrew Peacock – A Political Biography*. Angus & Robertson, a division of HarperCollins Publishers, Sydney, 1990.
Schneider, Russell. *War Without Blood: Malcolm Fraser in Power*. Angus & Robertson, a division of HarperCollins Publishers,

Sydney, 1990.

Solomon, David (ed). *Howard's Race*. HarperCollins, Sydney, 2002.

Stubbs, John. *Hayden*. William Heinemann, Melbourne, 1989.

Summers, Anne. *Gamble for Power: How Bob Hawke Beat Malcolm Fraser*. Nelson, Melbourne, 1983.

*Sydney Morning Herald* 1939.

Tench, Captain Watkin. *Sydney's First Four Years*. Library of Australian History, Sydney, 1961.

Tennant, Kylie. *Evatt: Politics and Justice*. Angus & Robertson, a division of HarperCollins Publishers, Sydney, 1970.

Thompson, John & Counihan, Noel (eds). *On Lips of Living Men*. Lansdowne Press, Sydney, 1962.

Waldren, Murray (ed). *Future Tense: Australia Beyond Election 1998*. Allen & Unwin, 1999.

Watson, Don. *Recollections of a Bleeding Heart*. Knopf, 2002.

Western Australia, Legislative Assembly 1921. *Parliamentary Debates*. Vol. 64.

Whitlam, Nicholas & Stubbs, John. *Nest of Traitors: Petrov Affair*. Jacaranda Wiley, Milton, 1974; reprinted by University of Queensland Press, St Lucia, 1985.

Every effort has been made to trace the original source of all copyright material contained in this book. Where the attempt has been unsuccessful, the publisher would be pleased to hear from copyright holders to rectify any errors or omissions.

# INDEX

## A
Affleck, William 'Wully' 47–8
Alfred Arthur George, Prince 28, 29-30
Anthony, Doug 159–160, 194, 226

## B
Barton, Edmund 53
Batman, John 17–18
Bavin, NSW Premier 87–8
Beazley, Kim 228–9, 261-2, 266, 275–6
Bent, Ellis 12
Bishop, Bronwyn 268–9
Bjelke-Petersen, Sir Johannes 249–250, 251-2, 253–4
Bligh, Governor William 6–9
Bolte, Henry 186–7
Bowen, Lionel 228
Browne, Frank 156–7
Bruce, Stanley 81–2, 103–4
Button, John 225–6, 237–8

## C
Calwell, Arthur 119, 129–130, 165, 169–170, 171–2, 198
Cameron, Archie 108, 113, 160
Cameron, Clyde 153–5, 198, 227
Cameron, Don 221
Carrington, Lord 38, 39
Chifley, Ben 95–6, 122, 123–6, 127–9, 131–2, 134–5, 137–8, 144–5
Chipp, Don 163–4, 173, 179, 207–8, 220

Clarey, Percy 147
Cohen, Barry 243–4
Connor, Rex 214
Cook, James Hume 50–1
Cook, Sir Joseph 65–6, 78
Coombs, Herbert 'Nugget' 120–1, 124–5, 174, 197
Cowan, Edith 79–80
Curtin, John 72–3, 98–9, 108–9, 114–5, 116, 117–9, 121, 122, 123

## D
Daly, Fred 132, 133–4
Darling, Governor James 15–6
Deakin, Alfred 34, 37, 40, 52, 58–9, 63–4
Ducker, John 230, 231–2

## E
Evans, Gareth 266, 268–9
Evatt, Dr H.V. 'Doc' 120–1, 127–9, 130, 131, 143–4, 147, 150–2, 153–5

## F
Fadden, Arthur 108–9, 113–5, 134, 136, 140–2
Falstein, Max 121
Fitzpatrick, Raymond 156–7
Fitzroy, Governor 25
Forde, Frank 98–9
Forrest, Sir John 63, 74–6
Fraser, Malcolm 207–8, 217–8, 220, 221–2, 223–5, 228, 229–230, 233, 235, 239

## G
Gair, Vince 175–6, 199–200
Game, Sir Philip 94
Garrett, Thomas 36–7
Gipps, Governor George 21
Glendinning, George 27-8
Goldstein Vida 49–50
Gore, William 7, 11
Gorton, John 174, 175–7, 180–1

## H
Hall, Thomas S. 27–8
Hasluck, Paul 167–8
Hawke, Bob 181, 205, 213–4, 231–232, 236, 238, 240, 242, 244–6, 247–8, 256–7, 258, 260-2
Hayden, Bill 182, 196, 217, 220, 228, 231–2, 236, 237–8
Haynes, John 45–6, 47–8
Higgins, Henry Bournes 59
Hewson, John 258–9, 263, 264, 265
Hinze, Russ 250–1
Hogan, E.J. 86
Holman, Ada 51–2
Holt, Harold 170–1, 173
Hopetoun, Lord 53
Howard, John 165, 235, 246–7, 249, 269–271, 272, 273–4, 275–6
Hughes, William Morris 'Billy' 40–6, 58–9, 60, 65–6, 68

## I
Isaacs, Sir Isaac 82–4

## J
Jack, William 137
James, Rowley 109–110, 139

Johnson, Lyndon Baines 171
Johnston, George 8

## K
Keating 195, 214, 218, 234–5, 240–2, 243–5, 247–8, 249, 255–7, 258–261, 262–4, 265–6, 267, 268, 269–270
Kelty, Bill 244–5, 257
Kemp, Judge Advocate 11
Kennelly, Pat 140
Kennett, Jeff 254–5
Kerr, Sir John 216–8
Killen, Jim 174, 185, 191, 227
King, Governor 5
Kingston, Charles 57–8

## L
Lang, Jack 48, 80, 89–91, 92–3, 94, 95
Lang, John Dunmore 21, 22–5, 30
Latham, John 78–9
Lynch, Phillip 194–5, 222–3
Lyne, Sir William 53, 61
Lyons, Joe 102

## M
Macarthur, Elizabeth 14
Macarthur, John 6, 7, 10, 12
McClelland, Jim 255–6
McEwan, John 'Black Jack' 189–190
McKell, William 126
McMahon, William 171–2, 182–4, 185, 187–190, 191–2
Macquarie, Lachlan 12–14
Mannix, Archbishop Daniel 160–1

Menzies, Robert  84, 102–6, 108–110, 111–3, 135, 136, 142, 143, 144–5, 157, 158–9, 160, 163, 164
Meredith, Louisa Anne  20
Murphy, Lionel  210
MacCallum, Mungo  240

O
O'Farrell, Henry James  30
O'Neill, Gary  261–2, 266
O'Malley, King  59, 60

P
Page, Earle  81–2, 101, 103–5
Parkes, Sir Henry  31-3, 36–7, 38, 39
Paterson, Lieutenant-Colonel William  12
Peacock, Andrew  207–8, 233, 254–5
Petrov, Vladimir and Evdokia  148–9
Phillip, Arthur  1–4
Pollard, Reg  123, 138–9
Putland, Mary  9–10

Q
Queen Elizabeth II  164

R
Reid, George  48–9, 57–8
Reith, Peter  246–7

Richardson, Graham  202–3, 212–3, 230, 237, 265-6
Robertson, Jack  27

S
Santamaria, B.A.  146
Scullin, James  82–3, 88–9
Sinclair, Ian  272
Snedden, Bill  200–2, 204–5, 242
Stone, John  241–2

T
Tench, Captain Watkin  1, 9

W
Ward, Eddie  161–2
Wentworth, William Charles  14–16, 18, 22, 26, 33
Wentworth, William Charles (great-grandson)  155–6, 177–8
Whitlam, Gough  161–2, 165, 167–8, 176–7, 180, 192–3, 195–6, 197–8, 205, 206–7, 208, 209–210, 211, 213–4, 217–8, 227
Wilson, Woodrow  77–8
Withers, Reg  229
Wran, Neville  230–8